Names You Never Remember, With Faces You Never Forget

Interviews with the Movies' Character Actors

by Justin Humphreys

Names You Never Remember, With Faces You Never Forget
Interviews with the Movies' Character Actors
© 2006 Justin Humphreys

Published in the USA by:

BearManor Media
PO Box 750
Boalsburg, PA 16827
www.BearManorMedia.com

Library of Congress Cataloging-in-Publication Data:

Humphreys, Justin.
   Names you never remember, with faces you never forget : interviews
with the movies' character actors / by Justin Humphreys.
      p. cm.
   Includes bibliographical references and index.
   ISBN 1-59393-041-0 (alk. paper)
   1. Character actors and actresses—United States—Interviews. 2.
Motion picture actors and actresses—United States—Interviews. I.
Title.

   PN1998.2.H79 2006
   791.4302'8092273—dc22
                        2005035243

Printed in the United States.

Design and Layout by Valerie Thompson.

TABLE OF CONTENTS

This book is dedicated to the memory of Royal Dano (1922–1994):
a remarkable actor, a hilarious raconteur, and a professional to the last.

ACKNOWLEDGMENTS

Special thanks are due to all of those who are interviewed here. This is your book, not mine. L. Q. Jones deserves a special commendation for his wonderful foreword. (L. Q. can *write?* And *read*, even?)

I would never have started doing interviews if John Agar had not first put me in touch with Royal Dano in 1994. John and his wife, Loretta, were a true joy to be around. I know that there are many among their other friends and fans who will agree that they are sorely missed.

Danny Siegel was a tremendous help throughout the creation of this book, lending moral support and extensive editorial advice.

This book would never have happened without the kind assistance of the following people: Tom Weaver, Peggy Dano, Dan and Kelly Roebuck, Bob and Kathy Burns, Dick Miller, Tom Khamis, Allaire Koslo, Mike Weldon, Fabrice Lambot, Peter Bogdanovich, George and Susan Garrett, Richard Fleischer, Dr. Darrell Cole, Fr. Brian Mulcahy, OP, Margaret Kartalian, Brian Penikas and the whole Apemania gang, Jeanene Skillen, Cinnamon Grabill, and my publisher, Ben Ohmart (Any relation to Carol?).

I would like to single out my friend, Mike Siegel, who has done an excellent job documenting the life of Sam Peckinpah, and whose archive of Peckinpah photos is unmatched. Make it a point to see his upcoming documentary, ***Passion and Poetry: The Journey of Sam Peckinpah,*** and check out his book on Peckinpah, as well. His website is at www.eldorado-film.de.

And with apologies to Jeff Burr.

FOREWORD
BY L. Q. JONES

Webster's II

CHAR-AC-TER
    adj. 1. Having the ability to act in roles emphasizing traits markedly different from those of the performer—

A GOOD ONE IS...

PEPPER TO SALT

BUTTER TO BREAD

THE SPARK PLUG THAT DRIVES THE ENGINE

UNDERPAID

OVERWORKED

UNDER-APPRECIATED

OVERLOOKED

SCARCER THAN HEN'S TEETH

A NATIONAL TREASURE!

& these (with the possible exception of 1) are GOOD ONES!!!

INTRODUCTION
THE CHARACTER ACTOR MANIFESTO

"There are two kinds of people in the world: those who love character actors, and everyone else. The ones who fit into the latter category have something to account for."
— Leonard Maltin. **The Real Stars.**

"All things considered, I'd rather watch Franklin Pangborn or Edgar Kennedy chew the scenery in a second-rate 1938 movie than sit through most of the entertainment Hollywood is dishing up today—not least because there is precious little screen time for anyone other than the stars."
— Jordan R. Young. **Reel Characters.**

"...I confess I have never had a defense—and neither, I suspect, have several generations of filmgoers—against the oldtime [sic] character actors. In their moments of glorious excess, the character actors came screaming off the screen, riveting our attention, securing their place in those precincts of our memory set aside for images of human overstatement...No station in life was safe from their distortions and commotions."
— Harold Meyerson. "The Case of the Vanishing Character Actor."
Film Comment magazine.

This book is about faces, personalities, and the character actors who inhabit them.

A movie's "name" leads provide the charisma and physiques that draw audiences to theaters. But, traditionally it has been left to the character people, cast in support, to make all of those stars' interactions on-screen and, more importantly, those stars' off-screen moments, as memorable as is humanly possible.

I will begin with what is, classically, the ultimate example of character actors' devious ability to overwhelm. Humphrey Bogart's portrayal of the merciless Sam Spade is, unquestionably, the backbone of John Huston's **The Maltese Falcon** (1941). But, as intense a personality as Bogie projected, he had to scramble to keep from having his many scenes with the inimitable Sidney Greenstreet and Peter Lorre stolen right out from underneath him. (And it was Greenstreet's cinematic bow, to boot.)

Critic Andrew Sarris once described the fortuitous casting of Greenstreet and Lorre as the unsavory Kasper Guttman and Joel Cairo, respectively, as "a coup of eerie accuracy." Sarris nailed it, just as Huston had done in casting: unquestionably, those two utterly embodied Dashiell Hammett's characters, as written. (Not to mention character titan Elisha Cook's performance as Wilmer, the gunsel.) Harold Meyerson, a highly astute judge of movie character talent, summed it up best and most succinctly: "The immutability of supporting characters—a given of classical cinema—became in the *Falcon* a source of wonder and delight." The pair were perhaps the character actor's nexus.

But the great, bygone movie studios never allowed chemistry *that* remarkable—and remunerative—to stay in check for long. Greenstreet and Lorre were such adroit character actors, and their personas so distinctive and well-loved, that Warner Brothers re-teamed them for a string of specially-tailored mystery vehicles, *The Mask of Dimitrios* (1944), *The Verdict* (1946), and *Three Strangers* (also '46).

Another unforgettable, archetypal personality whom Bogart found himself pitted against was the immortal Alfonso Bedoya, the Mexican "Gold Hat" of Huston's *The Treasure of the Sierra Madre* (1948). How many people (not simply movie aficionados, here—just ordinary people) can imitate Bedoya's insouciant challenge to Bogart—"Badges? We dun' need no steenkin' badges!"—and without ever having *seen* the film? Or without even having *heard it called by name?* Such is the resonance of extraordinary cinematic faces.

But Bogie could inevitably hold his own, even against stalwarts like Greenstreet, Lorre, or middling talents like Bedoya. With that said, not all stars have been so capable. Many a dashing leading man or sultry leading lady has been swallowed, whole, into the backdrop of a scene by some odd-looking and—acting journeyman character.

Case in point: when confronted with Steve McQueen (a fine actor, but more of a *personality*) and Ali MacGraw (a neophyte actress), Slim Pickens took a five-minute cameo as a scraggly, bandy-legged old cowboy in Sam Peckinpah's *The Getaway* (1972) and gave what was probably the film's most memorable performance. L. Q. Jones once said that Pickens "practically walked away with the picture." (L. Q. should know: he is an inveterate scene-stealer himself, and that is meant as the purest of compliments.)

Ranking up there with the inimitable Slim was the man who became the Costello to L. Q.'s Abbot, Strother Martin, particularly in the role that became wholly his own: the straw boss in *Cool Hand Luke* (1967). The people who could directly place the late, great actor's name to that character rank among a monumentally tiny minority. But thousands of others can instantly conjure up a phantom image of Martin, gloating over the broken Paul Newman, just by hearing someone imitate the actor's peculiar, whiney, gravelly voice, drawling out "What we have here is a failure to communicate," or explaining how Newman suffers from too much "rabbit in his blood."

Or, eschewing the obvious, the masterful Walter Brennan walks all over stars like Joel McCrea and Brian Donlevy in Howard Hawks' ***Barbary Coast*** (1935), the first of the endless Hawks/Brennan collaborations. Who that has seen it can forget Old Atrocity's (Brennan's) explanation for why he wears a patch over a perfectly good eye: "It makes me look more FEE-ro-cious!"

Most character actors' names elude the memories of everyone but their family members, co-stars, die-hard movie aficionados, and rabid tv addicts. Those same actors also possess some of the most instantly recognizable faces, voices, and screen personalities in movie history.

There was a wonderful time when the entertainment industry was not geared towards the most brain-dead among the young. Actors still resembled men—not the adolescents, eunuchs, or male models hogging screen time now. Actors were, very regularly, allowed to age.

Over time, their faces became more weathered and, simultaneously, more interesting—growing ever more deeply imbued with character. Craggy looks became a kind of left-handed asset. Think of it this way: where would Lee Marvin have been if he had had a facelift in the early '70s?

But, as fewer and fewer parts come up these days for older actors, and their decades of experience mean less and less to audiences being pandered to ever more crassly, this breed of honest-to-God, journeyman character actors are becoming frighteningly scarce.

There are innumerable differences between the older generation of character people—those whose careers generally began in the '40s and '50s—and the fleeting few new ones trickling in. Among others: many of these elder statesmen had led rich and varied lives and, importantly, had *experiences*.

These gifted men had fought overseas in World War II, or had actually ridden in cattle drives. Some of them had come from a rural America where electricity and indoor plumbing had yet to arrive. Some future actors had hopped freights, cross-country. Often, they had come of age in or around the Depression; some were impelled to chip in to their family's income.

The kinds of jobs that these actors were forced to take simply to survive would send a modern Juilliard graduate running in terror to his analyst. A perfect example is the magnificent Robert Ryan stoking coal in the bowels of a ship, long before he ever set foot on a soundstage. Bud Evans, brother of character stalwart Gene Evans, tells me that when his brother first began scrounging for bit parts, he swept floors at Bronson's Bar in Pasadena, and lived in a converted gas station ladies' room.

Since they knew something about life, many character actors—though, with exceptions—never ceased to be grateful for the opportunity to make a good living in a profession as comparatively undemanding as acting. Few of these men could also ever be deemed genuinely famous. Therefore, more than a few of them gracefully escaped that deadliest and most virulent of all Hollywood maladies: egomania.

What kept these men from developing god complexes? Simple: fifty or sixty years ago, innumerably more movies were being produced in Hollywood. That meant that acting jobs were much more plentiful than they have been for decades now. A working actor was special, but not *that* special.

Nowadays, Hollywood grinds out a pathetically small number of (pathetic) movies. The few actors who are working regularly—or at all—tend to think that they are somehow superior beings, immune to unemployment and their fans' eventual disinterest. Nothing could be further from the truth.

Essentially, these men had very real *character*. A facsimile of character taught by an acting coach can be picked up by any reasonably intelligent viewer within seconds. What Golden Age character men had was the genuine article.

And during Hollywood's seemingly golden age, the "genuine article" was plentiful. There was a veritable army of character actors available for any kind of supporting role the studios might demand. Contract players were kept on-hand to play hard-nosed drill sergeants, cabbies, desert trash outlaws, hillbillies, weak-kneed stoolies, ethnic characters, scientists, bikers, gangsters, crooks of all kinds, Nazis, slaves, mad scientists' equally depraved assistants, and, occasionally, the odd, ordinary working stiff and soda jerk. (And those types don't even touch on historical parts.)

The duty of a character actor, first and foremost, was to be a "face-maker." As Harold Meyerson put it, when the studios were at the height of the power, they "made enough films to give the character actor, even the uncontracted freelancer, a grand opportunity to encase himself in the career-bolstering armor of an ongoing identity."

When cast properly, a character man perfectly suited the way audiences felt a certain kind of character *ought* to look, however eccentric that conception was. Audiences seeking a representative of spineless, sweaty weasels everywhere found men on-screen like Strother Martin, Jack Elam, and Elisha "Cookie" Cook, Jr. To decades' worth of moviegoers' sheer joy, old masters like those three got to hone their sliminess to an advanced art over the course of dozens of movies. (As with all actors, moviegoers' belief in a character actor's cinematic persona often carried over into their actual lives. A story once circulated about an autograph hound greeting another great cinematic simperer, Percy Helton. She told him, "You see, I remember your name." Impeccably, he responded "That's very nice. Most people just call me 'That little bastard.'")

Or the studios might need someone for the part of a cigar-chomping soldier—weary, bitter, and hardened by combat. They need have looked no further than rough customers like Neville Brand (the fourth most decorated soldier in World War II), Aldo Ray, Gene Evans, or the extraordinary Charles McGraw.

Westerns were a magnificent stockyard for character talent, since glamour and age rarely factored into their casting. The incredible brotherhood of western character players became an inseparable part of the genre. ("The American West was 200 people endlessly recombined," Meyerson wrote.) A minute fraction of its invaluable members were Chill Wills, Walter Brennan, Edgar "Bucky" Buchanan, Ernest Borgnine, Andy Devine, Milburn Stone, Morris Ankrum, and Peter Whitney. Generally, character actors—especially western character actors—are among the most eye-catching parts of a movie because they don't tend to go out of their way to dress too well, shave too much, seem too brave, or act and speak too normally—all the things the leads were compelled to do.

Certain casts are populated almost entirely by stalwart character ensembles. Excepting the name leads in their casts, vivid examples of this phenomenon are John Ford's *The Man Who Shot Liberty Valance* (1962), Roger Corman's *The St. Valentine's Day Massacre* (1967), Phil Karlson's and Corman's *A Time for Killing* (1967), and Sam Peckinpah's *Pat Garrett and Billy the Kid* (1973). There are almost no green, kid actors in any of these movies, and some of the character people in their casts had careers stretching back nearly into the silent era.

In movies with casts like these, it is not unusual for a dedicated movie aficionado to not have a single scene slip by without feeling as if they have seen everyone in a given shot a hundred times before, appearing in that many different movies and television shows. Or for that same aficionado to recognize every last one of the first twenty names or so in the film's cast list. It should also be noted that three of the aforementioned films' directors—Ford, Corman, and Peckinpah—all famously cultivated their own personal stock companies, actors they regularly, almost reassuringly, recycled. Tersely—as usual—Ford explained to fellow director Bert Kennedy the reasoning behind this: "It's good to have actors you can trust, ones who will know their lines and be there." Simpler, and truer, words were never spoken.

Peckinpah, one of America's last truly great directors, had a particularly astute eye for casting his films' wall-to-wall character parts from among his personal acting stable. (Interviews with three of the members of his Wild Bunch can be found within these pages.)

In 1977, Harold Meyerson wrote elegiacally that these "alumni of late Wayne and early Peckinpah, these are the last characters to have practiced character acting in a manner that the original troupers would have recognized. By the mid-Seventies, however, the western, too, has substantially disappeared, and the character actor is deprived of the last hierarchy to have sustained him."

Hollywood's character actor roster became severely depopulated during the '70s for a variety of reasons, the main one being plain old age. By 1994, when I first started seeking out character people to interview, they were being snuffed out mercilessly. Very few of them had made it that far. Much to my dismay, even fewer lived to see the twenty-first century. Like most interviewers or film historians, there are dozens of interviews that sadly escaped me, for whatever reason.

This book is a selection of ten interviews that I conducted from 1994–2001 with various character men, which originally appeared in Mike Weldon's *Psychotronic Video* Magazine. The Jonathan Haze interview was also translated into French for Fabrice Lambot's *Atomovision*. Fabrice also assisted with writing the questions for that interview. Thankfully, all but one of the subjects interviewed here are still very much extant, and almost none of them have retired. That includes Marc Lawrence, well on his way to completing his first century.

Why are there no character *actresses* interviewed in this book? That, I genuinely don't know. My only explanation is that most of the actresses I would like to see interviewed, sadly, are doing summer stock in the sky: Aline MacMahon, Thelma Ritter, Rosalind Cash, and Minerva Urecal, among others. There are more than enough living, working character actresses to make up a companion to this book, women like Veronica Cartwright, Amy Wright, Melinda Dillon, Cloris Leachman, and Anna Massey. However, the subject of character women is one that longs for much deeper study than I can grant it in this little plot of paper.

Though I was never paid for my interviews for *Psychotronic*, its publisher, Mike Weldon, made up much of the difference by sending me crates-full of review books, videos, and magazines as compensation. And when I was in desperate need of the supremely rare John Agar monster movie, *Hand of Death,* who else but Mike Weldon would have shot a copy off to me within a week or so? Mike is also responsible for quite a bit of the research that went into this book, and duly deserves credit for it.

In closing, I would like to say that I have always been delighted to be able to bridge the distance to the long-departed, true golden age of movies that these interviews have permitted me. Besides, I wouldn't trade my experiences interviewing and becoming acquainted with these actors for anything. Having a friendly and loquacious interviewee must never be underrated. In a way, I am relieved that, though I was never an interviewer on the scale of Peter Bogdanovich, I was also never saddled with a bull-headed, interview-proof subject like Bogdanovich found in John Ford.

I hope that my readers will enjoy the lives chronicled and the anecdotes told in this book as much as I got a bang out of doing these interviews, and watching these men's unique performances. My parting advice is this: avoid seeing the computer-generated gibberish cluttering up your local cemetary-plex, and watch a sixty-year-old gem starring someone like Eugene Pallette, Guy Kibbee, Edward Arnold, or Thomas Gomez, today! Great character performances are everywhere, throughout nearly every decade of the cinema. You never know what irresistible talent lies curled up, waiting for you, well hidden in some esoteric movie, behind an elusive name with one hell of a face.

— JUSTIN HUMPHREYS

POSTSCRIPT/DIGRESSION: As of this writing, I nominate Dick Miller as the greatest character actor alive. Miller began as one of the hardest-working members of Roger Corman's acting pool, who all doubled as Jack-of-all-trades contributors to his films. From there, Miller went on to appear in dozens of different kinds of roles, in films of countless genres, made on endlessly varying budgets.

He is among the last of a breed of character actors, like the contract players of the '30s and '40s, whose credits reel off seemingly into the hundreds. Miller is so well known, he has his own running character, Walter Paisley, who he has reprised in at least eight movies by almost as many different directors. He is still going at it after close to fifty years. To people of a certain age, he is still just as recognizable as ever, even if his name might elude them. The only reason he isn't interviewed in this book is because so many other interviewers who have been at this a lot longer than yours truly, and are just as enthusiastic about Miller's acting as I am, have already interviewed him.

Viva Walter Paisley!

HERE ARE SOME OTHER BOOKS ON THE WONDERFUL SUBJECT OF CHARACTER PEOPLE, WHICH I HIGHLY RECOMMEND:

* *Reel Characters.* Jordan R. Young.
* *The Real Stars.* Edited by Leonard Maltin.
* *The Versatiles: Supporting Character Players in the Cinema 1930–1955.* Alfred E. Twomey and Arthur F. McClure.
* *The Bad Guys.* William K. Everson.
* *The Hollywood Hissables.* Greg Mank.
* *The Tough Guys.* James Robert Parish. (For his essays on Robert Ryan and Edward G. Robinson.)
* Any of Tom Weaver's long series of invaluable interview books from McFarland Press.

THESE MAGAZINES FREQUENTLY FEATURE INTERVIEWS WITH CHARACTER FOLK:

* *Castle of Frankenstein.* (defunct)
* *Psychotronic Video.* (defunct)
* *Filmfax.*
* *Western Characters.*
* *Film Comment.*
* *Starlog.*
* *Fangoria.*
* *Scarlet Street.*

Possibly the finest piece of writing on character actors is Harold Meyerson's article, "The Case of the Vanishing Character Actor," which I have quoted throughout this introduction. (It originally ran in the November-December, 1977 issue of *Film Comment,* pp. 6-15.) It is required reading on the subject.

A note on the text: Throughout the filmographies, I have used the abbreviation "tvm" to indicate "made-for-television movie."

R. G. Armstrong

"Well, if you're going to be an artist, just get prepared for heartbreaks all along the trail. And that's the way it's been."

I can think of few experiences more pleasant than sitting around and simply listening to R. G. Armstrong speak. He commands the English language uniquely, and phrases things like literally no one else I've ever known. And his statements are always delivered in his deep, booming Alabama accent, which Hollywood thankfully never shook loose from him.

He was, at one time, an English professor in North Carolina. R. G.'s original intention was to pursue a career strictly as a writer. He chooses his words carefully, with an enthusiasm for the Queen's English that is still very apparent.

R. G. was a stalwart presence, primarily in westerns, from 1957 onward. His stocky build and resonant voice suited him well for the gruff, overbearing blowhards he was so frequently cast as. He worked with some of the finest talent among western filmmakers, Howard Hawks (***El Dorado***), Henry Hathaway (***From Hell to Texas***), and Sam Peckinpah among them. But, of those three, it was Peckinpah truly became a catalyst for R. G.'s talent and creative drive.

Peckinpah, well known for deviously manipulating his actors, discovered R. G.'s background in strict, rural religion, and tapped into it by regularly casting him in feverishly religious roles. In what is very probably Peckinpah's masterpiece,

Ride the High Country (1962), Joshua Knudsen (R. G.), a zealot, acts as a foil to the even-minded, common-sense religion of Joel McCrea's graying Steve Judd. In *Major Dundee* (1965), R. G. improvised a line, which delighted Peckinpah enough to retain it in the finished film: he bellows "Mighty is the arm of the Lord!" as his character, a hellfire-and-brimstone preacher, clouts an enemy French soldier in the head with the butt of his rifle.

The most unforgettable and electric among R. G.'s performances for Peckinpah was in *Pat Garrett and Billy the Kid* (1973). He played Bob Ollinger, Garrett's fanatical deputy, who, with a single line, summed up the psychotic mood which the deteriorating Peckinpah imbued the film with. As R. G. flies into a rage and levels a shotgun loaded with "sixteen thin dimes" at Billy Bonny's (Kris Kristoffersen) chest, he half-threatens, half-implores him to "Repent, you son of a bitch!" This scene impressed enough people for it to grace the back cover of Bob Dylan's *Pat Garrett* soundtrack album. "Well, I know it's on the back of Bob Dylan's album," says R. G. "They don't say it's me, but that's me."

He had a more secular part in Peckinpah's criminally hard-to-find tv adaptation of Katherine Anne Porter's novella *Noon Wine* (1967). Also, he was Mr. Quittner, one of the many business-minded trolls in Peckinpah's universe, in *The Ballad of Cable Hogue* (1970). In the latter, Jason Robards (as Cable) pours a pitcher of ice-water down R. G.'s boot. R. G. then proceeds to toss the great man of the theater out of his office, ass over teakettle. Quite a way to make a living.

Not only was he justly a pet favorite of Peckinpah's, but R. G. won the admiration of Warren Beatty, and appeared in a number of Beatty's directorial efforts, including *Heaven Can Wait* (1978), *Reds* (1981), and *Dick Tracy* (1990). The latter afforded R. G. the chance to indelibly etch himself in the memories of new generation of moviegoers, in the part of Chester Gould's desiccated arch-villain, Pruneface. Rendered unrecognizable under layers of make-up created by technicians John Caglione and Doug Drexler, R. G. became a part of the media deluge that accompanied that film's release. One of the highest compliments an actor can be paid is having a toy made of him. There were several made of R. G. in his natty, pin-striped suit, tommy gun clasped firmly in hand. Don Post Studios even released a Pruneface mask.

Some of R. G.'s other outstanding credits, for various reasons, include his debut in an early nudist camp movie, *The Garden of Eden* (1957); the outstanding "Nothing in the Dark" segment of *Twilight Zone* (1962), starring Robert Redford as a disarming Death; Martin Ritt's *The Great White Hope* (1970); an adaptation of Manly Wade Wellman's superb "Silver John" fantasy stories, *The Legend of Hillbilly John* (1972); Jack Arnold's *Boss Nigger* (1974), which has been referred to as a straight-faced *Blazing Saddles*; Jack Starrett's drive-in favorite *Race With The Devil* (1975), which co-starred his Peckinpah cohort, Warren Oates; Wim Wenders' *Hammett* (1982); and in several '80s horror films, including Phillipe Mora's ludicrous *The Beast Within* (1982).

R.G., Justin, and Mary.

There are several unique memories that I always associate with R. G. and his wife, Mary. By the time I first met him, R. G. had grown a beard, and he bore a startling resemblance to Walter Huston in *The Devil and Daniel Webster* (1941). He had co-starred in Walt Disney's film of Marguerite Henry's *Justin Morgan Had a Horse* (1972), starring Don Murray as Justin. I once mentioned to him that my brother's name is Morgan, my mother used to raise horses, and that she always kidded that we were named after that novel. From then on, our phone conversations began with a standard, enthusiastic greeting: "Hey! 'Justin Morgan Had a Horse!'"

I vividly remember having dinner with the Armstrongs at a North Hollywood restaurant, then waiting for a cab with them on a bench in front of a Ralph's supermarket in Los Angeles. Mary was learning the words to the folk song, "The House of the Rising Sun," for a part she was up for, but never got. As we sat there, first she began to sing it, then R. G. joined in, and then I picked up the tune as best I could. It was an odd and wonderful experience and, sadly, it will probably be as close as I ever come to performing opposite R. G.

I was shocked to discover that R. G. used to trek out regularly to Watts in the '70s to collaborate on screenplays with Robert Beck, the former pimp and writer better known as Iceberg Slim. I have updated this interview with some fascinating stories that he told about their relationship. R. G. fell into acting for the same reason Vincent Price did: it paid so much better than his day job, which, in R. G.'s case, was writing. One of these days, his novels will be published. I, for one, look forward to poring over each and every one of them. To be sure, he has a hell of a lot more to tell us now than when he was a cub novelist in New York in the '50s.

(A brief digression: one of R. G.'s poems, "The Girl in the Black Raincoat," appears in the anthology, *The Girl in the Black Raincoat*. Edited by George Garrett, published in 1966 by Duell, Sloan, and Pearce.)

R. G., like L. Q. Jones, is a member of the Cowboy Hall of Fame and received their Golden Boot Award. He was interviewed extensively for David Weddle's biography of Sam Peckinpah, "*If They Move...Kill 'Em!*" and, Garner Simmons' Peckinpah bio., *A Portrait in Montage,* and is on-camera in Nick Redman's documentary, *Sam Peckinpah: Man of Iron* (1992). He and Mary were also guests at the Peckinpah film festival in Padua, Italy in September, 2000.

Sadly, in November, 2003, Mary Craven Armstrong died, still only in her fifties. She will be missed, and we can only hope that wherever she is now is an infinitely more loving and welcoming place than Los Angeles.

R. G. was born in 1917 in Birmingham, Alabama. "Pelham was the real little burg. It was a little steel mill town. That town was really the outskirts of the suburb of Birmingham, which later became incorporated in the city portion." The Armstrongs were a strictly religious family, and R. G.'s father intended for the boy to become a preacher. "Very hard, fundamentalist, Baptist, orthodox religion. We had even years of a lot of hard work, clearing up ten acres of land, new ground on a hillside, by creeks, putting it into gardening and raising food, you know, in Depression time."

Decades later, R. G. keeps his early family life private. "I won't go into that. I'm not interested in that. Just facts about my stepping stones to where I am now. The whole psychological behavioral system, studying all that is part of a mixed bag of tricks...Tricks of making adjustments to it in order to survive. So that's all gonna be comin' out in my novel. So I've been answering and giving interviews on stepping stones and where I am now on a *factual* basis."

The local schools that R. G. attended were strict, as well. But diligent studying freed him from a life sentence in the local steel mills. "I won a scholarship to Howard College, a Baptist-funded college. A small college, very prestigious in that area. And along across town, Methodists had funded Birmingham Southern. So we were rivals at football. The conditioning was to be a working person in the steel mills, mines, or farming. No alternative, unless you wanted to be a preacher or a teacher.

"In high school, I did a play. In college, they just put me in it. I wasn't trying to be an actor, but I would take a part, as part of a course of stuff, and produce some plays around in college. One-act plays, experimentals, inspired by a teacher who had been at the University of North Carolina and the Carolina Play-Makers. I went from there [Chapel Hill] after World War II, [on a plan] like the G. I. Bill, and got a Master's in dramatic art and English literature. And there's where I got in plays and cast in plays, but also writing plays. Played in outdoor dramas, like The Lost Colony [Theater in North Carolina], in the summertime."

From an early age, R. G. was a bookish, philosphical person. As a young man, he tried to erase his family's prejudices, "some of the Southern kinds of things about the blacks in the South. I tried to be ultra-liberal and tried to make friends with them, and I got tagged as a 'nigger-lover,' because I would be friends with 'em, would be seen around 'em. In the mill where I worked, I would make friends with the helpers, and was even invited up in their homes, up in the black district, 'colored' district they called it.

"And daddy couldn't understand that. Nobody could, not even my brother, why I was trying to make friends with black people, treating them just like white people. So I was known as that: 'Your brother's just a nigger-lover!' And I hated the term, any other way. I never talked about 'niggers' that way. I was conscientious then. I was gonna be a preacher, and all that kind of stuff and be as good as I could, to love all fellow men, sinners and all. To me, Jesus walked among sinners. 'Cause he didn't stay over here with the Christian element, and never associated with them—he actually went out and lived with sinners. A lot of them were rough characters. Even Peter was a rough 'ol cob…

"Jesus was a lover of the common man—that's what I got from the Bible. And the disciples were not picked from among the educated rabbi people. He was a young rabbi, Jesus was, when he broke off and started livin'…In other words, 'Love each another. Be a brother. Do unto others as you would have them do unto you.' To me, that was the main thing about Jesus. And to love your enemies— the main thing: to love your enemies. Not only that, but I would associate with people that was considered enemies of the church. Guys that were considered atheists in college, and all that.

"I was considered an atheist, but I wasn't an atheist. I believed in the whole thing of the universe, that it was all run by some higher level of energy. But, to me, I couldn't say whether that was God or not. To me, that was the localized version of the representation of delivering to man a way to live and a way to be, to be brothers. And, to me, the higher power infused everything. Everything— trees, the Earth, oceans, it was all part of an infusion of a higher level of energy that in certain manifestations of the physicality of the creature—whether it was a deer, or a rat, or a man, or whatever—they were all infused with this materialization from a higher level of energy. And each creature had its own limitations, or its own higher level of perception. Even a rat has that. So I became a kind of a 'Universalist,' in a sense. I went up to the preacher and told him, 'Take my name off the book in church. I can't be a preacher,' I did all of that. To live among men, like I thought Jesus lived among men, or Buddha lived among men, or Confucius lived among men. Any great leader or teacher of men—I didn't want to be a teacher, I just wanted to be *among* men, without saying that I was whatever I was, just manifest it in behavior.

The aspiring writer discovered that his brother was a talented poet. But coming from the impoverished, rural South crippled any chance he had of pursuing his gifts. His brother nicknamed R. G. "Squeaky," though it is hard to imagine anyone ever calling R. G. "Squeaky." "I started running around with my brother, and almost got killed, I don't know how many different times. He was a roughneck, but a poet. That was his reward. I'd been running around with him, and I'd been studying poetry, and he suddenly revealed that he was a poet. And I said, 'Yeah?

Well, quote me a poem then.' And he quoted me one of his poems, and I thought he'd copied it out of some book. I even made the mistake of saying, 'What book did you copy that out of?' And he said, 'You low-down son of a bitch, I didn't copy that out of any book. I wrote that myself.' And that's when I realized he was a poet. He was just ashamed of it. He had a whole yellow notebook full of poems. And he began to gradually let me read 'em, one after another. And, man, he was a real poet, like Mary's [R. G.'s wife] a real poet.

"I went in search of real poets, to know the truth, and to be a poet myself in living. Because I didn't have the lyricism, the lyric quality that I felt a poet needed. Brothers. Kinship! Kindred poets' spirits on Earth, that emerges on Earth with that kind of perception of [the way that] we really are infused with a higher level of intelligence and energy, and we can manifest it in our behavior in treating each other as if they had it, too—you're not the only one, you know." As he gradually learned more and more about the Protestant/Catholic Schism and its attendant bloodshed and discord, R. G. became disenchanted with the Church. "And that's when I began to say, 'I can't go Catholic, or Protestant, or Methodist, or Baptist. They're all sayin', 'The Methodists are goin' to hell because they don't salve 'em or baptize 'em"—This is where I grew up. I don't mean to be flip, but that's kind of the way it was...

"But, finally, I had this kind of secret thing, to go out and live the way I thought, regardless of any church or any religion, to live the way I felt it, and take the lumps. By goin' into honky-tonks with my brother, for one thing, when he invited me. And he was the one that got me goin' around with him, and I saw that he was gonna kill himself, the way he was drivin'. And did end up in the river." His older brother drowned during a car accident at age fifty-four.

"He's the one that started livin' kinda like I wanted to live with, because mama was saying he was lost and going to hell, because of the way he was living, drinking and running around. And I started runnin' around with him, because my brother asked me to. And I figured, if I'm gonna start livin' that way, I might as well start with my brother. I really thought that. And I almost got killed in two or three wrecks, and knife stabbin's, and pistols, and runnin' in-between him and a guy drawin' a pistol, and turnin' him around, and tryin' to get in front of him. That even happened one night in a honky-tonk. He charged a guy that drew a pistol on him, and I leaped up and caught him and turned him around—he was gonna be killed himself. I was there that night. See, I was there a couple of times that I thought I was gonna get killed, in a car, where he was drivin' down there and scrapin' trees with his fender just for the hell of it. He was a good driver. Women screamin'—he had three couples, six people, were in the car, all screamin', on the floor, prayin', and everything else. And him laughin' and beatin' the steering wheel. I said, 'He's crazy. I've got to die with him.' They weren't ready to die with him, see. And when he stopped, and slammed on the brakes, they all just got out of the car, and scattered like chickens from it. And I sat in the back and didn't get out. And he said, 'Ain't you gonna get out of the car, you yellow bastard?' And

I said, 'No.' And he said, 'Close the door then, boy.' And he started that '38 V-8 and just went down the road fast as he could, dirt road on the river, scrapin' trees till he got tired of it. And I said, 'I might as well get ready for when he wrecks. He's gonna drive it into a tree or somethin'.'

"He just stopped, and went back, docile as could be, and they got back in and we went home. I said, 'This is insane.' That was only one of the first times I ever went out with him. And from then on, I went the way of the world, according to my mother, just to be with him. I found out that's where you've gotta go: out among people. Out among people who are killin' themselves, and killing each other. Two or three of the people that I grew up with were killed, shot, killed in wrecks. Actually, they grew up and went wild, so to speak. In this real country village where I grew up in Alabama. I risked all that, came through it. And I put all that in every character I could, one way or another, that life I've lived."

One unforgettable incident from R. G.'s late teens worked its way into the 1960 film ***The Fugitive Kind,*** directed by Sidney Lumet and starring Marlon Brando. "Well, this was one of the bad boys, kind of, of the community, in Concord—Porter Gamble was his name, I'll never forget. His daddy was an operator in the mill where daddy worked. That's how I got to know him. And Porter was one of his wild sons. Porter had a good brother, too. [Porter] was a wild drunk and just hilarious, and wanted to have a great life, and have a good time. He had a personality, whereas the other guy was withdrawn, kind of, kind of a good boy. Well, anyway, Porter comes along one day and says, 'Let's go hoboin' down,' and see a friend that had just moved out of the community we all knew, and invited us down to stay with him. And we'd go catch fish for so many pennies a fish for bait, bait fishing, out of Tampa Bay, that area down in there. For some crazy reason, I went with him. I don't know how in the world to explain what it was. It was like my brother when I first went away with him to the river. This was another wild dude—fights, Porter had all kinds of fights, but had a good personality and he liked me, for some reason. So we went up to Birmingham, hoboing. I said, 'How are we going hoboing?' And he said, 'Let's ride in style. Let's catch a passenger train.' We went up there. First, we were going to visit my kinfolks in the Tennessee mountains. I said, 'Let's go up there, and we can spend [the night]', and so forth. I'd been wantin' to go up there. And he said, 'Ahhh, let's go.' So we came out at this big train station. We were gonna hobo a passenger train. There was a train that was goin' to Chattanooga, that was goin' up in to where my kinfolk lived, in the mountains, in Knoxville and up in there. And my mother came from Northern Tennessee. And when we were standin' there at 34th Street, where it had to slow down, where we were gonna catch the train—Where the train hit 34th Street out of Birmingham, going east, is where the trains and the tracks came along, one of them curved, broke off into Chattanooga, and the other to Atlanta. And, all at once, here come two trains, and we didn't know which one was which. We just hoboed the first one that slowed down, a passenger, we got right up behind the engine in the coal car, and just sat there. And it slowed down and then took off—'Woooo-Woooo!' All the way to Atlanta. By the time we got to Atlanta, we got off and walked to the station and looked for a train. Because these people lived in St. Petersburg and we were goin' to Tampa. And we decided we've got to catch a train down to Jacksonville, Florida. And that's the same way: we got on the train and went down to Jacksonville on one of these passenger trains. We were goin' in style. Up in the front, we were getting dirty. Then, finally, the conductor took mercy on us and said, 'Come on and sit in here, boys.' We went in and he said, 'Better not ride these again.'

"And in Jacksonville, we caught a passenger train. In Wildwood, Florida, the train slowed down. They'd already called ahead, 'We've got two of these guys hoboin'.' And that's why they were slowin' down purposefully, we thought. And in Wildwood, we jumped off and there were two of these big police. But they weren't dressed like police, they were like train policemen. And they grabbed us. And said, 'Alright, boys, we've got you.' And they took us over to this jail, little four-by-four jail, and threw us in there. They said, 'Stay there. We'll tell you what we're gonna do with you.' So, we waited about three or four hours. And, man, we were getting hungry. Then, they came and unlocked it—it was a real prison, steel bars and everything. We were just sittin' in there by ourselves, nobody else was in there. Four-by-four jail, four cells. So, he said, 'Come on over here, boys.' And he took us over to a restaurant and bought us a meal. He said, 'You all must be hungry.' We were starvin'! And he took us over on the road—this policeman in a police car—and let us out. On the road. He didn't mind us hitchhiking on the road. But he said, as he stood there before he got back in the car, and we were standin' there like two…We were bums, was what we were! Not-too-well looking, in a dirty kind of…But, anyway, he says, [in a gravelly voice] 'You boys see that railroad track over there?' 'Yes, sir.' 'You boys see that train over there?' There was a little passenger train or freight train that was changing cars or something, there in Wildwood, Florida. He said, 'Don't you ever'—I'll never forget how he said it—'Don't you EVER let me catch you on that train again. 'Cause if I do, I'm gonna put you *under* that jail. You got me, boys?' We said, 'Yes, sir, yes, sir.' 'All right, now. Ya'll get walkin' right down that road, and don't let me ever catch you in this town again.' I said, 'Yes, sir.' We started runnin' down the road, just to get away from him. Then, that's the way we caught rides hitchhiking. We hitched a ride with a drunk guy who was weavin' around, goin' every which way. We didn't know what we'd got into. 'Cause we were sort of on a tour, and he was out, wild, havin' fun drivin', and I thought we were gonna have a wreck before we ever stopped and got out of there.

"Somehow or another, we were able to catch another ride. We got into St. Petersburg, and we were starvin' to death. And we went up and slept under some stairs. We spent the night there—we were just dead. We were sort of hidden under some enclosed stairways to somethin'. And the next morning, we woke up, and there sat two big bottles of milk. The milkman had already come around. Man, we got those two bottles, he took one and I took one. And we took off away from there and drank that milk. We were *starvin'*. Actually stole it. I didn't like the idea of stealin'. But we actually went into a restaurant. I said, 'I'm not going to *beg* for something to eat, Porter.' And he said, 'Oh, I will, I'll beg. I'll ask for somethin'.' And we went into this one, and just this woman was there. And he started to beggin' her for somethin' to eat, and she said, 'You boys get out of here, you bums! GET OUT!' And we just turned and walked out like we were miserable specimens, the way she talked to us. It was awful. Wouldn't even give us a crumb. Then Porter asked for somethin' more, then said 'Just give us a piece of bread or somethin', lady!' And she said, 'Get out of here! You bums, you lice...' She didn't 'cuss, but she [said], 'Lousy bums,' you know. We felt like the lowest specimens. I did, I felt really bad to be run out of a restaurant. Porter didn't seem to mind too much, 'cause he'd had more experience in the world than I had."

Years later, R. G. convinced Sidney Lumet to let him use those memories of that Florida sheriff for a scene in **The Fugitive Kind.** He even used the sheriff's line about putting them "under" the jail, not in it. "Yeah. Oh, absolutely. Just the way that sheriff talked to us was the way I talked to [Marlon] Brando. Even the same kind of tone, very nice, but deadly. It really came in good stead, that experience in life, when I had to walk Brando down the street and talk to him. And I wasn't intimidated because I became that sheriff. I knew exactly how he acted and talked. Like a father to us."

Around that time, R. G. became friends with an unknown local actor and singer, Andy Griffith. "After I got my Master's in 1948, I taught a year at the University extension, English literature, freshman English, foreign language, Spanish. I didn't want to be a teacher. I wanted to be a writer, and I was getting close to thirty and I vowed I'd write a novel by that time. So I went to a friend's farm and worked and wrote a novel. It took eighteen months, plus working on the farm, plus living with a family, close friends. And writing that took...I had to sacrifice money and salary and everything to do that, you know, to be a writer.

"I was struggling to be a writer. And I went to New York in 1952 to see if I could get this novel published, and started reading plays around potential backers and got my novel in to an agent. But none of that paid off. I started getting jobs to be an actor, which I had to adjust to being after I got in the Actor's Studio in New York in 1952." When Rip Torn auditioned for the Actor's Studio, R. G. coached him with his audition monologue, a piece from "The Grapes of Wrath."

Though R. G. appeared in two of the first productions of Tennessee Williams's plays, he barely knew the playwright himself. "Well, Tennessee was very nice to me, kind, in terms of...I'm tryin' to remember a scene...I was sitting in a bar or something in Philadelphia, before [the play we were doing] went out on the road. I think it was either **Cat on a Hot Tin Roof** or **Orpheus Descending.** And he was sitting over in the booth. And he said—he had a high kind of voice— [Imitating Williams] 'You don't have to sit over there, Bob. Come over here and sit with us.' And he was sitting there with his friend, Frank Murlow. I was in one of his plays that was being tried, I think I might have been playing a sheriff—I don't know. And we got to talking, and he ordered me up a drink. And he started writing something, down on a piece [of paper], and signed it 'Tennessee,' and shoved it over to me." The author had drawn a caricature of R. G. on a coaster, and written "Bob Strongarm" below it. "And I took it, and I felt like I'd been honored with something. Because it was like he complimented me. And [Williams' partner] Frank Murlow, they both liked me. And I'd have to really go back in my memory to figure out that little conversation I had with Tennessee. That was about the only contact that I had with him.

"To me, Tennessee was one of the geniuses of the theater and play-writin'. And, at that time, I wanted to be a dramatist. I thought that he was more of a dramatic poet than Arthur Miller. Arthur Miller was a good playwright and all. Tennessee, to me, had more of the language, had characterization down. Actors love to play him [Williams's plays]. I found out actors, and myself, love to play [his works], 'cause I played Big Daddy forty-one times on Broadway when Burl Ives was out. [Normally] I played Doc Baugh, a small part. But that was like a major role while it was still a hit play. That was one of the biggest breaks I'd ever had. I got an agent out of his seein' me do Big Daddy."

While playing that now-classic part one evening, R. G. had one of his most profound experiences as an actor. He realized what every actor worth his salt should be striving for: to utterly fill the theater with his presence. "Oh, yeah. I was playin' Big Daddy that night, as a matter of fact. They had a raked stage. It was, like, slanted and then came to a point. And Ben Gazzara was over here, and I was cussin' him out, 'cause he was drinkin' himself to death over there. When Rip Torn was playin' it, Leo Penn played it, I've played it with all of 'em, got a chance to play it, when they played Brick and I played Big Daddy. And I was tellin' him about '25,000 acres'—I'd always turn to the audience when I said that— 'You've got 25,000 acres of the richest land, as far back as the Valley Nile up to here,' or whatever that was. And as I turned to the audience—I had never noticed this before and I had done this part before—I noticed a shadow was up this side of the audience, and I looked while I was talkin' to him, whatever the dialogue was. I saw that it was my legs. One of my legs was on this side, my torso was on the balcony, and my other leg was on that side of the audience—it was divided by an aisle up the middle. And my head up on the ceiling, like a giant shadow of me. And it so inspired me, I tried to fill that giant shadow. It infused me with how Big Daddy was talkin' to his son, about, 'Son, you've got the WHOLE WORLD I've built here for you!' And there was me, and that filled me with an emotion enough to fill that shadow to tell him about…I was far enough along that you use things as an actor, as they hit you. And it transformed me.

"I was there, working, playing Doc Baugh. Burl Ives was playing Big Daddy, and I was standing right close to him. And Big Daddy jerked the crutch away from Brick and said, 'Gimme that crutch! Stand up!' And he lost control of it and went down off the stage and down into the first level, down there where the audience was. And I thought, 'What is he gonna do now?' And Burl Ives went right over to somebody and said, 'GIMME THAT CRUTCH!' [laughs] I mean, the person got up out of his seat like was commandin' him and went up and got the crutch and handed it back to Burl! I said, 'Wow!' That's how, if somethin' happens, you carry it on through like that. And that was a lesson to me. He was Big Daddy tellin' that person to give him that crutch. And the person was so into it he said, 'Yeah, Big Daddy, here it is!' [laughs]"

R. G and John Barrymore, Jr.

He began acting in feature films in 1957. "The first one I recognize would be ***Never Love a Stranger.*** Steve McQueen was in it, John Barrymore, Jr. Harold Robbins wrote it, wrote it from his novel and produced it. Steve McQueen was unknown then. He was from an abused home, he was raised in juvenile delinquency homes, you know. He had an attitude, a chip on his shoulder, but he and I liked one another and got along. I recognized he was a good actor, but I also recognized he was in a whole... What had become a school of acting was—you don't act, you be it. So he was part of that school. Marlon Brando and a whole bunch of people in [the] New York Actor's Studio, which I fell in love with as part of my training in New York. That is, I call it training, going making the rounds just to see if I could get a job to help support myself, while I'd see if my novel was going to be accepted. It kept going from publisher to publisher and never got published. And I had fourteen submissions, you know. By that time, I was already involved heavily in acting. That is, getting the part out of this, out of this work group [that] Lee Strasberg, Ben Gazzara were part of, and did scenes.

"Actually, plays emerged from that group and were done on Broadway. ***End As a Man***, based on a Calder Willingham novel, was our first play on Broadway. I played the general in it. Yeah, that's way back there in 1954 or '53, I think. Ben Gazzara made a big hit as a psychotic killer of some kind [laughs], or a psychotic personality. Calder's a good writer, by the way." Willingham later became well known as a screenwriter, as well, on films like Stanley Kubrick's ***Paths of Glory*** (1957) and Arthur Penn's ***Little Big Man*** (1970).

One of R. G.'s earliest credits was Excelsior Pictures' nudist camp epic, ***Garden of Eden*** (1957). "Well, that was a nudist film. I don't know what kind of release it got, but Walter Bibo produced it. And the secretary of the studio called me up, and I hadn't done any acting by that time, except on Broadway. In film, I hadn't thought about doing movies, and she said, 'There's a part open in this picture that's going to be shooting in Florida if you want it. Fred Stuart dropped out.' He was in Actor's Studio, and so I said, 'Well, I'll go up and see about it.' So they gave it to me. There wasn't any question. I hadn't read the script, and it was $250 a week and it'd be two weeks. And I thought that was the biggest money I'd ever made. And so, we were to leave, I forget, the next day or two, going to Tampa, and I didn't know why or anything. They didn't tell me anything. When I got home, I was reading it, back at the apartment. I read about five pages, and it dawned, 'That can't be so. That can't be,' I said. And, finally, I looked. Those people are all naked, you know. This is a nudist colony, but it was a pretty good part, and my curiosity as a writer got the best of me, in one sense. I wanted to see what a nudist colony was really like, that it really existed, I mean. If they really carried this kind of process out. I never seen it, so I took the part. And in two days, I was down there in Tampa, Florida. It looked like a paradise place, you know, it was like an exclusive, rich club.

"A lake, trees, and orange trees, buildings, and people living…sort of up when they had breakfast communally. Only I was shocked everybody's walking around naked. Nude, you know? And it was being supervised by the Sunbather's Association of America, a national organization for nudist people in May's Landing, New Jersey, and I met them and talked to them. So it became an experience of being my first movie, and I don't like to tell people, generally speaking, 'cause the gimmick was it was the first nudist movie in color. I didn't know if it would even get out. So the very next year, I made **Never Love a Stranger.**

From Hell To Texas (1958) was a Henry Hathaway western in color and Cinemascope, co-starring a very young Dennis Hopper. "I was called to screen test for the movie, and that was out of the blue. The agent said, 'I want to represent you,' and she had something for me. They flew me out in 1957, October, to meet the people and have a screen test. This agent I was supposed to be attached to was attached to the agent in New York, which was upsetting me, drove me up to Twenty Century-Fox, and then to the office, and then to meet Henry Hathaway, and I was so scared I was shaking. I mean, that's an eight-hour trip. I wanted to get some coffee and settle down, but I was whisked right into that room, and there sat the writer and Henry Hathaway, chewing his little, short, stubby cigar. And he looked at me, and looked at me, and called in Don Murray. We got to talking, and, Don, he's from Virginia. And I said, 'Good, 'cause he's from the South, maybe I'll have a chance.' I felt I had an ally, because he was from the South.

"I didn't know anything that was happening behind-the-scenes. And, suddenly, Henry Hathaway looked at me and said, 'Hey, I believe you've got it, son. Go over there and get into wardrobe.' And there I was, in four days, ridin' a horse, galloping a hundred yards. Of course, I was from a farm and familiar with animals, and they didn't intimidate me. So I had to learn how to ride well. They did turn me out for lessons. We shot that up in Bishop out in California and the director was of the old time, but he was good at it, stationary cameras. He had a different way, instead of roving cameras around, you know, and I was scared to death, in a sense. I'd been on Broadway and so forth, but the movies was another whole scene, and [there was] the intimidation factor. It wasn't the type of direction I'd experienced in New York. He was one of the hardest directors in Hollywood. He was chewing a cigar, and he was yelling at everything, you know. But, as a matter of fact, I always felt that worked good for me, 'cause I showed a repressed nature. It came through. I was repressed, having to talk and everything. He was a good director, but I found out they all have a different style. But I couldn't believe my good luck. Eight weeks there, with this kind of salary. Just like out of the blue, things were just happening, moving me right along into something.

"It was a way to make money better than teaching. That paid the bills. Not only that, I was into writing. I was into O'Neill, and I got the [good] fortune to be in Tennessee Williams' plays on Broadway. Most of the movies, I didn't like. I was doin' my westerns, you know. I had to break all that artistic integrity up in Hollywood, make a living at acting. If you become a star, you sort of pick your own roles. But other actors have to sort of take what they can get and fight for the best, you know. It's a psychological fight, and you go crazy out here between jobs and stuff like that, 'cause I refuse to sign a contract. That was another problem out here. They want to own you. And they do want you to sign a contract. Till you get out of it, you do what they say."

One of Universal's premiere science fiction directors, Jack Arnold (**_Creature From the Black Lagoon_**, **_Tarantula_**) directed R. G. in **_No Name on the Bullet_** (1959), starring Audie Murphy. "I knew Jack. I'd worked with him before. He was like a studio director. I mean, he could really turn it out on time and the film in, and he wouldn't go overtime, you know, and a terrific presence on the set.

'Come on, guys, now let's get it goin'!' I liked working with him. He was different that Henry Hathaway in terms of his personality. He was friendly, talked to you right. Henry didn't know how to talk to actors, [was] the way I felt about it. The experience was working with Audie Murphy. I mean, I heard about him being the number one World War most-decorated war veteran, see. I related to him. He had a quietness about him that really made you be curious. You know he could explode. He walked around very nice, very polite. It was fascinating for me to be working with an actor who had been a war hero, from my minor perspective at that time. And seeing him the way he was acting, and the whole nervous tension that he caused, caused until finally the real killer showed himself.

"I got a kick out of it. Well, the thing about the movie was in learning about Hollywood and what to do. The scene in the blacksmith's shop that Jack wanted me to do, he says, 'Take that anvil,' which seemed about three hundred pounds, something like that. And it looked real as hell, and I thought, 'That's it,' you know. It didn't even enter my mind it was fake. And so, when we rehearsed, his character crossed the scene and set it down over there while I was talking, doing the scene, and I picked it up, and I almost fell backwards because it was light. So, I say, 'Hey, can't we have a real anvil here? I mean, 'cause this is light.' I realized, out here, you don't ask for things like that, you know. Jack looked and said, 'You mean, you can lift an anvil? A real anvil?' I said, 'Yeah, I worked at the mill driving 250-pound kegs around and stuff.' And, anyway, they put a real anvil down there, and when I picked it up, I had to carry through. I struggled and carried it like my daddy said he carried big bales of wire in the wire mill, and just sort of…waddled over, set it down and stopped, and got through with the scene. I said, 'All right, Jack, you were right. It's too heavy to do a scene with.' But when you see that scene, I had that real anvil going across there. You work with props and learn how to make them seem heavy. I couldn't get the real things all the times that I wanted, and I had to adjust to that. That was a big adjustment. That doesn't bother me at all now, you know. But that's like being trained into something."

R. G. made several appearances on **Alfred Hitchcock Presents**. "I did five **Alfred Hitchcocks**. The one I remember ["What Frightened You, Fred?" (1962)] real good is the one I did with Ed Asner, where I was a convict who did real good in prison. And the warden, Ed Asner, let me go, and said, 'I know he'll make it good.' And I get out and look up my old girlfriend, and then I got the call she was underground. Really means the mob, that whole kind of business, the way Hitchcock was establishing it. I didn't get to work with Hitchcock personally, but I worked with Paul Henreid, he was an actor turned director. Anyway, that whole feeling of getting to play a lead role of a convict like that began to appeal to me.

"I began to get parts that I enjoyed. The psychology of those kind of roles were very rewarding for me. Another one I did ["Final Vow" (1962)], I played a rich guy who was the fence that Carol Lynley…And the nuns, something was stolen from the nuns, a sacred statue. And she had to come out and try to find it, and I was the one who was fencing it, the power behind it all. So all of those things were helping me adjusting to my fate as an actor out here, [if you] like to put it that way. Working with Hitchcock.

"In the early '60's, I began to find somebody like Sam Peckinpah. I began to see that they were real artists under the challenge of working with limited money, limited script, and having to do it and trying to work through until you get something good. Maybe out of ten, you get one real good one. So this is the kind of fate I began to adjust to and accept, and it helped me to make peace with my whole life."

Ride the High Country (1962) marked R. G.'s first role in a Sam Peckinpah movie; it was only Peckinpah's second feature. He played Joshua Knudson, a hard-line Fundamentalist who lives on a secluded farm with his sheltered daughter, Elsa (Mariette Hartley). "Well, it wasn't the first thing [I did with him]. I did *The Rifleman*, the pilot film for *The Rifleman* [which originally aired on *Dick Powell's The Zane Grey Theatre*.] I played the sheriff, and Sam Peckinpah created the series. Wrote it, with the provision he could get a chance to direct some of the episodes. And I didn't want to do it, and my agent tried to talk me into it. Yeah, I'm turning down a half a million dollars or so of money. I'm not stupid. That is…I'm still thinking I don't want to be typed in westerns. And so, I turned it down. They said they've got to kill you off then. The fourth episode, they killed me off, and brought in the young director, and then is when I found out that Sam Peckinpah had written *The Rifleman*. And when I got through, he came and he told me, 'I'm gonna get a stock company, like John Ford.' He says, 'I want you in everything I direct.' And that almost happened. I did four, five things [with him].

"I didn't want to take the part [in *High Country*], but I did, you know. The fact is, Sam Peckinpah saw me as a self-righteous, religious figure who carried shotguns and could kill. But trying to be good, but it's dangerous, and that's the kind of part he wanted me to project in that father of Mariette Hartley. The big bonus for me was to work with Randolph Scott and Joel McCrea, 'cause I'd seen them as a kid in movies. And here I am, seeing them and how they act and relating to them and relating to Mariette Hartley, who's just beginning. And [Peckinpah was] sending me into these religious dialogues with Joel McCrea, and having me try to manifest this incestuous relationship with his daughter, without injuring my religious principles. I was totally dominating her, and when I had to slap her, and when she had to slap me, we were practicing outside. She said, 'I can't hit you hard.' I said, 'Go ahead and let go. Make it real, go ahead and slap me. Not try to do what stunt guys do.' Anyway, I went in, and when she slapped me, it stunned me in the scene. It fired me up to some kind of reality that I did the rest of the scene walking around quoting the scriptures with an experience I never had, that strong in front of the camera, which I began to realize is what actors are supposed to be doing—living it. Experiencing it for real. And that's what I began to learn in Hollywood, that this was a chance for me to experience it for real, whatever it's in, in a creative effort if you can repeat and do it. You were there, you were doing it. I began to accept movies and television shows to practice doing that, 'cause I realized that I'd been acting general emotions, and that you could actually trigger yourself to really experience something. And that's a bonus for you, yourself, in doing a scene, 'cause you feel like you're not quite giving it the depth and dimension you have for that."

Major Dundee (1965) was Peckinpah's post-Civil War epic, starring Charlton Heston, Richard Harris, James Coburn, and an enormous cast of character people that included L. Q. Jones. It was badly truncated by producer Jerry Bresler. "It made sense, at that time, and structures and everything. It was just beautiful, and *Major Dundee* was to be Sam Peckinpah's epic. Oscar Saul worked on it, and I read the script. I called and told him, 'This is like *Moby Dick* in the desert.' And he said, 'You son of a bitch—you and Oscar Saul are the only ones who recognized that,' you know, that he's capable of adapting…ideas and major things like *Moby Dick* into a whole run of things, in another setting, another character and all. Good writers can do that, and so it was with great eagerness I went down [to film in Mexico]. Four different costumes, four different kinds of boots—they were prepared to be there a long time. Three months it turned out to be, and when we landed in Durango, it was like landing in another land.

"Let's put it this way: we landed in Torreon, and Richard Harris was on the plane, Charlton Heston, and all. We got off to stretch, catch another smaller plane up in the mountains of Durango. And here was one of those mariachi bands, and that sound of Mexico hit us. And we stopped off the plane, and it was exciting, like entering fantasyland. I might as well have entered down like Alice in Wonderland, going down the hole into another world, when I got out of that door of that plane and stepped down and around and smelled the country. And there's the Mexican population all around, gathered to see these stars coming in. I was part of the party, you know, and then that feeling never left me that I was experiencing another whole world for the first time. And that the music constantly followed us. When we got to Durango, in parties, they have a mariachi band, or just two or three [musicians], you know what I mean?

"Everywhere was that whole feeling that Sam had become like our guide explorer, which was really the way we felt, and then we got ready for anything, almost. We was ready to go out and ride down that creek and come close [to participating in the real thing]. The closest thing I've ever seen was riding down the Tuxtla River, and there's real Yaqui Indians they hired coming down there to charge us, the Army brigade that Charlton Heston was leading into this foot water piece of river and holes, potholes, and Yaqui Indians they had stationed up in the trees. And I'm on the back of my horse, and they're startin' to yellin', and this is not damn acting: this is real. I mean, my horse started rearing, and I'm holding on to the horn of the saddle and I'm shooting up into the trees. The shotgun was [in] sort of weird positioning—BAM!—and you see the Indian fall out of the tree. And [firing] the full blanks of the shotgun is not easy, you know. The gun will go off on you.

"Anyway, my horse was rearing around. And a stunt guy rode by, Chuck Hayward—I'll never forget his name—and said, 'R. G., R. G., that's old Rosie, she's a rearing horse, you're giving her the signal to rear. Do the lines this way.' And I did, and she settled down, and I had no problem. And nobody warned me that this was a rearing horse, and I'm a son of a bitch, I could have been thrown in the river and trampled and everything. I was hangin' on that saddle for dear life, let's put it that way. By the time we got to another scene in the river, near the end, we had all lost about fifteen pounds, worn out two, three wardrobes, and I'd worn out three pairs of boots. And laying on the banks of these rivers, and turning rocks over for scorpions, and the nights and the smells. And it was like I'd been taken to the land of…danger. And, yet, tremendous, paradise-like kind of conditions. These trees, and little shady streets, river running, rushing through the night, and things like this.

"All of that was like this was not making movies, this to me was a way to live, do you know what I mean? I mean, I couldn't tell you how…to have the experience of transcending acting. Being this character in this safari across Mexico. At several different places, really being close to death. Like, in one place, we went out one night and I saw one guy and two guys come in to get him, and took him and drug him. They went out and he shot them both before they could turn around and shoot him. Right outside the window, I mean on the set, one of the people who was working on the set came in and caught his wife with another of 'em, and shot him. All this was happening in and around the making of the film. It was something you just don't experience very much when making films. A whole other world, Sam Peckinpah set that for you. Like many other directors wouldn't."

The film had around forty-five minutes cut out of it. "I knew Jerry Bresler. He was Mickey Mouse. Here the stuff was going on, and he was flyin' over to Acapulco and directing Lana Turner and Cliff Robertson in some little 'ol love epic [*Love Has Many Faces* (1965)]. And that is way we all felt, and Sam was glad to get rid of him. And he came back, finally, in a week or two. They said Sam was gonna be replaced. And [we] said, 'Hell, we're all gonna quit. To hell with that son of a bitch.' And, suddenly, all the nice guys around, he has never been somebody who was a head guy, and has come down to relieve Sam. And we found out all these things going on, and Charlton knew what we were gonna do. And [Heston] heard that and walked in and says, 'Look if you're gonna fire Sam, you've got to give this man a chance. He's really good. I like his work and I'll give you back my salary, and you keep Sam, you understand? Otherwise, we're all gonna quit and take the consequences. We're behind Sam.' And so, they backed down. Then we knew we were working with the real article in Hollywood to get that done, and Charlton Heston gave back his close to half a million salary. And we went on and got ours.

"And we were renewed to die for an artist, and for this we went on for three months. And one of the breaks in it was Sam Peckinpah was gonna be given the...Mexico's Academy Awards down there, comparable to the Oscars here, were being given, and they were giving Sam Peckinpah the Best Foreign Film in Mexico to him while he's down there.

"So he said, 'I want all the guys in *Ride the High Country* to come up and accept it with me.' So they had tuxedos laid out for us. We came down, waddled up to the hotel where the award was being given, walked in there, and there was just all the luminaries of Mexican film on award night. And when they called Sam up to give him the best foreign film of the year, we were all sittin' there at the table in our tuxedos, looking silly at him. And so we all got up, and he said, 'I'm not going to accept the award unless my boys are up here with me.' So we got up and walked up and stood there with him while he accepted the award, you know, Warren Oates, L. Q. Jones, and me.

"That was all part of us getting behind a real artist. That made Hollywood palatable: for me to get, every once in a while, a film where a real artist can work and they let him at least get some of this done. And then to see a Jerry Bresler do that, take out the wonderful music, the transitional moods and transitional scenes that made sense out of things. And cut out 'Laura Lee,' that old Civil War ballad that was sung by Brock Peters and [backed with a] harmonica. And that crashing military music [by Daniel Amfitheatrof] wasn't right for that movie. When we first saw it, Sam stomped out, mad as hell. He really wanted to shoot Bresler, and wanted to take his name off the film, and we all felt down. We went with great expectations, and felt down. What have they done to this movie? They chopped it up. There were transitional, stitching things between scenes, which were very important to go from one to the other to open up, keep opening up. The actors got in with him, Peckinpah. They robbed him of making a terrific epic."

He went on to make several movies with one of the finest actors from Peckinpah's repertory company, Warren Oates. "Warren Oates was from Kentucky. We had to room in the same apartment, kind of like two rooms in a motel kind of thing. We were on that film that Sam Peckinpah shot on *The Rifleman*. Warren Oates was one of the guys that I watched grow and get more confident [as an actor], and until he did *Bring Me the Head of Alfredo Garcia* (1974), of Sam Peckinpah. [Oates imitated Sam Peckinpah in his role as Bennie, the piano player, in *Alfredo Garcia*.] He had all these little things goin', like I play my daddy. I played my daddy in a lot of films. I did, 'cause I could do that. But, anyway, Warren Oates was, to me, like a country boy making good, like a friend of mine, Andy Griffith, did. That is, he's growing and he was getting more confident. It wasn't the fact they underestimated him at first. The fact is he was given a chance to grow. So this is what I shared...like a brother. He was like a brother in Hollywood. Like a brother [or] comrade, coming out of the country and out of the South, working out here, like our dream was fulfilled. My God, we both got lucky, didn't we?

R. G. was in Peckinpah's television production of Katherine Anne Porter's masterful novella **Noon Wine**. He didn't appear in either of Peckinpah's next two films, though, either the aborted **Cincinnati Kid** (1966) or **The Wild Bunch** (1969). "Oh, yeah, that [**Wild Bunch**] was a classic film. People, they sort of remember I was in it, anyway. They just assume, 'cause I did four or five pictures with him. Peckinpah didn't call me for that. I had turned down **The Cincinnati Kid**. He wanted me to do the father of Tuesday Weld and Steve McQueen, when they were running...Just one scene, and I turned it down. And it pissed him off. However, he was fired from that picture, and this good director Norman Jewison took over. And I would have stayed in it, even if I had taken the part. But I called him. He told me he'd read a screenplay I'd written and he was in production on **The Wild Bunch**. And I called him, and he came to the phone. I couldn't believe it, and the first thing he said to me, he says, 'You wouldn't work for me, would you, you son of a bitch?' I said, 'Sam, that wasn't a big part.' He said, 'Oh, screw you. You just don't know structure. That was an important role,' and we went on about that. And he says, 'Alright, you send that goddang script down here and I'll read it. But don't you ever turn me down again, you son of a bitch.' This was the way he'd talk to me, so when he offered **Pat Garrett**, I said, 'Okay, okay,' you know. **The Wild Bunch**, I could have been in it, and that's just my fate about a lot of things. **The Wild Bunch**, that was a hell of film. I think Sam was a great director."

Over the past forty years, R. G. has acted in nearly a dozen films with L. Q. Jones. In fact, L. Q.'s character, Dakota, does a very unflattering (and excruciatingly funny) imitation of R. G.'s character in **Lone Wolf McQuade** (1983). "He's the only one I know who could talk to Sam Peckinpah on the set. 'All right, Sam, let's get this piece of shit on the road. What do you think you're gonna do? Make a masterpiece on this kind of budget and script?' He would talk that way to Sam. I'd look around and then say, 'My God,' and Sam would take it. Nobody else would dare do that. They had a weird kind of relationship, and it was great. He and Warren Oates were buddies. Peckinpah and Warren were buddies, and they'd go hunting and go off, whatever. They were all buddies, but L. Q. had a little different niche...as I did, in terms of Sam, and we each had a part to play. L. Q. could do that, and get away with it, and Sam wouldn't let anybody else do that. He'd say, 'Get the fuck off my set—you're all fired.' Really. And they were, twenty of them."

R. G. made a biker movie for New World, **Angels Die Hard!** (1970), directed by Richard Compton, co-starring biker movie king William Smith and William Baker. "I got involved in that one because of my agent, who had put up money in that. And that was the first cheap-budget movie I did, and it was a motorcycle movie. I'd never done anything like that, a motorcycle movie. And there were friends of mine in it, Bill Smith. We were actor buddies and also worked out in a gym together many years ago when we first came out here. Well, not buddies. On the set—I'd never see him personally. Most actors' acquaintances are on sets. So I just went out and did it because they took a friend of mine on, and gave him a job. We went up to Kernville, in the little town of Kernville. It was fun. Every set has been fun to me, but it was done a shoestring basis. And it was the only movie I was able to get any deal to where they would give me a percentage of the gross."

During the early '70s, tv westerns waned in popularity and began gradually to disappear from the airwaves. "Well, I was ambivalent. It was like, I'm sick of doing those, you know. The opportunity and what you might say...classroom, where I could learn how to act, I used that for exercise. I needed to get the practice to get, in a sense, diminished self-consciousness, which it did. Once you do something like that over and over and over, pretty soon, you feel like you go on and you don't worry about that self-consciousness of being an actor. You just get freer in front of the camera."

Director Philip (*The Right Stuff*) Kaufman's *The Great Northfield, Minnesota Raid* (1972) was a revisionist version of the story of Frank and Jesse James. It co-starred Robert Duvall, Cliff Robertson, Elisha Cook, Luke Askew, and Royal Dano, among many others. "They re-did a town, and made a western set out of it. And it was my chance to work with Phil Kaufman. I really trusted him. I felt my trust was correct, because I think he's one of the top poets with the camera and making movies out here. He's a poet. I mean, his sensitivities and his sense of transitions, and his sense of things. Like that dance in the house of ill repute after the bath. We were sittin' there, and all that weird, old-time music was playing, and we were dancing around. It had set such a mood, that I hadn't seen or felt before. They were goin' out and do a job and get killed. It was almost like a dirge...Sending them out, into the unknown. And Phil Kaufman, we parted with him, and he did that movie with Warren Oates up around the North Pole [*The White Dawn*]. You know, he actually wrote the script for *The Outlaw Josey Wales*, and [Clint] Eastwood took it away from him after about two weeks and finished it himself. But he kept the film that Phil shot."

The Legend of Hillbilly John (1972) was an adaptation of writer Manly Wade Wellman's "Silver John" stories, about a traveling Appalachian minstrel with a silver-stringed guitar who constantly encounters the supernatural. It featured stop-motion animation by special effects great Gene Warren. "Yes! I just had an experience with that. I'd almost forgotten about it. Barney Rosenzweig produced that. His daughter was directing a *Biography* show. They were doing one on Andy Griffith, and they asked me to come in and be interviewed, because I put him in my play when he was about twenty-one years old, at the University of North Carolina. I chose him to do that. I saw the talent in my mind, you know.

"And that *Hillbilly John*, he produced that, and Alfred Ryder was in that. I remember we did that out in Concord, Arkansas. [It was a] Terrific attempt... It sort of failed commercially and all that, but it attempted to catch something in the South that has to do with mystical kind of things, people way back in the hills, the superstition that could be communicated through songs and influences on people that really exist down there. It did, which I got from my mother. She was from up in the Cumberland Mountains of Tennessee. Nelson Rockefeller's brother was the Governor of Arkansas, owned the big mountain out there. And we shot that on top of this mountain, overlooking the whole valley around. And I enjoyed doing that. Although it was a small part, it was a chance to go down in the South, and I like to go on location."

White Lightning was a drive-in classic, also shot down South, starring Burt Reynolds as Gator McKlusky. Bo Hopkins co-starred. "Burt, I've known for a good while out here, before he ever got goin' as a star and everything. Burt was like, to me, he wanted to do all the work, not all the parts, but all his work, the work, and everything. He got so involved in it. And I liked working with Burt. We were like kids working together. When I was working with him, I'd say, 'There's old Burt, there!' It became part of the character I was playing, the old white lightning guy. That's about the only time I really did work with him. I did one television show. We were down there five weeks or so, I think. And Burt, that was his first big grosser, started makin' money, being a star in that picture. He didn't make that money on ***Deliverance*** or become a star…But that's ***White Lightning***. Then he did a whole bunch of them after that, that character, Gator.

"We made that out of Little Rock [Arkansas]. Yeah, found a place, it looked like this little house that was in there with a bootlegger where I'm supposed to be living. They actually found this little abandoned house, way out in the country there. And the experience is there, you know. We were making a picture about white lightning.

"This guy was on the set, who was, like, well-to-do, kind of like a big rancher. He'd say, 'Let's go out, come on out in the truck, Let's have a drink.' It was hot and everything. I thought it was white lightning. He had a jug half-full of white lightning, like water. He also had a can of grapefruit juice we used. I don't drink that, but I drink it just to be sociable. But, boy, was that good stuff. I mean, in terms of homemade stuff. 'Cause I was raised out in Alabama, out in the sticks where, during the '20s, before prohibition was repealed, there were deacons of the church being sent to prison for a year. They were discovered making whiskey. It was hard times. You had to make a buck."

My Name is Nobody (1973) was a popular Sergio Leone spaghetti western. It starred spaghetti hero Terence Hill and Henry Fonda as rival gunfighters, and featured an Ennio Morricone score. "Yeah, well, it was a great trip over there, to Granada [Spain]. We shot out from Granada on a western set out there. It was a beautiful western set. Henry Fonda was in it. I got to meet Henry Fonda. We went out, in New Mexico, Silverton or Silver City or somewhere, and shot some of that stuff. And I got to know Sergio Leone pretty good, working with him. They had a director, but [Leone] was constantly interfering with that director. I didn't particularly like that. But, of course, it was his stuff.

"I had to drive a big wagon, which I think is four horses or something like that. And I pulled into a little narrow place, in to a barn-looking place, and, man, I'm not an expert, but I did that and drove it. Boy, I just made it perfect, and he came yelling up, Sergio, and said, 'You didn't go in far enough,' you know. But I thought I done a hell of a job, and I had to do that again, and it really kind of pissed me off. It was like…inconsideration. I'd done a hell of a job, for being an actor. Slim Pickens, now he could take six horses and drive a stagecoach. I saw him do it. There weren't many actors could do that."

In the early '70s, back in Los Angeles, R. G. became writing partners with the notorious pimp-cum-author, Iceberg Slim (*nee* Robert Beck). "I went to a party up on Mulholland Drive with a friend of mine, who is a black actor—I can't remember his name. We were havin' a pretty good time. He's married to an actress from Canada, this guy was. And in walked this guy, with this hat and dressed to the nines, and had this classic kind of Roman nose profile, and big eyes, and really dressed. And had a classic presentation about himself. And I said, [Whispers] 'Who is that?' 'Man, that's Iceberg Slim.' [laughs] And I said, 'Iceberg Slim—who is that?' He said, 'Why, he's the greatest pimp in the world. Didn't you ever hear of his book, *Pimp*?' One of the people up there handed me the book *Pimp* for me to read. I think he did, as a matter of fact, went out to his car and gave me a copy so that I could read it.

"When I started reading, I had no idea what a terrific writer he would be, and how good he really was. He had said that he had whipped that off in six weeks, because another person he had been talking to about his life and career was rippin' him off and tryin' to write it and get it out before him. And he went and he wrote it quick as he could and gave it to this publisher, who ripped him off, anyway. I don't think he got over $1,500 for the whole time with *Pimp*. It became a sensation underground. Kinda rough book, but it was really about a pimp, a real pimp.

"And he was invited to colleges and everything to speak, when he was really recognized. And he wrote the second book, which was *Trick Baby*, out of which the movie *The Sting* was adapted, and stolen from, in a sense. The two white people [with] a black con man teaching a white guy the con game. And then, [in] the movie, they made it Robert Redford and Paul Newman. And essentially kept to the story. And they didn't give him anything for that. They tried to get him to come out there and sign a contract at Universal. He told me this story, about the head of Universal. And he decided, 'No, I'll just go it alone and write my books,' and so forth, and so on. And he could've been under contract, but he turned it down. That's how much they thought of his writing, and his flair, and what he would mean commercially to them. And so they just sort of stole his books. I couldn't believe it when I saw how writers out here, when you get to know 'em, how they get ripped-off. They really do.

"I was at a party, and he actually invited me to come down to his place. He wanted me to collaborate with him in adapting this, I think, his next novel. I forget which one it was now. He lived down in Watts, right on the edge of Watts, in Compton. And I went down there for months and wrote two screenplays…He wanted to write a screenplay based on *Pimp*, that's the way it was. He said, 'Since you're in the movie business, and have written screenplays"—I told him I had written screenplays. I've written several screenplays and didn't get 'em done. And he read one of 'em, and he said, 'Would you help me adapt *Pimp* to a screenplay?' So that's the way it started. So I went down and started writing a screenplay to *Pimp*.

"He even got it optioned. It went around, but it was sort of rough trying to get a movie out of it, at that time, about a black pimp. It was the tenor of the times, kind of. Then, after we did that one, we worked so good together, writing scenes and developing the whole screenplay, 'cause I have a structure sense of a screenplay, he asked me to work with him adapting, I think it was the 'white con,' called *Trick Baby*.

"I helped him adapt two of his novels into screenplays. And it took three months or more, sometimes off and on, 'cause I couldn't get down there all the time to work on screenplays. One of the main things, to me, was, in writing, to see how brilliant he was. To see him improvise dialogue, to see his poetic, real sense of literary-ness—he wrote great, literary scenes. He could also write pimp talk and all that down in the low-level kind of 'street talk,' he called it. But he was really educated…Iceberg was a master of language. I don't know how he did it, but he said, 'I read everything in the damn libraries where I went, when I was in prison.'"

Beck, says R. G., was "*Very much* a gentleman. Eloquently spoken. He'd speak to you like a college professor. And he had huge black eyes. They could just rivet you, and almost hypnotize you. And he could laugh. He told me about how he used to, down in Watts, how the gangs would get around him and try to [pester him]…And how he had to talk himself out, and said, 'I'd just act like I was a poor old black man,' and did a little thing. In other words, he could talk the street talk, the rhythm. He even got down and did a little scene, the way he'd talk to 'em. It was a fantastic experience for me, just to have the experience to write with a person that long, and get to know a person from that element of life that I never had any chance to contact anybody who had really been, lived that kind of life. And did four terms in prison.

"To me, if I ever run into a genius, who had the ability to improvise dialogue right off the top of his head, and fluent in language, and narrative description, I'd be writing it down as fast as I could. I've got books around here, notebooks I've got here somewhere, where we'd dictate and write these plays. His wife typed 'em up. She wasn't that good of a typist, but she typed 'em up…

"Iceberg was very intelligent. As a matter of fact, I've been around college professors, and I've even got a Master's Degree, but he was one of the most intelligent people that I've ever been around."

Boss Nigger (1974) was a black western starring Fred Williamson and D'urville Martin; Jack Arnold directed. "They took away the word 'Nigger' [from the title]. When I was doing *Stay Hungry* (1976) with Bob Rafelson and [actor] Roger Mosley, I had a scene in that where I was doin' a number, peeping down on Sally Field. And I yelled out, and he opened the door on me and caught me,

Roger Mosley. And when I said, 'Get out of here, nigger,' Bob Rafelson stopped me and whispers, 'I don't want you to say 'nigger.'' I said, 'Why? It's what this guy would say, and I'm playin' the character.' He said that doesn't make any difference. He doesn't want too hear you say you are a Southerner, and something comes through. Other actors pronounce that 'nigra,' and all that. I said, 'That's the way they say it down here.' They got too many actors that don't know the South, go down there [and badly impersonate] Southern accents. It beats me.

"But Fred Williamson is like a real charming and charismatic personality, by the way. I'm not saying that much for his talent or anything. He's great, talking something so he can make money out of movies. He was very nice, and it was a trip to Santa Fe. It was during a troubled time for me, my wife leaving. I was really down and out. I'd given up everything I wanted to be on a film somewhere, writing, which I wanted to do and I got tapped into doing movies. I couldn't teach anything to make money, to what I wanted to do, so I kept doing movies when they came up. I didn't have the proper representation. It was one of those hardship trials, and trying to make a transition from western movies. That's exactly what those movies were: *Devil Dog: Hound of Hell* (1978), *Boss Nigger*, and *Angels Die Hard!* All those movies of me trying do a part of, trying to do something different. I wasn't in with a social scene. I didn't get the kind of peak parts that I should have been getting. So I started just using it to set myself up to do what I wanted to do, and which I did."

R. G. made his final appearance in a Peckinpah film in *Pat Garrett and Billy the Kid* (1973) as Deputy Bob Ollinger. Like Peckinpah's *Dundee*, it was eviscerated by its studio, MGM, at the behest of its loathsome then-head, Jim Aubrey. Working with Peckinpah, says R. G., was "sort of like an apprentice[ship] to a dictator. I mean, he was somebody who's a total tyrant. He believed he'd run the set, and he did, you know. I'd see him run producers out of the set, and so forth. He had a lot of problems. But he respected me somehow, because…there was some kind of connection. 'All right, go ahead,' and 'Tell me, take it to the edge,' that is, depth. Some of those scenes I was in, I was very, very risky doing them. But, anyway, when he really did a jolt was in *Pat Garrett*. I got up out of the chair in the corner of the room, which he spent hours lighting, just lighting the whole thing, to go over and embrace Kris Kristofferson. It was a good walk of fifteen feet almost, across to get to him. Right in the middle of it, I had a couple of lines thrown at him, back and to, and before I jumped, one after. And he yelled from behind the camera while the cameras was going, and says, 'I don't believe a God damn thing you're sayin' or doin'!' And I stopped dead in my tracks.

"Nobody'd ever done that to me, not even in life, and I was in absolute, insane rage, whether to go over and stomp him, [or] just let it go. He humiliated me, I'm from the South, you know what I mean? He always had led me in the other movies very nice and respectful and so forth. Then 'cause he had me playing preachers and so forth, that were half killers. But, anyway, I stood there and I says, 'That son of a bitch, I'll show him,' you know what I mean? I mean those

R.G. in *Pat Garrett and Billy the Kid.*

were all little voices now. I stomped back, and sitting down on the set, I heard the director say 'Action.' Even the way he said, 'Action,' I stomped across there, and I was supposed to miss that chair and let Kris take his own fall. But I just tipped off the edge of that chair, he went a-flying, tumblin', and I went around and grabbed him by the hair of the head, and ripped him up and…His eyes were bulging out at me, and I shoved the shotgun, and said, 'Repent, you son of a bitch!' I was really feelin' it, and Matt Clark, he stuck his gun right into my face and he said, 'Stop it! Stop it, Bob!'

"It was real, it was real, man. I mean, I slammed him down, and I stalked up, past the camera and everything. Sam Peckinpah leaned over, he leaned back and says, 'God damn! Print!' And he fell backwards in his chair [laughs]! That was somethin' that happened. It happened on the set, both the director and us, and that doesn't happen very often. But from then on, I realized they ain't gonna be satisfied, no good director out here, [they will] demand you give your whole soul, heart, and bottom of your feet to him, and let him mold it the way they want to. As an actor, you've gotta have something they want to work with." One of R G.'s many memorable lines—"I'll make you walk across hell on a spider's web" was taken from the title of one of his late brother's poems. R. G. added it on the set.

An actor couldn't ask for a more dramatic death scene than R. G.'s in ***Pat Garrett***: Kristofferson shoots him with a shotgun loaded with dimes. "Sixteen squibs in all. They got the pad against me, about a quarter of an inch thick, and an undershirt, and a short shirt, and a vest. Four squibs on my right side, and four on my left side. And four on my back, and four on my, you know, and had all these copper wires running out down my leg, over to this detonator over on the side. A. J. Lohman was—I will never forget him—the special effects man. He had an aura of confidence, and you could trust that you're not gonna get hurt. I'm really tense, and not 'cause I never had that many squibs on me. I had to look up and say the line, you know. It's like you're chained. And he [Kristofferson] let go on me. And when they detonated me, it was like I was being shot, how being shot must feel, 'cause I went up in the air with it, backwards, in reaction. I didn't have to do much acting, it sort of propelled me. It was really shocking. I mean, I'm constantly being shocked doing things in movies that are…borderline being, getting dangerous and hurt, doing this in life and [to] willingly get out there to do it because of the art. If you want to be an actor, you reach hell-raising kinds of feelings."

R. G. was the sheriff in *Race With the Devil* (1975), about four dirt-bikers in an RV (played by Peter Fonda, Warren Oates, Loretta Swit, and Laura Parker) and who are pursued by a satanic cult. "That was interesting, the way that came about. That was, again, my agent who was involved in money in it. And he called me and says, 'Jack Starrett is sitting here,' he says. 'Wes Bishop and somebody else want Jack to direct the movie, and [they] said they wanted to know if you'd play the sheriff for him.' And I always wanted to work with Jack. I knew Jack and saw his *Run, Angel, Run* (1969) and he was pretty good. He had been parking cars out here for ten years, but he knew the camera, he knew how to pace things. And this script was lousy when I saw it, so he worked with me like an actor. And he says, 'Okay, R. G., look for signs around the tree, and just improvise whatever you want.' I felt freer and freer with him and Peter Fonda and Warren Oates. I had fun with them. I had fun with those guys. They were good actors. Warren's a hell of an actor.

"So I threw [a] western sheriff at 'em for real, and had a ball doin' it. And when I saw the movie, it became Fox's second biggest grosser that year. Jack Starrett's direction had put that pace in it, and that chase in that motor home…They hadn't seen anything like it. I saw it once or twice in the theater, and when one of the women in the motor home opened the door, one of the doors above the kitchen, and that rattlesnake was laying there and sort of moved around the head to strike, and the audience screamed. This is what amazed me during the time, in the '80s or whenever after that, most of the time, people, when I go on location and go around, they recognize me from that movie and another movie. I thought surely it would be [from appearing with] Marlon Brando in *The Fugitive Kind*, where I did one of the first things that got me typed as a sheriff. And that was a hell of a chance, a hell of a part, and a hell of a movie, but it was a 'down' movie. Tennessee Williams…It's a classic now, just because it's Tennessee Williams and Marlon Brando. And so, *Race With the Devil* was one of those movies that surprised me, seeing what the American public would buy. That was sort of disillusioning. Of course, that was a different time, too. I had to take it all…I was growing, understanding about what I was involved in.

"Warren Oates was, to me, one of the actors that could have been a big star, that I'd worked with on a character level, and really could have done it if he'd gotten the right part. And Sam Peckinpah was getting ready to…Well, he did, with *Alfredo Garcia*, and he was really gonna do some movies with Warren as a star. Warren died first, I think, and then Peckinpah. Warren was getting' set to emerge out of that character category like Lee Marvin, and I believe would have done it. I think, probably, Warren was a better actor. His ***Dillinger*** (1973)—you would have thought he *was* Dillinger. And that ***Two-Lane Blacktop*** (1971). A friend of mine wrote that, Will Corry. That was another thing…they were beginning to get more of a humanity that Warren had in his movies. I think he was one of the top five or six [most] sensitive actors I worked with. He had that inner reality of some kind. And, also, Brando had that. He had an inner reality, though it was on a quieter level. In Warren, it was more phonetic sensitivity."

Heaven Can Wait began R. G.'s running association with Warren Beatty. "Warren Beatty wanted to meet me for ***Heaven Can Wait***, for a big part in that. I had a meeting with him on a Thursday. And they called me on Tuesday and said they already cast the part to a star, and it was Jack Warden, who got the part of the coach. And a little luck, three or four days later, they called and said, 'Warren wants you to do a small part in it. Would you do it? He wants you real bad.' My agent says, 'Well, I advise you to do it.' I said, 'Okay,' and I did it. Wasn't much of a part, to play the owner of a team and everything. But when I reported to work one day and I walked out on the field where they were shooting the football stuff, and Warren Beatty was already in his football togs and everything. And I'm standing on the sidelines, and he looked up between the shot while they were rehearsing some plays, and he looked up and I saw him turn and trot to me. I couldn't believe he was heading to me. He headed right to me, and he said, 'R. G., I'm so glad you came in to do this part. We'll get some good stuff for you. Ever since I saw you do that sheriff in ***The Fugitive Kind*** with Marlon Brando, I've watched your work and I like what you do, and I'm glad to work with you.' Gee, and that flattered the hell out of me. Then, I went in with gusto!

"He even let me in the room where all the football boys, to give him the news there's more than it'd take in a week, and he'd bought the team, he's gonna do it. He let me improvise that whole scene. Buck Henry was co-director, and he came up beside me when I was getting' the camera over my shoulder on them. And I had two paragraphs to say, and he came up and slipped the pages out of my hand. The camera's running, they don't know it, so I just start talkin' to 'em. So that scene came out of that. I was glad to have the confidence to do that on a big picture. I finally worked it up to where I could do that. That's victory in Hollywood. It's been my whole, big reason for having done it. I got free, where I could do work like that without just trembling and shaking and having reached that stage to improvise it. [laughs] Whether it was a big part or not, I felt sort of a triumph and gain at what I had been working for, because I didn't like that feeling in me. Charles Grodin was there. I didn't need him, I was just around him, saw [him act like] a crazy guy. He's a good actor, but he's got some cables shorted out.

"But, anyway, that led to the next one, ***Reds*** (1981). Warren said, "I want to work with you a lot." And he called me for ***Reds***, to do that one big scene, an interrogation of a witch-hunt in 1917 or 1918, the Bolsheviks, and I got to go to England on that, a place I never visited. I was over there over a week. It was great."

Where the Buffalo Roam (1980) starred Bill Murray as writer Hunter S. Thompson. "They wanted me to come in and do the judge out there, and I never done a judge. I'm constantly trying to do different parts, and I went out there and I really enjoyed it. I had no idea these guys were getting the movie together as we were doin' it. It was just crazy. I mean, Peter Boyle and Bill Murray and [director] Art Linson. But I had fun just being around those actors and seeing how they did comedy. They were dead serious, I mean. I read Hunter S. Thompson's book about being in a motorcycle gang, ***Hell's Angels***. But, yeah, I sort of liked his writing. That's one of the reasons I wanted to do it, as a matter of fact. I now realized why I did that, besides playing a judge. I knew I could play a lot of judges, but I haven't played a judge since. Bill Murray was taciturn around us, you know what I mean? And he was almost like he does in his parts, you know, in the situations he comes off funny or kind of interesting. I think he's a very interesting kind of an actor. I was up for a part [in a movie] that he was in [***Larger Than Life*** (1996)]. Went over and actually did a scene in a thing he did recently, where he inherited an elephant. I never saw that, but I was up for the part of an old circus kind of guy...drivin' nails in his head, and he's a retired freak kind of guy, in the script. And I thought that'd be a good part to do, but I think Pat Hingle did it.

Hammett (1980) was a tribute to the pulps, directed by Wim Wenders and starring Frederick Forrest as Dashiell Hammett. The excellent supporting cast included Elisha Cook as a revolutionary cabbie, Sylvia Sydney, Sam Fuller, and Royal Dano as the proprietor of a newsstand. "Well, that was interesting, too. With Brian Keith playing the partner of Frederick Forrest, who played Hammett. The story is [by] Wim Wenders. I forgot how many months before the picture, [Wenders] had married this girl who played in Bob Altman's ***Nashville***, the singer in it, dark-haired girl [Ronee Blakeley]. It was noticed that, little by little, the script was being rewritten. She began with a small part, and it ended up being almost as big a part as Mary Astor had in ***The Maltese Falcon***. They shut the picture down and got Bob Thomas, a writer, to work on a rewrite and recast it. They brought in Peter Boyle to play the part that Brian Keith had. They kept me, and I didn't expect to be retained in that part. And a year later, I did it after I'd already done it with an Irish accent. And when I made it again, they said, 'Knock out the Irish accent.' So, I did. And I enjoyed seeing it again, yesterday."

Lone Wolf McQuade (1983) was directed by R. G.'s friend, Steve Carver, and starred Chuck Norris as the titular Texas ranger. "I was looking forward to working with Chuck Norris. I had become friends with director Steve Carver, that had done ***Moonbeam Rider*** or ***Fast Charlie***, about this motorcycle race in 1918, [with] David Carradine and Brenda Vaccaro, and I thought it was a cute script. It came off pretty good. It could have had a little more pace and everything. That was my first movie with Steve. I've done six movies with him. He hasn't done

R. G. and Brenda Vaccaro.

anything in a while, and that was one of the ones he had an interest in to do, and he wanted me to do it. And we went to El Paso. I had a lot of fun doin' that picture. I enjoyed goin' to El Paso, I enjoyed goin' across into Mexico, and I enjoyed L. Q. [Jones] in it. I always liked L. Q. being in a picture. We'd get off in some long, far-away location, and go out and eat dinners together. It's like going on a safari, doing a picture like that, and all of 'em away from L. A. It was sort of a success for Steve Carver, and also Yoram [Globus], he was an Israeli producer, part of Cannon Productions. I think they got a suit in it, against when they did *Walker, Texas Ranger*. They used the same character. They cut Steve out of it. They used the whole idea and everything. Ramification.

"L. Q. and I went down and did one of those [*Walker,*] *Texas Ranger*s. About one-and-a-half weeks, I enjoyed being down there, I like the location. I've gotten to see the world, which I never would have if I'd have been a teacher or something. I've been all over the country. I've been in so many different little towns in this country. In 1985, I did, with Willie Nelson, *The Red-Headed Stranger*. I really enjoyed doing that part. It was the kind of part I could have been doin' out here all the time. They didn't promote it right after they got it together. It was faultily constructed, and I think…it might be classified as a example of primitive making of movies by somebody I liked, Willie Nelson, and the money he raised to do the movie the way they wanted to do it."

R. G. had a small part in *Predator* (1987). "I did that movie *Stay Hungry* with Arnold Schwarzenegger. It was his first movie over here. He had done Hercules and they had dubbed his voice, but Arnold had worked real hard on things. And Joel Silver that produced it, I'd done a small part in **Pursuit of D. B. Cooper** for him. And when they sent me the script, I said, 'I don't want to do it. It's not a big enough part.' You know, I had to work with Arnold after having the part I did in **Stay Hungry**. They said it would be one week's work down there, maybe two weeks in Mexico and Puerto Vallarta. I said, 'Puerto Vallarta? That sounds great.' Really, that's the way it went. [laughs] I still turned it down. And Joel Silver called me from Puerto Vallarta and says, 'Get on down here.' So, I said, 'Okay,' and they paid me good money, and we stayed in one of those chain kind of motels in Mexico, sort of really ritzy. Camino Real, or something like that. But I did that, a lot of these things, to get the location. [laughs] And John Huston had his little island over there. He was my hero, John Huston. I've read his autobiography. He's my favorite actor. I thought he was the greatest actor."

He was a semi-regular on **Friday the 13th: The Series**, as a pivotal character, Uncle Lewis. Footage of him appeared at the opening of each episode. "Oh, yeah. [laughs] Canada. They offered me good money to do that. They had tried to get Peter Cushing, but then they offered it to me. Made a deal, and I lived in real good quarters in one of the big hotels, and I needed a little money at that time, making the transition to that. So I went up and did it. Well, I did four more of them! [laughs] I had a ball, in some strange way. See, I didn't look at myself, my acting career. This was all grist for the mill for me to write about. I never got around to writing. I might still get around to writing stuff about myself. Then, I asked for a little raise if I was gonna keep comin' up there, because I had gotten pretty hurt on it, and I was sore for three months as a result of it. And they said, 'Oh, no.' And I said, 'Well, forget it, then.' [laughs] But I coulda kept on doin' it. I was glad to get out of it, in reality."

R. G. was given a tremendous amount of exposure in a part he was virtually unrecognizable in: Pruneface in Beatty's **Dick Tracy** (1990). "Yeah. Three-and-a-half hours [getting] in that make-up. William Forsythe [as Flattop] was sittin' next to me, four hours in make-up. He was doin' Flattop. It was a good experience, but it was miserable to sit there. I sat there all day one day in that make-up, and they didn't get to me. That was a real good-paying job. [Beatty] came over and asked me for a personal interview. He's a lover. That is, he loves and strokes you. And he called, 'Could you possibly consider doing a small part for me in **Dick Tracy**? One of those characters?' I said, 'Sure, Warren. Which one?' 'Well, I don't know. Do you remember Pruneface?' I said, 'Not really, but I remember Mrs. Pruneface.' 'Oh, yeah, she was even meaner than Pruneface.' Well, he laughed and said, 'Well, there's Big Boy and…' he threw out some [character] names. And I said, 'Well, all right, whatever you think I can do, I'll do it.' And the next day, his agent called and said they want you to do Pruneface. So we made a deal. Al Pacino did Big Boy. Anyway, that was an experience, and getting to work with Warren again. He's really great to work with.

"I did one scene with Al Pacino [as "Big Boy" Caprice], where he discovers they're looking down upon him, and that they had a bug on him, and then at the

R. G. as Pruneface.

end, when they killed him. I was glad about that, being free. I was sitting there, and at the end of the scene, there was a bowl of English walnuts sitting in front of Al Pacino. I wondered what that's for. And on the whole big table, it was the only thing on there. [laughs] And so, at the end of the scene, Al Pacino took a handful of the walnuts, and, one by one, he'd slide those English walnuts down the table to each other. And it irritated me. And, as my character, I'm having to come under to him. And as one of them sailed by me, I had an impulse, and I reached out with my left hand and— BAM!—smashed it right on the table. I can't tell you how good it made me feel, to be free enough to do that. So every time he'd do one again, I'd smash it! Then, when they'd come up to another angle, another shot, Warren said, 'R. G., don't forget to smash that walnut!' [Laughs] It's like a transition to another scene. I felt free to do that with him [Al Pacino]. He's the lead in the movie—a big lead! I felt free enough to do whatever he wanted to do with it. I smashed it! [laughs]

"They gave me a really good part in *Warlock 2* (1993). And I knew the guy who produced it was the son of that trio who did *White Lightning* and also did *The Rifleman*, Four Star [Jules Levy, Arthur Gardner, and Arnold Laven]. His son, Robert Levy, called and asked me, wanted me to do that part in *Payback* (1994), in the second movie, since I'd done the other one. So I said, 'Okay.' You know, it was more like a favor, and I also wanted to see how I could function with my eyes. It was the first movie I did where I thought…I had macular deterioration…how it could affect me on the set. And with all the lights, it didn't bother me. I found out then, that *Payback* helped me to understand I could do movies the way I was, and not feel limited by it.

"I played Eric Stoltz's grandfather in *Don't Look Back* (1996); it was for HBO. The guy who wrote it was there, also playing the villain in it. It turned out to be Billy Bob Thornton! That's when I knew what an actor he was! He did a hell of a job as a sort of a drug kind of guy, comin' in to get his money back, had this gang with him. After it was over, I went up and shook his hand, and said, 'Billy Bob, I sure enjoyed workin' with you.' 'Yeah,' he says. 'Me too. I got something in October, and I want you to be in it. And we'll go down to Arkansas,' or somewhere down there. I said, 'Okay,' and we parted. But I never heard from him, and the movie that came out was *Sling Blade* (1996)! I coulda been in that. Robert Duvall was in it. I have eyes sort of like him. So that was my fling with one of the top moviemakers now. He did that movie, called *A Family Thing*, with James Earl Jones and Bob Duvall. Now, he's a hell of a talent. And, so I got to work with him again, I think. *Sling Blade* just knocked me out. My God! That was something I would have liked to have written about, exploring the whole symbolism of the way a lot of people in the South have been looked at for a long time. I think he should have got the Oscar." In 1999, R. G. brushed once again against his past work with Peckinpah when he appeared in *Purgatory* (1999), written by Gordon Dawson. Dawson, amazingly, probably worked on more Peckinpah films than R. G.

"I'm still available. I'm going to keep working. Everybody says, 'You've had so many different phases in your life, so many different lives!' from when I worked in the steel mills and all that time, out in the sticks in Alabama, which I don't wanna talk about. Well, if you're going to be an artist, just get prepared for heartbreaks all along the trail. And that's the way it's been.'"

THE FILMS OF R. G. ARMSTRONG

1957	*The Garden of Eden*
1958	*From Hell to Texas*
	Never Love a Stranger
1959	*No Name on the Bullet*
1960	*The Fugitive Kind*
	Ten Who Dared
1962	*Ride the High Country*
1964	*Bullet for a Badman*
	He Rides Tall
1965	*Major Dundee*
1967	*El Dorado*
1969–80	*Steps to Jonah*
1970	*The Ballad of Cable Hogue*
	Angels Die Hard!
	The Great White Hope
	The McMasters
	Tiger by the Tail
1972	*The Great Northfield, Minnesota Raid*
	J. W. Coop

1972 *(cont.)*	*The Legend of Hillbilly John*
1973	*Pat Garrett and Billy the Kid*
	White Lightning
1974	*Boss Nigger* (aka: *The Boss*)
	Reflections of Murder
	Manhunter (NBC tvm)
1975	*Race With the Devil*
	White Line Fever
1976	*Dixie Dynamite*
	Stay Hungry
	Kingston: The Power Play (NBC tvm)
1977	*The Pack*
	The Car
	Mr. Billion
	Texas Detour
1978	*Heaven Can Wait*
	Devil Dog: Hound of Hell (CBS tvm)
	The Time Machine (NBC tvm)
1979	*The Villain*
	Good Luck, Miss Wyckoff
	Dear Detective (tvm)
	Fast Charlie, The Moonbeam Rider
	Last Ride of the Dalton Gang (NBC tvm)
	The Legend of the Golden Gun (NBC tvm)
1980	*Steel*
	Where the Buffalo Roam
1981	*The Pursuit of D. B. Cooper*
	Reds
	Raggedy Man
1982	*Hammett*
	Evilspeak
	The Beast Within
	Shadow Riders
1983	*Lone Wolf McQuade*
1984	*Children of the Corn*
	Jocks
1986	*The Best of Times*

1986 *(cont.)*	*The Red-Headed Stranger*
	Oceans of Fire
1987	*Predator*
	LBJ: The Early Years (NBC tvm)
	Independence (NBC tvm)
1988	*Bulletproof*
	War and Remembrance (ABC tvm)
1989	*Ghetto Blasters*
	Trapper County War
1990	*Dick Tracy*
1993	*Warlock: The Armageddon*
1994	*Payback*
1996	*Don't Look Back*
	Invasion of Privacy
1998	*The Man in the Iron Mask*
1999	*Purgatory* (TNT tvm)
2001	*The Waking*

TELEVISION

R. G. also made an uncredited appearance in Elia Kazan's **Baby Doll**. R. G. was a regular on **Texas John Slaughter** and played a recurring character on **Friday the 13th: The Series**. He was on **Lawman, The Rifleman, Alfred Hitchcock Presents,** and **Have Gun, Will Travel** twice per show. He was also on **Twilight Zone, Maverick, Rawhide, Cheyenne, Laramie, Bonanza, Great Ghost Tales, Gunsmoke, The Andy Griffith Show, Wyatt Earp, Maverick, Death Valley Days, The Big Valley, The Time Tunnel, Daniel Boone, Cimarron Strip, Starsky and Hutch, The High Chapperal, Darkroom, Beauty and the Beast, Quantum Leap,** and **Millennium.** His tv western credits are far too numerous to list here in their entirety.

DICK BAKALYAN

"Everything I've ever done's been fun. I've never been on a film where I didn't have a good time. So if I keep saying that, it's true."

Just as Frankie Avalon became a figurehead for the '60s "Beach Party" series, and William Smith became, as Paul Koslo has said, "the king of the biker movies," Dick Bakalyan was possibly the most recognizable face in the '50s' "J. D." (Juvenile Delinquent) movies. This genre dealt with the youth-gone-wrong of the time. Sex, drugs, rock 'n' roll, switchblades, doing a stretch in "juvie," chicken runs, and thirty-year-olds playing underage criminals were its key ingredients.

The growing drive-in theater market thrived on these adolescent crime melodramas. Bakalyan appeared in what may be a record number of them: Robert Altman's **The Delinquents** (1955); **Dino** (1957), starring Sal Mineo; **The Delicate Delinquent** (1957), a genre parody starring Jerry Lewis; **The Cool and The Crazy**; **Hot Car Girl**; and **Juvenile Jungle** (all 1958). He also had the honor of being one of the first post-holocaust hoodlums glimpsed in the nuclear war drama, **Panic in Year Zero** (1962), starring and directed by Ray Milland. When the publishers of the **Re/Search** book series ran an interview with him, they aptly described the Armenian-American actor: "Bakalyan's beady eyes and smart-ass smirk helped make him the quintessential delinquent."

Bakalyan's tough upbringing near Boston is something that he doesn't particularly relish recalling, but it gave him the background he needed for playing the various hoods that would earn him an honest living. While he was growing up, he would watch old, Italian men in his neighborhood while they played bocci ball. He acquired some of their mannerisms, which has fooled countless viewers into believing that he was Italian. He was also a boxer; like John Huston—his flat nose attests to that. In Roger Corman *The St. Valentine's Day Massacre* (1967), he played John Scalisi, one of Al Capone's real-life hired killers, who is eventually rubbed-out personally by Capone (Jason Robards). In Roman Polanski's classic *Chinatown* (1974), he famously traded barbs with Jack Nicholson. He thickened his Boston accent for the voice of Dinky the Sparrow in Walt Disney's *The Fox and The Hound* (1981), one of a string of films he worked on for the studio. He also appeared in several Frank Sinatra vehicles, including *Robin and the Seven Hoods* (1964) and *Von Ryan's Express* (1965). He will be also be seen in Terry Zwigoff's upcoming *Art School Confidential*.

The thug parts that he has been typed in for so long give no indication of Dick Bakalyan's immense amiability. Bakalyan is one of the only people that I know of in Hollywood who stresses the utter importance of integrity. He is one among many examples of how, nine times out of ten, no actor possesses a disposition with one scintilla of resemblance to his on-screen persona.

Boyd Rice did a brief, but good, interview with Bakalyan in *Re/Search #10: Incredibly Strange Films* (1986). He also had a documentary made about him, *Dick Bakalyan: The Face is Familiar*, though it is currently unavailable.

Richard "Dick" Bakalyan was born January 29, 1931, in Watertown, Massachusetts. "My mother's Canadian, from Nova Scotia, and my father's from Armenia...My father's name was William Nishan Bakalyan, and my mother's was Elsie Florence Fancy Bakalyan." Their neighborhood was mostly Italian. "It was a tough neighborhood. It was a factory town, a water town, just on the outside of Boston on the Charles River, where the arsenal is. You maintained your cool by being ready to duke it out if people wanted to do that. It wasn't that you went around doing it, but if it was there, you took care of business. That was the attitude then.

Bakalyan had a tough upbringing. "Oh, well, I got in some trouble, yeah. It's not something I like to talk about, though. You get in some trouble and you deal with it, and it makes you a better person if you have the right guidance. But my mother was a widow, and she brought up three boys by herself." He served in the Air Force for "Four years. Discharged honorably as a staff sergeant."

He was also a boxer, "When I was a kid," he says. "I was probably the littlest guy around, and you get in a lot of street fights, 'cause you scuffle. It's all part of growing up; it's not like the gang stuff today. If you had a problem, you duked it out—couple of punches, drew a little blood, went in and had a Coca-Cola or a Pepsi and that was the end of it. Sometimes, the guy became your best friend.

But you had to do that to maintain. It was part of growing up. Of course, my early years were maybe in the late '30s and early '40s. As a kid in the '40s, growing up, the war was on, they had other elements that were interesting in our growth period, because our bubble gum, baseball cards, were war cards! They were training us to go, figuring the war was going to go on for some time. So, we all took part in the patriotism within in the country. I guess the films of that period influenced a lot of us.

"Even the bad guys had some honor, and there was a certain kind of integrity in the arena you played in. People were good to their mothers, they respected the churches, and that carried over even in the way they were identified on the screen, and then carried over into our life, because a lot of guys were killed during the war. There were a lot of families…every house had a flag in the window or a star when they lost someone. It was an interesting time to grow up, the '40s.

"You're always looking for it, a spotlight to do your thing. I never thought I'd be an actor. Absolutely not. That all came down afterwards. You know, some people say you're always an actor! Once you are, you are, that's it. So, I probably was. I know I was in the junior play in high school, in a small part."

After his discharge, says Bakalyan, Anthony Quinn "started me, really" as an actor. While a neophyte actor, Bakalyan had a firsthand opportunity to watch Quinn work, many times. "What Anthony Quinn would do [was] he would go through his mind, when he's lookin' at you, then he'd say it and do it. He had unbelievable body language. So we learn from that."

"He had a workshop, with a guy name Raiken Ben Ari. They had a workshop at a place on La Cienaga, called The Coronet Theater. And I met Quinn, and he invited me to go there. I went, I saw some wonderful actors in the room— They were all workin' on stuff. And he invited me to go. And I told him, 'I can't afford this. My wife's workin'. I'm just out here—I gotta figure out what I'm doin'." He said, 'Nah, nah. You won't pay. You don't pay here. Just spread it around.' What he meant was "Pass it on," whatever I'm gonna learn there. But he liked my physicality—That was the way he put."

Bakalyan stresses how important it is for an actor to hone his "physical" skills: "A lot of times people talk—their tongue's sayin' somethin' that their body isn't."

Quinn's workshop was "wonderful," he says, "We got to do scenes, I worked with people. There was some terrific talent in the room. Not too long later, I got my first interview. I did a scene an agent saw it, and she signed me."

His movie debut was as a tough in **The Delinquents**, directed by Robert Altman, who, at the time, had only directed industrial films and was unknown. It was made in the summer of 1955 in Kansas City. "Yes, with Robert Altman. Well, that was interesting because I had done a showcase where you do some scenes, and an agency had seen me there and signed me to represent. Betty Wookey, terrific agent, she had some clients that were going up for this film, and she sent me up for the part. And I met Robert Altman, did a reading for him, and I got a different part. He said, 'Read this part,' I read it, and I was signed to

do the film. Then, I flew to Kansas City—several weeks later, of course—going through all the procedures of making the deal, and proceeded to make this film with several actors, Tom Laughlin, who proceeded to become Billy Jack, Tina Miller, who had come out of *Blackboard Jungle*, and a lot of local people. We had a lot of fun. And that was the early days of making film. We shot, I think it was four weeks in Kansas City."

Altman, Bakalyan says, was a "Very good director, and, of course, for me, I depended upon guidance from a director, and I know he wouldn't let me go too far, because I was brand new at it. And when you're brand new at it, you want to try everything, but I didn't want to go too far and make a fool of myself. So I was very fortunate to work with a director who had an eye for storytelling, and an eye for keeping you within. You know what they say, 'Less is more, unless you're talking about your check.' We had a lot of fun on that one. And the producer was a man named Elmer C. Rhoden, who, a couple of years later, I did another film for, *The Cool and The Crazy*."

One of his co-stars played a practical joke on Bakalyan during filming. "Oh, yeah, well, that was Peter Miller, and that was in Kansas City...What happened was, we had an apartment. They put us up in these wonderful buildings. And, across the street, there was a pharmacy you went downstairs into. There was a soda fountain in there. Pete was always saying to me he was going to go for his lemon ice cream soda. And I thought, I never heard of that, I never heard of a lemon ice cream soda. Lemon to me was always sherbet. He convinced me to go in there with him, and I did. Now, I'm in there and I'm waiting for my food, and a cop comes in. Anyway, they put me against the counter, I started laughing at the cop. I thought it was a gag from the get-go, he didn't think it was funny. Anyway, he pushed me into the counter, and I said, 'Wait a minute, wait a minute. I'm here with my friend here, Peter Miller.' Pete says, 'What? The guy followed me in, officer. I never saw him before in my life.' The cop said, 'What are you doing here?' I said, 'I'm making a movie here,' and he said, 'Nobody makes movies in Kansas City.' It was one of those things.

"Of course, we all had a good time afterwards down at the station. Evidently, somebody had run away from a reform school, I don't know. Whatever happened, I was wearing a certain color shirt the guy had been wearing, that they were on the lookout for. And he was making a check on me. It went further when I started to laugh, because he thought maybe I was ridiculing him, I don't know, but that was not it. I got scared because they took me in! Of course, later, the cops came down on the set, and we all had a good time." Several years later, Bakalyan appeared on one of Altman's *Combat* episodes.

Allied Artists' *Dino* (1957) starred Sal Mineo, who was then cresting on his fame from *Rebel Without a Cause.* "Yeah, nice guy [Mineo]. Sal was one of the good guys, and everyone else that was in that film—Brian Keith, terrific actor to work with. Let me put it this way—a terrific man, who happens to be a very good actor. But Sal was very sensitive. You just knew he was going to go further than the roles he was just playing at the time. I believe a television show [was] the first time I'd seen him, and *Dino* was a television film he did first, an hour show, I believe so. And, anyway, they made this film and I was fortunate enough to play...my character's name was Duke. The gang was called the Golden Dukes, or something."

Bakalyan was in a parody of J. D. movies, *The Delicate Delinquent* (also '57), starring Jerry Lewis. "*Delicate Delinquent* was the first one Jerry Lewis did without Dean Martin; Darren McGavin was playing that [Martin's] part. Originally, it was called *Damon and Pythias*, based on that legend. Of course, then they changed it, and I was lucky enough to be called in...

"I was in the office with my agent. She was there on some other things. And Eddie Morris, the casting director at Paramount, saw me. He came out of his office, we chatted a minute, and then he took me over, and said, 'You better tell your agent why you're thanking me.' We told her he was taking me over to meet Jerry Lewis and Don, the director, McGuire. And I sat with them a bit, I read something for them. And they put me in, they said right away, bingo. We went back to the office and made the deal. I loved working with Jerry at the time. You know, he was extremely creative, and I was always in awe of the guy. I was a fan of his and Dean Martin's before...It was a great joy for me to be on the set and watch people like this perform. Especially when he [Lewis] did the knife thing with Martha Hyer. We used to kid around because Martha Hyer never made a mistake. We used to bet money that she would make a goof somewhere in there. She never did. She was always on the money.

"I enjoyed everybody on the thing." Bakalyan says, of his co-stars. All of the actors playing the delinquents in the film were cognizant of the serious J. D. movies "that came before us," movies like *City Across the River*—"Those were heavy pictures. And we didn't want to be too gritty. We had to be what we were,

without playin' the result. But indicating, 'This is what goes on with us.' Today, they'd all have Uzis, to keep up with the times!"

The Brothers Rico (1957) was directed by an exceptional "B" director, action specialist Phil Karlson. "Yes, with Richard Conte and a friend of mine still to this day, Jimmy Darren. That was fun, that was a lot of fun...Well, everything I've ever done's been fun. I've never been on a film where I didn't have a good time. So if I keep saying that, it's true. I like Richard Conte, we had a mutual respect. In fact, I almost hurt him, because I had to drive a new Lincoln at the time, and they had power brakes, which was a new thing for me. I had to stop at a certain spot, because they had these stands with lights and things on them, sandbags to hold them in place. I had to pull up—he was in the backseat—I hit the brake and he was in the front seat with me! It was one of those. From that point, I learned to always check a vehicle before you drive it. Same with a gun: if you're going to use it, you go outside with the prop guys and test it. That was fun, we had a good laugh on that one."

He was never a studio contract player. "No, but *working*, just freelancing...It wasn't a deal where you signed a deal at a studio. Those days when they had a contract, where they had character people under contract—they had gone out in the '40s. In the '50s, the studios had some people, but mostly they were the young lads, and they were training them, in fencing and all the other areas that they utilized them in films. But tv was new then, so it was great for us, to start doing some of the newer shows that came along. You couldn't take time to think about what you were going to say. You had to say it, because you're dealing with time now. And tv is like radio, with pictures added."

The Cool and The Crazy (1958), starring Bakalyan, became one of the archetypal J. D. movies. This story of dope-crazed teens was produced by Earl C. Rhoden, Jr., producer of *The Delinquents*. It found Bakalyan once again back filming in Kansas City. It was directed by one of the finest low-budget western and movie serial directors, William (*Master of the World*) Witney. He directed Bakalyan in four films, beginning with *The Cool...*"Bill Witney, he was great because he could see the action in his head. He knew how to do that, because he came out of doing serials for years. So, whatever he approached, it had a rhythm like waves hitting the beach, because of the Saturday afternoon serials. That was his training ground, if you get me. So, he could put together a good piece. I liked him, 'cause he was a man who did his work. And he didn't take any guff from anybody. He didn't let anybody pressure him, so I learned a lot from watching these guys what they do. The big key was watching the crew when you went on a set.

"Like I just finished a thing I did with David Hasselhoff, called *Baywatch Nights* [Circa 1994]. When I walked on the set, I knew he was a good guy, though I had never met him before. But you knew from the demeanor of the crew—there's an attitude that goes around. And I used to watch the crews a lot, in the films I did, in the early shows. I'd look for a crew guy to see his reaction. If it was okay with him—to them it was a job—if they gave you the high sign, you know you're sent in, that's all. If I could make them smile, or they hung around then they could have gone and just goofed-off, they hang around to see what you were going to do in a scene, and you knew you were doing something okay."

Dick Bakalyan as Tic-Tac in *Juvenille Jungle*.

Dick Bakalyan as Tic-Tac in *Juvenille Jungle*.

The actor's other Witney films were all shot in 1958: *Juvenile Jungle, The Bonnie Parker Story,* and *Paratroop Command*. "Well, *Paratroop Command* and *The Bonnie Parker Story,* they were produced by a guy named Stan Shpetner, who was a dynamite guy. He'd come out of television, he'd been with CBS and he decided to make some films. He wrote them, and we made them. And, again, fun people to work around, Dorothy Provine and them in *The Bonnie Parker Story*. *Juvenile Jungle* was fun...In fact, yesterday, I had coffee with a guy named Joe DeReda, who was one of the co-stars in that movie. Yeah, he's a big writer now."

By 1962, the J. D. movies were *passe,* bypassed by, among other things, AIP's "Beach Party" series. "Well, you know what they [J. D. movies] are. They weren't really about delinquency, they were just reflective about some of the rebellion that was coming out of the young people at that time. It was an interesting time in our country. But they weren't in the full sense of the kids today that are involved in gangs, these shooters and drive-by guys. I mean, it was nothing like that. I mean, we were just kids, breaking the law in our own way, smoking a marijuana cigarette, or doin' whatever. Today, they shoot, and they're doing all the other things. It was a training ground for me. It gave me a chance to really learn a craft, and play some interesting characters. It probably helped me as a man, because I had a chance to let a lot of things come out of Dick Bakalyan through those characters, you know. You're not even aware of it as it's happening. You reflect back years later and go, 'Ahh! Look at that—I learned from that character's behavior.' Also, they're cult films today. And a lot of the lobby cards and the one-sheets I have from the old days that, you know, you just throw in the closet—They're now quite valuable. They're in demand in foreign countries, especially in England. They love those films over there."

Jack Webb directed Bakalyan in the 1959 newspaper drama, *30*. "I enjoyed working with him [Webb]. He was a nice man. I liked working with David Nelson…Bill Conrad, who was terrific. Years later, of course, I did a couple of *Cannons* with him; they were fun. But it was a pleasant set. I played a copy boy in that movie, I remember, I was bopping around. Jack Webb was in it. An interesting man, because he wasn't a showbizzy kind of guy. He was a man who knew what he wanted, and he got it. He had a certain style and a rhythm about him, and he imposed that. And if you delivered it, you worked with him—That's it. A good director, but he wanted everything, you know—he liked to hear the periods and the commas. They had teleprompters, also. I can't work with those. I don't do that. When we did *The Bobby Darin Show*, we had guys with cards off to the sides. That was a live show, you had a live audience. But television, you had teleprompters, you do it. You can't read and perform."

Bakalyan and Warren Oates worked closely together on Gordon Douglas' World War II submarine picture, *Up Periscope* (1959). "Well, Warren, I knew years ago, a wonderful guy. We used to have a lot of laughs together, played some nickel/dime/quarter poker together with a few of the other guys around at that time. But I enjoyed doing it, because Jimmy Garner was in it, Edmond O'Brien was great to work with, and I like Gordon Douglas, the director, one of the good guys."

There was a major fight scene on a submarine between Bakalyan and Oates in the film: "Oh, yeah, that was fun. We had a thing, though—the director yelled at me—I think it was the day before that, too—because we were in the middle of a shot, and we were running out of oxygen, and one of the guys was smoking a cigarette. You know, you get in character, and you look around, and a guy's smoking a cigarette, that means he's burning up your oxygen." In character, Bakalyan got angry and responded to the smoker by improvising a hostile response, "ruining" that take. "Then the director got on my case, and then, of course, he got on the case of everyone else, once he realized why I had blown the take.

"But, working with Warren, we knew what we were going to do. We did it and we tried to do it better than any stuntmen were going to do it—stuntmen interpreting our characters would do it. The way they had it set up in the close quarters, you couldn't really double it. So we'd rehearsed it like you would a good sword fight, and then we did it. It was fun, we laughed. It was great. It was such a release, too. The other guys got a kick out of it. They had no idea what we were goin' to do."

In *Alcatraz Express* (1959), a theatrical release of an *Untouchables* two-parter, the marvelous Neville Brand starred as Al Capone, with Bakalyan playing support. "Neville Brand, what a nice guy he is. One of the highest decorated soldiers [in World War II]. I liked Neville Brand; he was a sweet guy, really nice. And when I say it, I mean it with the utmost respect. Anyway, we had fun on that. I had to stab him with scissors, I think…I was lucky enough to do a few of those *Untouchables*."

Bakalyan worked with several future stars on *The Untouchables*, including Charles Bronson. "Yeah, 'The Death Tree' [featured Bronson]. And then I did...'Blues for a Gone Goose' was the name of it, [with] Robert Duvall. It was the last *Untouchables* we shot. He played a trumpet player, [who] gets involved with my boss's lady or whatever, so I had to shoot up the bar [he plays at]. I like Charles Bronson. He always had an element of danger about him as a man, and that's nice, because it came through in this character. He burned me in that one. He didn't burn me, but he shot my coat. There's a scene where he has to kill me, and we're in three-piece suits, the overcoats on, the whole thing. But the spark came out of the gun when he fired it, and it stuck on my coat, I guess. So we're there, and it's like happening, and, all of a sudden, I'm burning, smoke's coming up."

Bakalyan was one of the many character actors who appeared in cameos in *The Errand Boy* (1961), which Jerry Lewis wrote, directed, and starred in. "Yeah, I'd been hurt at that time. I was limping in that, I think. I couldn't move too well, because I had cut my knee and it was pretty well bandaged-up, but Jerry gave me the gig anyway. He was a good guy. That was good, I liked working with Jerry Lewis. Some years later, he got a little bit 'out there.' I guess we all did."

American-International's *Panic in Year Zero!* (1962) was directed by and starred Ray Milland. Milland plays a suburbanite on a family camping trip, suddenly forced to contend with surviving a nuclear attack. Bakalyan and two other young actors played genuinely scurrilous looters, who rape Milland's character's daughter. "We filmed that all here in the Los Angeles area," recalls Bakalyan. "Ray Milland directed it. We were the gang that was robbing people after the bomb went off...Milland was terrific, I would like to have worked with him again. I enjoyed being around the guy, and then I talked to him later about it. I saw him in New York, as a matter of fact, with his daughter and a girlfriend at a club or restaurant in New York. I was there with Frank Sinatra; we were getting ready to go to Europe to do *Von Ryan's Express*. That was the last time I saw him.

"Milland was a classy guy, and he treated everybody with respect...We had fun on the set. And nobody really dealt with, 'What would the reality of this be, really?' We were making an entertainment, and we knew that. It wasn't something to upset people, even though it was about a heavy thing. We didn't deal with it that way. His approach was, 'Let's just entertain with this.'" Carl, Bakalyan's character in *Panic*, was easily one of his vilest roles. It was somewhat of an acting challenge for him: "You try and find justification of the window you're looking out of. You rationalize behavior, and then it becomes okay. It's like a contract killer. That's what he does. He's not just killing people, murdering people, he's doing his job. These guys were out there. You remember incidents, on films. I feel like I'm on the O. J. trial here—they want to know everything!"

He was in *Pressure Point* (also '62), produced by Stanley Kramer and starring Bobby Darin. "I was in this work gang, and we had to take over a club," Bakalyan recalls. "We played tic-tac-toe in a saloon. And then Bobby and I ended up playing

tic-tac-toe on a guy's wife, played by an actress named Mary Monday. We used her lipstick to play, and it became a key spot [in the film, used] in the sales of the film. I met Bobby Darin on that one, and we became friends. He's a great guy. It was directed by Hubert Cornfield. It was under the auspices of Kramer's company, but it was called a Kramer film."

From 1964 to '66, Bakalyan appeared in three Frank Sinatra movies. The all-star *Robin and the Seven Hoods* also featured Dean Martin, Sammy Davis, Jr., Peter Falk, and Edward G. Robinson, with Bakalyan as one of the hoods. Sinatra produced, directed, and starred in *None But the Brave*. Mark Robson directed *Von Ryan's Express*, a World War II drama. Bakalyan was brought in to audition for *Robin...* "Well, the great thing was when I went in the interview, they were there, you know, to cast the whole thing. Frank Sinatra was in the office, and [director] Gordon Douglas was in the office, and Howard Koch, Sr. And we had a nice interview. Anyway, Frank Sinatra said to me, 'I seen everything you do.' 'Cause I knew his daughter, Nancy, and every time I had a show on, she would tell him, 'Daddy, watch this, watch that.' And that was great, my wife and I are friends with Nancy. Nancy used to say, 'Come on, I'll introduce you.' I said, 'I'll meet him one day. He's a great guy, he's a great talent...' You know, I was working, and it worked out nice...And, anyway, the windup is he said, 'Look, you'll be with us.' I think he asked me, 'Do you sing?' I said, 'Not as well as you!' Anyway, he said, 'You'll be in my gang.' So, they put me in this gang, and that's why I was hanging out with...the gang was Sammy Davis, Dean Martin, Bing Crosby was trying to get into the gang, Phil Crosby, Hank Henry, Sonny King...I mean, you know, just to be on the set with these guys was a thrill.

"Bing Crosby was a nice guy. But I remember when we were doing some audio pick-ups, we were all there before he got there, and then he got there, and they went to him first. We said, 'Look at this—They go for the money even on the sound!' But a nice man to be around. I didn't hang out with him.

"Years later, when I did *Never a Dull Moment* at Disney, I worked with Edward G. Robinson. And I was fortunate enough that he invited me for lunch one day. He and I just sat down and talked, and that was kind of nice. I always liked Sammy Davis. Great guy. I knew him before that. I met him on a couple of social occasions, and what impressed me was, I met him once, and, then, the next time I saw him, he remembered my name! Great talent. When we did *Robin and the Seven Hoods*, I was fortunate enough to be their guest in Las Vegas at the Sands Hotel where Sinatra, and Dean Martin, and Sammy went on stage together. And that was wonderful. And then I did *None But the Brave*, that he directed in Hawaii. And while I was doing that, they signed me for *Von Ryan's Express*. It was nice. I saw him do some nice things for people, a lot of people don't know about it. It wasn't for the press, the grandstand, it was nice stuff.

"*None But the Brave* was an interesting film, because, on that one, Frank almost drowned. It was not when we were shooting. 'Cause he had a house right over [from where] we were staying, at a place called the Coco Palms. But it was over on Oahu; that was on the island of Kauai, where we filmed it. And I was in Oahu with Nancy and Tommy Sands; she was with Tommy, at the time...

"It was beautiful there. It was before all the hotels had gone up. I had no idea: I used to think Kauai was just a little island. I had no idea they had a Grand Canyon there, black Angus cattle ranches, rice fields—it's a big place. And we had the wrong impression of the islands. We thought it was all palm trees and coconuts. I liked working out in the mornings with Clint Walker. We had a guy named Howie Young; he was a hockey player. He had a part in it. He was a wonderful guy, too. Rodeo rider, hockey player! And some of the other guys...Tommy Sands, of course. I don't think anybody appreciated Sands' grasp on his character, this young lieutenant who's trying to be all balls. It sustained him, which was good. I like Tommy. I saw him the other night...We were over at my friend Mickey Callan's house, we watched the fights, the Oscar De La Hoya fight.

"*Von Ryan's Express* was a pleasant experience, 'cause I got to go to Europe!" RKO graduate Mark (*Isle of the Dead*) Robson directed the film in Italy. "He knew Europe," Bakalyan observed about Robson, "he'd been over there before. I like working with him. At first he thought I was just some [Sinatra] flunky that was there with my gut." After seeing Bakalyan perform an especially demanding scene, Robson realized the depth of the actor's talent. "It seemed like I had the shakes from Malaria, when I got caught stealing Atrobines. Then he said, 'You're really an actor.' I said 'What do you think I'm doing here?!'

"It's tough, though, to be with Sinatra. Other people respond differently. They think you're a flunky. It's like Frank Sinatra will go get a cup of coffee, and everyone says, 'What a great guy.' And you get one for him, you're a gofer. And he tries not to let that happen, because he's sensitive to that. He can see that. It's just how other people respond around him. He was good to me, though. He's a good guy."

One of the few major historical characters Bakalyan ever played was Dismus (later, Saint Dismus), the patron saint of thieves, in **The Greatest Story Ever Told** (1965). Along with Max Von Sydow's Christ, Bakalyan is crucified. The film was directed by veteran George Stevens, who Bakalyan says rarely interacted with his cast: "He was more interested in making pictures—he just assumed the actor 'brings it.' I had a sequence, where I was on the cross, and the rain was comin' down. I'm blinkin', 'cause it was hittin' my eyes! It was hurtin'! And he was on a big crane with a loudspeaker, and all the extras were movin' around. 'Cause after the character Jesus dies, the sky opens up, and the rains come." At this point, Bakalyan imitated Stevens' gruff voice: "'All right, Mr. Bakalyan, that's enough acting. Cut!' One of those…And I tried to say, 'I'm not—It's hurtin'!' We did it one more time, they printed it, and it was a Friday night. On Monday, we were told we had to do it again, because the raindrops were bouncing too high on the wood of cross. Not on my eyeball. It was comin' down too hard. So they had to lighten up the rain. Because he was more interested in the visual picture. And then, we did it again, and we got it."

Stevens was "not maybe 'hands-off,'" Bakalyan explains, "but if he's lookin' in, tryin' to set somethin' up, he's got no time to talk to ya. When he signed me to do Dismus, I didn't have a beard—they built a beard every day. 'Cause I said, 'It's gonna take me a while to grow it,' and they said, 'No, no. We put the wig on him, and bring me Dismus.' That's all he said."

Dick Bakalyan as John Scalisi in _The St. Valentine's Day Massacre._

The St. Valentine's Day Massacre (above and below).

Bakalyan played Scalisi, one of the actual gangsters responsible for *The St. Valentine's Day Massacre* (1967) in Roger Corman's film of the same name. "Well, I like Roger as a person. He's a good director. He knows what he wants. He doesn't have to shoot for it. He doesn't over-shoot. Some guys, they shoot twenty-to-one ratio or something, and you're just burned out from doing it over and over again. You don't have to. If a guy knows what he wants, sets it up— boom—do it. 'Cause in film, there's nothing to do with acting. Film has to do with matching your master [shot], then you've got to do your coverage. And you gotta match, physically, everything you did at the time you did it, so they can cut it.

"I'll tell you, I haven't seen that film in a long time, but I remember doing research on the character Scalisi. He was a real hit man; he was loaned to Capone. I don't say one word during the movie. Scalisi went to High Mass every Mass before he went out to do what he did. He was one of those guys who could rationalize or justify their occupation, so it's just a matter of fact." Capone caught Scalisi and his partner, Anselmi, in a plot to poison his salad. Bakalyan used Scalisi's strong religious feelings as a means of creating business for the character. "So, when they came down, when they tried to get the salad chef [to poison Capone], where [Capone's men] are planning on taking out Scalisi and Anselmo, when they get caught. When he realizes he'll get killed, you don't run, you bless yourself, you go to your knees, and you take the hit. You know, films have changed today. I haven't been to a movie in a bit, but there was a pleasantness on the set. People weren't running around with major egos like a lot of people today. I guess why were old enough to handle the success. That's harder to handle than losing out, much more difficult. Some people, it makes them better persons. And some, they just go by the wayside."

In early 2005, Bakalyan elaborated further on why Corman appealed to him: "Roger was good, because everything was…easy. In other words, you knew they were cuttin' corners, you knew it was not easy for them. The guys were running, doing, pickin' up shit, workin' hard. Roger never lost his cool. No matter what went wrong. Same with his brother, Gene Corman, 'cause I did *Hot Car Girl* for Gene. They were well brought-up people, because they were delightful to everyone around them."

Bakalyan began a long association with Walt Disney Productions with *Follow Me, Boys!* (1966). "Oh, yeah, with Fred MacMurray. That was at Disney, and I remember the casting guy told me, 'I want you to do this. It's only for a couple of days.' It was a sergeant or something, a military sergeant. It had to do with war games, and some boy scouts. It turned out to be a fun piece. Anyway, the windup for that is, the casting director told me that they'd bring me back. And a couple of months went by, and I'm going, 'Nobody's gonna bring me back,' so I forgot about Disney. Two months later, boom, I go over to do a thing, and I was there fifteen years doing a lot of different stuff."

In Disney's *Never a Dull Moment* (1968), Bakalyan played Bobby Macoon, a punch-drunk boxer. Its stars were Dick Van Dyke, and Edward G. Robinson as an art forger. "You know, Robinson is just extraordinary," says Bakalyan. "The man is a legend. I grew up seeing him in films, but I was more enamored by the man than the characters he played, because he was such a class act. And, one night, when we finished the film, he had us all to his home for dinner. Around a long table, a bunch of us, Dick Van Dyke, all of us, with our respective mates. And after dinner, we all had a big cigar he handed us. You didn't want to refuse it. Of course, you took the cigar. And then he took me through and showed me all the artwork that he had collected over the years. It was wonderful."

Disney's *The Computer Wore Tennis Shoes* (1969) starred Kurt Russell as Dexter Riley. "Oh, yeah, well, Kurt Russell was a kid then. Originally, we did it as a two-part movie of the week, and then they decided to release it theatrically. And, then, we did two other films following that up, which was Now You See Him, *Now You Don't and The Strongest Man in the World*. Russell's father was a nice man, Bing Russell, who was also a good ball player. I remember when Kurt was just a kid, he was under contract with one of the major league clubs, Cincinnati, as a second baseman. Good athlete, nice young man—good actor! He's doing some good stuff today. Every time I see him, I love him. He's a man, a good guy."

In Disney's *Return From Witch Mountain* (1978), the sequel to the popular *Escape to Witch Mountain* (1975), Bakalyan was Eddie, a cabbie. "Right, that was with Bette Davis and Christopher Lee. I played a cab driver, who had a perfect record that I blow in the course of this thing. It was a nice piece of business they wrote in for me. I had a good time. I remember telling Bette Davis, 'All these years, I've admired you, I wanted to work with you. Here we are on the same set, we're sitting down in your chairs, and I don't have one scene with you.' She said, 'Let me ask the director. Maybe I could take your cab.' That was great. What a lady. I liked Disney. Everybody was great to me over there. And then I did some voices for them."

In 1981, Bakalyan could be heard in *The Fox and The Hound*. "Yeah, I do the voice for Dinky the Sparrow." "Dinky" was a kind of reprise of his avian role in *It's Tough to be a Bird*." *It's Tough...*was directed by the late, great Ward

Kimball, and won the 1969 Academy Award for Best Short Film. "I played a character called M. C. Bird, and he's animated and he shows you live-action footage of birds, 'cause he tells you the history of birds, and with a Damon Runyan voice. And then we did a similar voice, but lighter [for *Fox...*]. Pearl Bailey played Big Mama the Owl, and Paul Winchell was Boomer the Woodpecker, and we were the three birds who ran through that movie. And it was fun, too, because [they had] the voices of Mickey Rooney, Kurt Russell...Fun, just fun."

Bakalyan explains why Ward Kimball ("A wonderful man. One of Disney's ten original guys, you know.") hired him to play M. C.: "When he cast me to do the voice, I remember sayin' to him, 'You can get anyone in the world. Why me?' He said, 'You have a unique sound. And when we put a face with it—if someone's out of the room and they hear it, they'll remember the face, from the sound." On voicing cartoon characters, Bakalyan relates, "When you do a big animation, you do the voice first. It's not like you dub it. And you try to animate the sound, so that they can do something with the character."

In an entirely different vein, Bakalyan wrote and produced *The Animals* (1970), a violent western: "Oh, that was a thing I wanted to do. They wanted me to write a movie about violence and this and that, and we did it. [*The Animals*] was a waste of time.

"I'll tell you the truth: you make a movie now, you gotta fight for distribution. MGM had it for fifteen years—that was on the international market and they made some money with it. That's a whole other ballgame, distribution and stuff. You gotta chase people for the money, you gotta threaten them to get it. It's crazy! So, I said I don't want any part of that end of the business. That's why we made one film and that was the end of it.

"Henry Silva and Keenan Wynn starred in it. If I were to do it today, I would do a different film. I would get more into the psychological elements. But I was dealing with the violence and the animal instinct being inherent in every man, every woman, every child, and how it'll take over. And that's what happens. And the Indian, who's the key character, the symbol of savagery in our society, is the only one that acts with any semblance of humanness in the film! Everybody else is a rat."

He a regular on *The Bobby Darin Amusement Company* (1972), a summer tv series. "Bobby Darin called me on the phone, and said, 'Dickey, are you interested? I'm gonna do a show, we're gonna do a thing here for the summer. Are you interested in doing it?' I said, 'Whatever you want to do, come on!' He said, 'I got an idea. The guys from NBC will call you.' So, they called. And I went to a meeting, and I remember they were saying they wanted a comic to play the part. And Bobby told them, 'Hey, name the comic, Dick'll play the comic doin' it, but he's doin' it, or we don't do it, guys.' And that was it. We did the neighborhood spot, and it was unique for a musical variety show, of course: two pals on a stoop in the Bronx. It was about friendship, and about two wacky guys. And I loved it, it was wonderful for me. Because it was something unique on this kind of a show, and they didn't understand it—You couldn't rehearse it. You had to just do it. The last couple, I was working intellectually. I remember, because I would start to say my line before the audience finished laughing. I wasn't used to that. It was fun. I had a good time on that show. The actual title was *Dean Martin Presents The Bobby Darin Amusement Company*. I did altogether nineteen of them, and there were twenty shows. But the last one was Bobby with Peggy Lee doing a concert." Bakalyan was also a regular on the short-lived *Bobby Darin Show* (1973). After seeing Kevin Spacey's recent Darin biopic, *Beyond the Sea*, Bakalyan reported that—though he thought that Spacey did a fine job, technically—he failed to catch Darin's spirit, or the essence of the man.

One of Bakalyan's best-known roles was as Perry Lopez's police partner, Loach, in Roman Polanski's *Chinatown* (1974). The snide banter between Loach and Gittes (Jack Nicholson) is unforgettable (particularly Gittes' comment about how Loach's wife "closed her legs too fast.") "Oh, I liked working with [Polanski]. Because, though there was a language barrier, there was a problem there, he'd do what he wanted. It took him a while to get to it, so he had some difficulty articulating what he was looking for. I remember him saying, 'Find it, bring it back a bit.' 'Cause he always had me moving. It was a 'talking' script. Bob Towne wrote a brilliant script.

"I enjoyed working with Jack Nicholson. As a matter of fact, Jack was in *St. Valentine's Day Massacre* with us. He had one line in there. He's one of the good guys, also. I had a falling out with…it was just bad communication on *The Two Jakes* (1989), on the sequel to that. That's why I turned it down. It had nothing to do with Jack Nicholson. I loved Faye Dunaway. What an actress. But, again, on the set, everybody is equal. They say, 'Action, action,' there's no movie stars there. It's wonderful. You're talking about John Huston. I remember he's sitting on the running board of the car, shooting the breeze on the street. And listening to him tell stories about his old days. Great."

In the film's classic final scene, the only scene in the film actually set in L. A.'s Chinatown, Bakalyan shoots Faye Dunaway, a typically bleak Polanski ending. "It was interesting. It was set up nice. Let's see: Perry reaches to shoot, Jack blocks him, and he's handcuffed to me, a shot fires, and then we run. I tell you, the special effects make-up was unbelievable. I had no idea what she was going to look like, when we came up into that scene where she's there, and Jack looks at her, her eye's blown out. But they took an eggshell, the inside liner of an egg, they put that there. Then they put the blood and all the other stuff there. Unbelievable. It gave me a strange feeling, I must say. It helps the actor when they do that, because you're really responding to that. I mean, we weren't killers, we were cops, but, you know, it was interesting to do that. Of course, he never forgives me. That's why, in *The Two Jakes*, he was supposed to carry on, but I didn't do the film." Nicholson and Perry Lopez, among others, did appear in the forgettable sequel, which Nicholson also directed.

H. O. T. S. (1979) was a *risque* teen/frat comedy. Bakalyan appears as a recently-released crook, who, along with his partner returns to an abandoned house were they stashed their loot. In the meantime, it has become a sorority house, and a battleground between two feuding sororities. "I had fun," says Bakalyan, "because there were all [these] pretty girls, and it was a chance to do comedy in a movie. The only place where I was getting to do that was in Disney." Bakalyan dresses up like a robot in one scene. "Oh, yeah, we did anything to get in the house. And then the scene in the air balloon with the bear! Oh, God! That was fun."

Once again, Bakalyan played a cop in ***The Man With Bogart's Face*** (1980), starring Robert Sacchi. "Andy Fenady produced it. Andy Fenady was one of the guys I worked with over the years, and we're still friends. His first film was ***Stakeout on Dope Street***. He went on to do "The Rebel" series and a bunch of other things. And he produced that one. It was always pleasant on the set. Bob Sacchi was amazing as the Marlowe character. I remember George Raft had a part in it. Joe Theisman had a part in it. He played a gunsel* that was working for George Raft. But I enjoyed it. We had a good time, and I got to go to Catalina, where we did some shots."

Another '80s role was in ***Blame it on the Night*** (1984), starring Nick Mancuso. "Right. I had to get a natural for that, I remember. I played the road manager for a rock star. Nick Mancuso played the rock star. The story was by Mick Jagger. That was fun, 'cause that was around other people...music people. I got to be in the studio and listen and watch guys like Tom Scott play the sax. But it was a different beat for me, let me say. So, I had a good time, but there was a lot going on in those days. As a matter of face, I was supposed to do a Broadway musical with them, called ***Pandemonium***. It's ***Peter Pan***, but as a rock musical. I was the only one on the cast who would not be singing, because I do not sing. But they would put some music behind me when I was talking. And we were going to do ***Peter Pan*** today, in the streets of New York. Captain Hook is a captain in the juvenile squad, and I played his assistant. But, the producer/director that was behind the deal got sick and died. It would have been great for me, because I never worked in New York. It would be nice to go there, and everyone thinks that's where I'm from."

"And then, of course, I just recently did this thing with the ***Baywatch*** group, called ***Baywatch Nights***. But I'm doing a lot of writing. And a couple of projects I'm working on, we've had some meetings now—We didn't get turned down yet!—on some interactive cd-rom stuff, and a character that I had an artist draw for me, called Benny The Book Bug. He knows everything because he's in and out of books his whole life. And, hopefully, he's going to be the Smokey the Bear of words. That's what we're trying to do at the moment. But I've been in meetings with a company called Digital Magic out here. They do a lot of the special effects stuff. And, hopefully, I'll be talking with Warner Brothers in the next two weeks. They have a whole new department, interaction, CD-rom stuff.

"Somebody asked me once what's the best role I've played, and it's always the next one. I enjoyed working on **The Greatest Story Ever Told** (1965), way back then, playing Dismas. He was still a crook, he was still a thief, but he was the king of them, at that time. I've been lucky. I've been working for forty years. There's a lot of stuff I turned down because they don't want to pay your salary, and they want to insult you. Or they're buying meat, and then you know if you go on the set and everyone's working for these prices they want to pay, they're not going to know what they're doing—half of them, not all of them, 'cause a lot of them do and they really need the gig. And you know you're going to have to do the take over and over and over again. They forget the sun moves or something. They're working outside, you do your master. By the time you get to the coverage, for the close-ups and all that, the sun has moved, so the shadows will be long if you didn't cheat your looks and move with the sun. Anyway, that's stuff you learn over the years. And you can't get that—a lot of times, they'll buy actors who give a good reading, but don't understand film. Acting is one thing—finding a character, and being able to understand him and give him a back story. But matching is a whole other ballgame.

"You play the same scene differently on a live tv show, or on a filmed tv show, or in a movie. You play it all differently. Even though it's the same words, *etcetera*, because the style of presentation has to be for the medium you're working in. In a film, you can take time and think. you can let the wheels turn, and then say or do something, or respond. In tv, you can't. If you got a filmed show, you've got to match. If it's a four-camera show, you don't have to match anything, you can just send it in, 'cause you don't have to remember what you did or where your finger was when you said that line. That's all.

"Anyway, I enjoy it. That's my playground, and I'm thrilled to be a character actor, and I know that the guys that came along with me, or along on the same ride, respect me. All you have to do is understand what you're doing and be good at it. That's all. If I can't do it by this time, I'm in the wrong business."

Recently, Bakalyan delightedly reported that he had "worked in a fun movie: **Art School Confidential**." It is directed by Terry (**Crumb**) Zwigoff, and is scheduled for release this year. "What a wonderful guy Terry is. He's a sweetheart, and Dan Clowes, who's the writer.

"I don't play a big part. I play a cranky security guard at the art school, where all these characters are doing their thing. And it's like it's *my* place. But there's murders goin' on…And then I do a character in a film within the film, for one of the guys. But it's a nice little role. I was very pleased to be aboard with these guys…I work with the young kid who's the lead."

Bakalyan calls Zwigoff "the best." The actor gave Zwigoff a copy of a recent documentary on him, **Dick Bakalyan: The Face is Familiar** "to look at," he explains. "There's a cut [clip] from **Chinatown**, where I shoot Faye Dunaway at the end. And I'm handcuffed to Jack, so when he reaches to stop Perry Lopez from shootin', he pulls me forward and then I fire. So it's a very drawn-out shooting, where I'm leaning forward to fire. My point is I'm getting' ready to shoot at this guy in the film within the film. And, now, Terry looks at me, and he says, 'Shoot him the way you shot Faye Dunaway.' And I knew exactly what he wanted, for me to exaggerate just a fraction. We did, and it was 'Bingo!' We printed."

Zwigoff was "great to work with," he continues. "He's very easy. I told him, 'Listen, I'll carry your bag next time.' He said, 'You'll never carry my bag. We'll work together again.' First of all, he won't settle for anything. He'll shoot till he gets it. Not the way Polanski did; Polanski would shoot until we *found* it. He knows what he wants, over here. And not that Polanski didn't, but it was easier for him to convey to his people what he was lookin' for.

"We had some people on the set, the one day that I took the disc over to give him, that I hadn't seen: the teenagers that are goin' to this art school—With their earrings, and with their this and their that…And their red hair—blue, green. Outrageous. I don't think much of it. I go, 'This is an interesting film I'm in.' Dissolve—I go down to San Diego with some friends, to their comic book convention. And I'm a guest on there. And walk through there, and EVERYBODY looked like that! The people that came! It blew me away!

"Recently, I did **Cold Case**, Jerry Bruckheimer's series at CBS. And the [lead] girl is just elegant, and the kids, they're great to work with! I told them, after the first day, I said, 'It's so nice to meet young people that are starrin' on a series that don't think they know every fuckin' thing!'

"Sometimes I go on interviews with casting people. And I say to them, 'Before we start—'cause I've only got six pages, I don't know what happened before here—But do I like the guy I'm talkin' to here? How long have I known him?' And I had one of 'em say, 'Why? What do you mean, 'Why'?' ''Cause it's gonna affect the 'HOW'!'"

He has several concepts for television shows and projects that he is currently shopping around. One is "'Grey Matters, because Gray Matters," says Bakalyan, "And it's a senior citizen news show…. News of the day as it affects seniors. Watch this if your young, because, if you're lucky, you'll live long enough to be a senior. So whatever's botherin' us today, fix now, so when you get there, you won't have the problem!" "Benny the Book" is still gestating, as well.

Since he first became a working actor in 1955, Bakalyan has seen respect for his profession steadily decline: "The industry—everyone's moving up the scale. But actors, they're trying to hold you at scale. I don't want to work for scale—I don't do that." But, Bakalyan insists, "It's not about money—it's about the respect they show by hiring you. It's your worth."

Dozens of extremely competent, trained directors and other film technicians are currently out of work, as a result of Hollywood's "age-ism." Of this appalling trend, Bakalyan notes, "I talk to directors now, like George Fenady, people like that, who are brilliant. They'll give you seventeen set-ups without even thinking. They *deliver*, which you gotta do, every day, [Shoot] 'So' many things, for them to cut. But they can't get an interview, let alone a job anymore. They don't want a director over 40. And even that's pushin' it."

He says that he tells "all the young actors" that "less is more, unless you're talkin' about your check." In other words, says Bakalyan, "Don't try to do too much."

"If you know your craft," he says, only half-jokingly, "you can make it look so easy that people think you're stealin' their money. And we try to give 'em that impression."

As everyone knows, Bakalyan says, actors are "out of work most of the time. However, when I'm out, I'm lookin' at developing *character*, by watching people. I watch people eat, I watch 'em wait for a bus, I try to figure out what they're talkin' about from across the street, the body language of people. That's the fun of being an actor, 'cause that's what we're workin' with. And then, when you get a part, you make choices that will indicate to the audience, or the guy in the twentieth row, what the hell ya got goin'."

As keen an observer and communicator of human behavior as ever, Bakalyan has absolutely no interest in retiring: "I'm gonna be 74 in a couple of weeks, and I still look forward to gettin' a gig. I could be a multi-millionaire. It wouldn't make any difference. Someone sees you, and they want to buy your talent—they know you can ride the horse." On acting professionally, he concludes, "The idea is, we're always retired—it's when we get a job that we go to work. That's when our life starts."

---

* Bakalyan makes a very common error (among writers, at least) here. Dashiell Hammett first used the term "gunsel" in its correct meaning: the lower half of a homosexual relationship between convicts. However, over time, the word mistakenly became synonymous with "gunman."

THE FILMS OF DICK BAKALYAN

1955	*The Delinquents*
1957	*Dino*
	The Delicate Delinquent
	The Brothers Rico
	Hear Me Good
1958	*The Cool and the Crazy*
	Hot Car Girl
	Juvenile Jungle
	The Bonnie Parker Story
	Paratroop Command
1959	*30*
	Up Periscope
	Alcatraz Express (Comprised of *Untouchables* episodes)
1961	*The Errand Boy*

1962	*Panic in Year Zero!*
	Pressure Point
1963	*Operation Bikini*
1964	*Robin and the Seven Hoods*
	The Patsy
1965	*None But the Brave*
	Von Ryan's Express
	The Greatest Story Ever Told
1966	*Follow Me, Boys!*
1967	*The St. Valentine's Day Massacre*
1968	*Never a Dull Moment*
1969	*The Computer Wore Tennis Shoes*
	It's Tough to be a Bird (short)
1970	*The Animals* (producer/script)
1972	*Now You See Him, Now You Don't*
1974	*Chinatown*
1975	*The Strongest Man in the World*
1976	*The Shaggy D. A.*
	Marathon Man (voice)
	Woman of the Year (CBS tvm)
1977	*Pine Canyon is Burning* (NBC tvm)
	Black Sunday (voice)
1978	*Return from Witch Mountain*
1979	*H.O.T.S.*
1980	*The Man With Bogart's Face*
1981	*The Fox and the Hound* (voice)
1983	*Shooting Stars* (ABC tvm)
1984	*Blame it on the Night*
1985	*Heart of a Champion: The Ray Mancini Story* (CBS tvm)
1994	*Confessions of a Hit Man* (What year?)
2000	*The Mask Maker*
2001	*Discord*
2004	*Dick Bakalyan: The Face is Familiar* (documentary)
2006	*Art School Confidential*

TELEVISION

Bakalyan was a regular on *Dean Martin Presents The Bobby Darin Amusement Company* and *The Bobby Darin Show.* His other tv credits include: *Bat Masterson, The Deputy, The Untouchables, Batman, Branded, Wagon Train, Laramie, The Girl from UNCLE, The Partridge Family, Kolchak, Kojak,* and *The Rockford Files.*

DON PEDRO COLLEY

"I had planned on my character to be sympathetic. He was just protecting his little group of mutants. [But] I've had so many people tell me, over the years, 'You know, when I was ten years old and I saw you, you just scared the shit out of me!'"

Beneath the Planet of the Apes (1970)

After several years of working onstage and in television, Don Pedro Colley broke into features with two very memorable performances. He was in the single bleakest "G"-rated movie ever, ***Beneath the Planet of the Apes*** (1970), the first of four sequels to ***Planet of the Apes*** (1968). That same year, he played a gregarious hologram George Lucas' first feature, the similarly grim and dystopic ***THX-1138***. An early standout guest spot was as Forrest Tucker's assistant snake oil salesman in the "Dr. Stringfellow's Rejuvenator" segment of ***Night Gallery*** (1971).

Next, Don popped up in two of ex-football star Fred Williamson's black action films, starting with ***The Legend of Nigger Charlie*** (1972), a western. (As little as he probably relishes remembering the film, Don at least had the thrill of seeing a hulking 41" by 81" image of himself, Williamson, and Martin on the film's three-sheet poster.) In Larry Cohen's ***Black Caesar*** (1973),

Don was given a fine, theatrical death scene as the nattily dressed gangster, Crawdaddy. Seated in a swank restaurant, he is seen ordering dinner. "Can you recommend anything?" he politely asks the waiter. He lays down his menu, and, a moment later, is rewarded for his fine table manners with a bullet in the chest.

His performance as the suitably imposing post-nuclear mutant inquisitor of the far future in *Beneath the Planet...*gave Don one of his showiest parts, as limited as his screen time was. Over thirty years later, Don can look back with extreme satisfaction at having crafted what is *easily* the film's most nightmare-inducing performance, in the finest Margaret Hamilton tradition. Some of Don's catchiest dialogue in *Beneath*—"Mr. Brent, we're a peaceful people. We don't *kill* our enemies, we get our enemies to *kill* each other"—even found their way into the film's trailer. Like Buck Kartalian (interviewed elsewhere in this book), Don was given the chance to mistreat one of America's great leading men, Charlton Heston. In the film, his character uses his superhuman telepathic powers to force Heston and James Franciscus into a duel involving their fists, teeth, feet, and enormous, spiked clubs. The two turn the tables on Don, though, and gruesomely do him in by clamping him between a prison cell wall and its door, both of which are studded with massive iron spikes. *Beneath...*is exhibit "A" for the case that the "G" rating meant *nothing* in the '70s.

Don's overwhelming performance as the piratical, swaggering Baron Samedi in Paul Maslansky's *Sugar Hill* (1974) is one of his finest. Gaudily dressed in a sash, top hat, and spats, and commanding an army of pop-eyed zombies, he is the supreme highlight of the movie. His dialogue is also a joy: "I am Baron Samedi! This is my domain! A kingdom of the DEAD!" When Sugar Hill (Marki Bey) herself asks if he's troubled by jealousy, Baron Samedi beams, then replies (none-too-innocently), "Me, Sugar? *Nothing* troubles me!" Sugar convinces Samedi to put her cop boyfriend out of commission briefly, but the Baron is crest-fallen that she won't let him do-in the nosey flatfoot. "Much easier to kill him," pleads Samedi, visibly disappointed. Samedi appears in various guises throughout the movie:

as a construction worker, cabbie, gardener, and bartender (serving up a "zombie," naturally). Voodoo has almost never been this much fun.

I first encountered Don Colley's name and likeness in issue #5 of the '70s Marvel/Curtis Magazine, *Tales of the Zombie*, which featured a story-in-photos version of *Sugar Hill*. Don Pedro Colley, the copy ran, was playing Baron Samedi, one of the Haitian loa, in the film. His name begins with *Don*, I noticed; there's a *Pedro* there, so he must be Spanish, I further reasoned; and he is playing a character named *Baron* Samedi. *He must be an authentic exotic nobleman*, I concluded, *And he's been typecast!* Afterwards, as I began placing Don's name to his face in his movies, I was led into further delusions along similar lines by his orotund, courtly voice. A voice like his was made for the stage, as was his commanding, barrel-chested, 6' 4", 250-pound frame. (Like the late William Marshall, Don is an *ideal* Othello.) If he isn't the changeling son of a prince, I thought, he sure *seems* regal. When I finally made Don's acquaintance, I had long since found out that he was as exotic and/or royal as Waylon Jennings.

With their usual tact, logic, and charm, casting directors regularly gave Don the same kind of runaround that Robert Townsend's character faces in *Hollywood Shuffle* (1987). "Sorry, you just don't sound *ethnic* enough," was one example Don gave me of the static he would get. Just as Buck Kartalian suffers in casting for being a robust older man who isn't stereotypically feeble, Don Colley suffered for being a black man who didn't sound like Mantan Moreland or Jimmy Walker. Shortly before he retired, Don lamented of his profession, "It seemed more like a gift that I might have to give back."

Don's official website is at www.donpedrocolley.com. He was also interviewed by the *Planet of the Apes* fanzine, *Apesfan*. He briefly discussed his one *Night Gallery* appearance in *Night Gallery: An After Hours Tour* by Scott Skelton.

Don Pedro Colley was born in August 30, 1938 in Klamath Falls, Oregon, the son of Pete and Muriel Colley. "Actually," Don says," my Dad's name was Edgar

Allen, but everybody called him 'Pete.' Mother's name was Muriel Elizabeth, but she insisted she be called 'Merle.'" He calls his childhood "average," and though the Colleys weren't rich, he says, "We did very well. When my parents came west from Kansas in '35, they settled in Klamath. I think there was one relative there at the time.

"Klamath Falls was kind of a wild western town and it lies halfway on the railroad between Portland, Oregon, and San Francisco." There was a lot of "troop movement," Don explains, during World War II, between Portland and 'Frisco. Soldiers "used to overnight sometimes in Klamath," recalls Don, "which had some gambling houses and houses of ill-repute, and things like that. And dad was a piano player, like Nat 'King' Cole—he played and sang. So he did really well there.

"My mother got very involved in local politics, PTA, and things like that. And, some years later, there was the NAACP and she was northwest regional chairman of that for the states of Washington, Oregon, and Idaho.

"I was accorded the best of things around my school years," Don recalls. Though he played some football and basketball, track became his specialty in high school. "I was a discus thrower. I guess that's because where we lived in the country, we had lots of horses and cows and you used to get yourself a cowpie that was dry, and you'd sail that sucker away [laughs]."

As far as he can remember, he was the only black enrolled in Klamath's schools: "I think there was one girl. She was around high school age. But, poor child, she wasn't what you'd call a beauty, and we didn't socialize much together. I had a lot of friends, casual acquaintances, and most of the white kids that I was really most friendly with were the ones that nobody else would be friendly with [laughs]."

Like Paul Koslo, Don's attraction to acting began with an excess of the best kind of childish imagination. "I had one neighbor, his folks had come from Oklahoma, and he was kind of a loner kid, too." The two would play at an "untilled" field at the end of their road, Don says, a "huge sagebrush field that had a river or two running through it. We used to go there and we would imagine we were in the Amazon, or wherever. We'd build a little raft, and raft down this little river. We would build forts out of sagebrush, and some of the other kids would come out into the field and join us."

As a boy, Don's parents mainly socialized in Klamath's main black district of the period, Broad Street. "We lived by the airport and, occasionally, when I was a kid, we would go up and have a big barbecue [on Broad Street], and they'd gamble and play music and drink booze." The barracks of a local World War II airbase were later recycled as a secondary school, which Don attended.

The actor's closest friends included Modesto Jiminez, "a full-blooded Modock Indian," which was not surprising considering his mother's activist bent: "My mother got very involved in Indian politics and tribal doings there, to try and help people put their lives on the right track. There were a few educated ones.

But, basically, everybody got heavily into drugs and alcohol. And during a long period, it was really sad to see the Indians. They were more discriminated against then than I or my family were.

"I never dated in school. There was nobody to date. I had female friends, but I could never date them because it was just the sort of thing you didn't do. And we're talking from '52 to '56, when I was in high school. But it wasn't something that I missed, because I didn't have any frame of reference for it. Now it bothers me [laughs], *then* it didn't bother me. I was pretty bashful, anyway."

Don attended the University of Oregon in Eugene, he explains, "on a track scholarship as an architecture student. And it was such a wonderful new experience, I'm afraid I forgot to study a bit. [laughs] After my second year there, my grades were kind of down, so I had to transfer to a smaller college, Southern Oregon College in Ashland, for two-and-a-half years.

"I had a lot of credits, but couldn't get a degree." He remembers becoming intrigued by a music appreciation class, where he was exposed to the finest of classical composers. "I also got into some pretty heavy art classes," he says. "By then, there was group of us, interested in jazz at the beginning of the beatnik era. There was Greenwich Village in New York and North Beach in San Francisco. A lot of people began to migrate to San Francisco, and I ended up going myself in '61. And I was a beatnik in North Beach."

In 1966, he moved to Los Angeles, where he stayed with a buddy from Oregon: "He was in San Francisco at that time, and in the theater, and I was the only one who had a car. He needed to get to the theater one day, so I said, 'Hey, I've got a car. I'll take you.' I took him down there, and I asked [wonderingly], 'What do you *do* in there? What do you call 'legitimate theater'? What goes on in there? Can I see?'" His friend begrudgingly let Don observe them rehearse Jean Anouilh's *Caligula*, but made him sit in the empty house. "I was just astounded at what was going on. I remember sitting there with my mouth open and…drool was running down my chin, I was just so intrigued." Don's interest was piqued enough for him volunteer as an assistant with costumes, sets, lighting, and even ushering. He was far from disappointed: "Golly, it was just great, just grand."

"The Firing Squad," a splinter group specializing in improvisational comedy, formed from this theater company. The group's name arose from their base of operations and rehearsal space, an old firehouse. Among other venues, Don explains, "We were doing cabaret theater in local nightclubs."

Not only was Don's life changed drastically during this period, but his appearance, as well: "To earn money, we would paint Victorian houses, as a group. While painting a house, I fell off a fifteen-foot scaffold. It took sixteen stitches to close my head wound. They had to shave my head, and, since I couldn't wear a wig while acting, I've kept it that way ever since.

Young Don had chosen his career. "I was totally addicted from that point on," he explains. "It was amazing. It was wonderful. And other plays came around." Don was able to appear in the works of, among others, classic 19th century playwrights, like Chekhov, Ibsen, and Shaw. "If you could do the part, you did the part," he enthuses, "it didn't make any difference whether you were black, or white, or Asian, or Mexican, or whatever.

"I did thirteen different shows, one after another. I eventually worked my way up to the Actor's Workshop, which, at that time, was very big. Bertolt Brecht came all the way to San Francisco to oversee a play of his that we were doing. All of that period was really exciting, electric." Don took a succession of odd jobs, including mopping floors, working as a bouncer, and driving a cab. "I was mostly out of work, sleeping on the floors of hotel rooms, where we beatnik kids were hanging out. Somebody would have some money, and they'd open up a hotel room, and there'd be six or eight of us sleeping on the floors of the place.

"So I had this little raggedy car and I drove to L.A. And I remember coming in on the 101 Freeway at night and seeing the lights of Universal Studios...Every hair on my body stood straight up. 'Here I am in Hollywood!'

"I got off of Highland and went down and crossed Hollywood Boulevard and said [stunned], 'God, this here's HOLLYWOOD BOULEVARD! This is it! This is IIIIIIITTT!'" As this star-struck young man traveled around Sunset and Hollywood Boulevards, he recalls, "I saw this HUGE warehouse kind of building there, with pillars and steeples and filigree, and there was huge golden lettering on the front of the building, and it was all lit up at night. It said 'Samuel Goldwyn Studios.' And I stopped my car and I just sat there. For about twenty minutes, I just sat there, looking at it. It couldn't be true, but it was true: here I am."

His friend, Garland, was appearing in a production of Harry Segall's **Heaven Can Wait**, starring Jack Palance. It began at the Theater in the Round at Disneyland, and later traveled, closing in Anaheim's Melodyland Theater. During its initial rehearsals, Don recollects, "I sat down ringside and watched 'em rehearse and move around on the stage. And, God, I was just thrilled. I was within an arm's distance of touching Jack Palance.

"There were only three of us blacks in the show: my friend, Garland, and myself, and [famous ex-boxer] Archie Moore." It was during the heart of the '60s Civil Rights struggle. Anaheim was full at that time, Don says, of bitter, bigoted Okies, leftover from the "Dust Bowl days." These "old crackers," Don says, were more than happy to take potshots from nearby freeway overpasses at the blacks, Mexicans, and Asians passing below. "Hell, yeah, it was scary, very scary," he recalls, apprehensively. "And people were very hostile towards us. But we made a pact: hold your head up and keep going."

On a more upbeat note, though, Don's dearly enjoyed his stint working with the amiable Archie Moore. As the show was being rehearsed, Don says, "Archie grabbed me and Garland, and he said, 'Come on, guys. I need some help learning this part. I'll tell you what: they've given me this suite in a hotel room. I'll have them move some beds in, and you guys stay with me, and help tutor me in this part.' 'Well, you got it, Archie! Let's do it!' So Archie and I would have a little joke. He'd say, 'Hey, Don, close the doe.' D-O-E. And I'd say, 'Okay, Mistuh Moe!'

M-O-E. [laughs] He was very much like my father. He was that kind of gentle, warm human being. He was a really swell guy.

"I remember one time he had to come into town, so he'd acquired a limousine and he said, 'C'mon, Don, I'm going to take you with me.' 'Really? Okay!' So I got in the back of this limousine with [sounds like he's announcing the president] AR-CHIE MOORE! We're driving through one of the black sections of Los Angeles, and, I swear to God, traffic stopped, people came out of their stores and out of their businesses, and they lined the street like we were a parade of one or two. Archie would open the window, and he'd wave out or he'd stand up through the open roof. And people would yell, 'Yay! Archie Moore! We love you! My God! Oh, you're the greatest!' Sometimes people would come up and he'd sign a few autographs, not many, because if he really started in one spot, he'd get inundated and never get out of there. And I'm sitting in the backseat, and I thought, 'I WANT SOME OF THIS! I want some of this celebrity thing! This is just grand'

"Jack Palance was cool. He was like a big 19-year-old kid that was out of control. One night, we had a folding chair onstage, and the damned thing started collapsing. So he picked it up, took it like a frisbee, and tossed it over the orchestra pit, about fifteen or twenty rows up! Of course, he was pissed about the people and their attitude, because they gave us a bad time, because we were the blacks in the show." This fit of anger, Don says, was Palance's retaliation against the locals ass-backwards attitude. "And with Jack's craggy face, and this wild look in his eyes, and this crazy laugh of his, he had everybody totally mesmerized and scared to death.

"Closing night, we all said, "Please, Jack, just say your goodbyes and don't do anything insane, and let's get the hell out of Dodge, 'cause it's scary here.' But, that night, he got up there and he gave those people a piece of his mind about their attitude. Oh, man! And we hid out in the bus, because we were sure they were gonna lynch us that night! [laughs] It was marvelous that he stood up for us."

Their production of **Heaven Can Wait** traveled to Salt Lake City, with Don replacing Archie Moore. "We checked into the Mormon Tabernacle Temple Hotel, right across the street from the Mormon Tabernacle enclave. They started checking in everybody, until they got to Garland and me. They asked us, 'What are you two doing here?' 'Oh, we're part of the show.' 'You can't stay here.' 'But we're part of the show!' A quick phone call to Jack Palance. Jack came downstairs and he picked up the desk clerk by the collar, and lifted him off his feet. And this poor guy turned about forty-four shades of pink, green, and yellow. I know he had brown marks in his pants, too. Jack said, 'If you don't put my people in this hotel, we're leaving town right now.' He also threatened to bring in the newspeople, and to put out press releases and the whole nine yards. They didn't know what to do. They ended up calling in the mayor. They finally ended up putting us up at the hotel. It was fun.

"So now it came time to go find some food. Garland and I said, 'Well, let's see. We're gonna have trouble. Hey! Let's go where the black folks are. We know we can get some food there.' And they're usually down either by the bus depot or by the train depot. So, cool, we took off walking down to the train depot, and we got close to the [black] district, and we ran across a barbershop. 'Hey, brothers! What's happening?' 'Hey, man, where's a good place to eat?' 'Well, Mama Ophelia's Cafeteria's right around the corner.' 'Mama Ophelia…Okay, we got it!'

"We went down by the tracks, around the corner, and there's Mama Ophelia's. And she serves us a HUGE sausage patty, three or four eggs, biscuits with honey and jelly, and she reached up under the bar, and pulled out a little bottle of whiskey, and she put some in our coffee. And we had—Aaaaah —grits, all for about two dollars! And we told her we were in town doing this show, and if she had a chance, come out and see us. And she said, 'Well, I'd like to, but I don't think they'd let us come and see the show.' 'Well, it's kind of sad, but it is a free country, and if you want to, if you feel like you can handle the pressure, we're there and we're doing it. Please come see us.' In the meantime, they treated us just like royalty, so it was great.

"So, we go on back to the hotel and some of the other kids in the cast said, 'Well, where did you guys go eat?' 'Well, we found a place down the street…What did you guys eat?' 'It was kind of bad. We went around the corner and they turkey sandwiches on white bread and butter. It cost us about six bucks. [laughs] What did you guys eat?'" Colley described their massive meal. "'WOW! Can we go with you?' 'Noooo, I don't think so.' 'How come?' 'It'd sown by the railroad tracks where the black folks live.' 'But we could…' 'You forgot: You're in Salt Lake City, man. WE can't come up here, and YOU can't go down there!' 'That's not fair!' they said. This was one time [Garland and me] didn't mind things not being too fair [laughs]."

Don and Garland decided to walk over to a college jazz club one evening during the show's run. "All of a sudden, this carload of thugs drives by and starts calling us all kinds of ugly names and spitting on us, and shit. I said, 'Man, don't pay any attention to them. Just ignore them like they're not there.' We went to the club and had a great time. We had to walk back. The same carload of assholes came back. They'd gotten a fire extinguisher. It's midnight, and it's February, and it's cold. And they started spraying us and calling us more ugly names. A police car went by and we didn't even attempt to wave it down or anything. We decided not to tell Jack about it. He'd just make a big stink and there'll be more pressure. Nobody got hurt."

The stringent local standards of decency were quite a shock to Don: "One of the locals involved with the show said, 'The show is great, but your language in the show is so rough.' We had to take out everything that was 'bad.' Every time we said 'hell,' it had to be 'heck,' and every time it said, 'damn,' it became 'darn.' In the meantime, some distant relatives of Brigham Young took us around to some historic places that had belonged to him…They were certainly nice people, and treated us right."

One of Don's earliest tv appearances was on the popular exotic adventure series, *Daktari.* "They had a sequence on this episode where I had to do a minor stunt," Don says. " They didn't know from having black stunt guys. There weren't more than two or three around, at the best. There was not a stunt guy my size, black or white, and they would have had to put a skull cap on them. I went up to [producer] Leonard Kaufman and said, 'I'll do it for you. Let's keep going. This is costing us all money.' He was impressed.

"I was wearing this leopard skin thing. I was playing a tribal chieftain, and I was running away and I run across this tall grassy field. And the camera was down in a ditch, filming through the grass, and I ran in toward the camera. And I laid down and slid down this grassy incline, and rolled over and looked away from the camera. They said, 'Action,' I ran, and slid down on my butt. And the shot was great, and they said, 'Cut.' Then I heard somebody gasp, 'Oh, my God!' I began to feel my back. This gravel underneath the grass had shredded my back. I began to bleed. Now he's having a hissy fit and a panic attack because somebody else would probably sue, sue, sue big time. I just said, 'Just get your nurse over here. I said I'd do this for free.' They should have given me some compensation, though. So they doctored me up, and we went on with it, and I forgot about it."

After appearing onstage in Joseph Tuotti's *Big Time Buck White* in L.A., then understudying James Earl Jones as boxer Jack Johnson in Howard Sackler's *The Great White Hope* in New York, Don was cast as a hologram in George Lucas' feature debut, *THX-1138* (1970). The film's extraordinary cast included the fledgling Robert Duvall as THX, Donald Pleasance as the treacherous SEN, Sid Haig, and the ubiquitous, snowy-haired character man, Ian Wolfe. "I lived in a theatrical residence hotel in Los Angeles, called La Resido. Many of the performers who came west stayed there. In this hotel was Robert Duvall, Vincent Gardenia, Julie Harris, and several others. We all used to go to the swimming pool and swap stories and swim and tell lies. Just kids on a lark, having a great time. Duvall got the part with [George] Lucas. They apparently had auditioned everybody they could find in San Francisco to fill the part that I eventually got. Robert suggested that they bring me up to audition for the part, and they did. And I gave them a reading, and they hired me on the spot. They said, 'Are you ready to work? We'll need you for ten weeks.'

"In the meantime, this lady and I were great friends in San Francisco, because I had lived in San Francisco for six years. So, here I am, back in San Francisco, working. It was great. So, I arranged that I could go and live at her house in Haight and Ashbury, on Ashbury Street, a beautiful four-story Victorian. She still lives there. She's the mother of my twenty-two year old daughter, who's about to graduate from college in education and law."

The lengthy chase scene that concludes *THX* and other sequences were shot in the then-unfinished subway system between San Francisco, Berkeley, and Oakland. "We were on location for ten weeks there," Don says, "then we shot some scenes in the SF International Airport. And, then, we came to L. A. and we shot at Los Angeles Airport. There's a tram that runs down these long hallways. One side of the hallway was all kinds of mosaic tile. We had hundreds of extras. Many of them in San Francisco were from Synanon [drug treatment center]. They had to shave their heads, even the girls, and dress in white. We were up in Berkeley at the physics school, up on the hill; it was a NASA thing. We shot a bunch of scenes in that."

THX's highly irregular shoot continued in Los Angeles, in a studio formerly owned by Elvis Presley. Don was amazed by the unusual 1,000-millimeter lens that Lucas was using, which "took five people to operate. The aperture opening was about eighteen inches in diameter. It took two people to focus that. Then, there was one person focussing the camera, and, then, the camera operator. All four of those people wore headsets.

"They took a whole soundstage, and curved the sides all the way up to the catwalks, like sixty-five feet above the floor. They painted everything white in it. If you walked out in the middle of this huge soundstage, you found yourself lifting your feet and legs like you were walking on sponge or eggshells. You lost all sense of balance. It was weird—you had no frame of reference. You finally got used to it.

"And we put another man up on a catwalk. He had headphones that were connected to the four guys on the camera. This lens was so powerful that you could not shoot anything inside a distance of 250 feet. You had to be 250 feet away from the lens to focus on an object. They put marks on the floor at 75, 125, 175, and 200 feet." The cast rehearsed their lines with "little, tiny microphones that are picked up by short wave, with wires running down your costume. It's so you don't have to use sound booms."

"George Lucas was sitting on a six-foot stepladder just out of camera range, watching everything progress. As the actors would walk forward crossing a mark on the floor, the guy on the catwalk would call the distance to the camera focusers, and they would focus the huge lens. As the actors passed the next mark, he'd call out the next distance, and the next, and the next. Then, the actors would turn around and walk away from the lens, and the guy would call the distances. When you see the film, in that particular segment, where Duvall and Donald Pleasance escape from the jail cell, and Pleasance is saying, 'We can't do this. I can't breathe. Don't you feel it crushing down on us? Nobody has ever done this before. Where are we going?' The images of the characters shimmer like they're way, way away from you, and you're looking at them through a telephoto lens.

"George is sitting on this ladder with these big horn-rimmed glasses, and I'm watching George. And I swear to God, I saw this golden halo around his head. He looked like one of those cameo pictures of Jesus. It was kind of weird. George has a real problem with actors. He's a technocrat. He knows all about the technical parts of filmmaking, but actors confuse him because they're not static. He'd really rather have people like chess players on a board and do his thing.

"Between Duvall and George and myself, and his co-writer, Walter Murch, we used to have to sit and talk for hours, trying to get the subtext out of the script.

The things that would make the movie a movie, not just another one of his pieces that he would use to pass his grades in film school. And he often didn't understand where we were coming from, because we were talking theater, and acting, and life, and blood. And it was confusing to him, because he's thinking about angles, and lighting, and types of film, and types of lens. We had to make some compromises. He had to compromise and we had to compromise and work toward the end results. I think it was new to him at that time, being the kid who was in control of every part of the film, he had to release some control and work with others around him, not just his own imagination. We had to into his imagination and make it live for him.

"I remember they called me back to add a scene. It was a scene where Duvall and I are in this little control booth, looking at these bottles of blue liquid with these little, shapeless forms, bodies. I had a line, something like, 'Although it happened so slowly, nobody realized how it happened, and how man evolved into cybergenics…' He would say, 'Cut, cut. I want you to do it this way.' So, I'd do it again, and he'd say, 'No, no, cut.' We did twenty takes. I told George, 'You are asking me to act a reaction. It's impossible. It can't be done. The actor acts the action. The audience gets a reaction.' But, 'No, no, no.' He was trying to give me stage directions, and they were all wrong.

"Finally, I said, 'Please, let me do it my way just once, please.' We'd been there almost six hours. It was supposed to take one hour to complete. The bill was running and the clock was ticking. He wasn't happy about it, but he got what he wanted. We called it a wrap and went on home. In those early stages, he didn't know how to relinquish total control in everything and work as a film director, as well as a producer. You have to let the actors do their thing." Despite any qualms Don may have had with Lucas' directorial style, the actor and director were reunited recently at Lucas' gargantuan Skywalker Ranch. There, Don was housed in high style, and filmed an interview for **THX**'s expanded dvd release. In conjunction with the dvd, Don will be appearing with other major **THX** alumni at a screening at New York's Guggenheim Museum.

In his first film role for a major studio, Fox, Don played the post-nuclear, bomb-worshipping mutants' torturer in **Beneath The Planet of the Apes**. (He was unceremoniously dubbed "Negro" in the film's credits.) "I didn't have to audition," he recalls. "My agents were very powerful at that time. I got the script and then I got a call to do a costume fitting at a special seamstress. And then they called me in and started the whole process of doing the masks out of molds. We had to be at the make-up department at Twentieth at 4:30 in the morning, the five of us mutants: Victor Buono, Natalie Trundy, Jeff Corey, Paul Richards, and myself. We each had our own make-up assistants. They stuck straws in my nose and said, 'We're going to have to stick your head in this plaster. And if you get claustrophobic, you're gonna have to be in there for at least a half-hour. Just give us a holler and we'll break it off your head and get you out of there.' They took this warm goo and they put it all over your head, clear down to your shoulder

blades, front and back. You sit there while it hardens. It was so nice and comfortable in there, what the hell, I went to sleep! [Eventually] they had a perfect mask of your face, just like a Halloween mask. Then, they painted it to look like the under-skin, under your epidermal layer." A second, normal facemask was then made, to be worn over the mutant make-up. "By the time we had the

first mask glued on and another mask over us, a wool hood, a tee shirt, a wool jacket, wool pants, and wool gloves. And then they put a wool outer robe over [it all], with the headpiece that went over the top with a big medallion down one side. Eventually, when we were in the cathedral, singing the songs, they had another robe with a hood piece that went over the top. The object was to sit in all of this stuff and not sweat, because it would loosen the glue on the mask and the mask would look all weird." (Note: Several years ago, Don's ornate mutant costume came up for auction on eBay.)

"Before we were in the final costumes and make-up, we were brought in the studio and started script rehearsals. We started in a large conference room, then they moved us to the set, so we all had a chance to see it. It was wonderful, because it was like doing a stage play in this great, huge soundstage. We had our own dressing rooms and it was marvelous to be at Twentieth and in the major production going on there at the time. Other stars around the studio would sneak in to watch us work, which was kind of exciting, to see [famous] people peeking around the corner. Sometimes, they also had a red-light set. After a while, they said, 'Nobody can come in and watch. It's a secret. [In a mock-diabolical voice] You can't come look. Stay out—Nyaaahahahaha....' [laughs]

"I made friends with Victor Buono. He was such a nice guy. And he was an inveterate game player; he had all these little games that he liked to play, little word games, little board games. One day, he says, 'Don Pedro, come into my trailer. I've got this new game I want to show you!' We go out to the trailer. We had these little two-wheeled trailers for our dressing rooms at the time. And we go in the back and sit down on a bench, and the trailer tips up—boink! [laughs] He was a big guy and I'm not little myself, so here we are. We overbalanced this damned trailer, and the doorway is sticking straight up in the air, and we're in there shouting 'HELLLP! Somebody get us out of here!' And nobody came. We're sitting there cracking up, because it was funny, I must admit. So, I said, 'Victor, you sit here, and I'll work my way up alongside the wall and see if I can't get up to the door.' I start crawling back, I get halfway, and—BOOM!—the trailer comes down! All the mirrors come off the walls, the lights all break and explode in a cloud of sparks. It was hilarious. I don't' think they were too happy with us [laughs]. The set carpenters came and built a foundation around the trailer, so it wouldn't tip up after that. God, it was funny."

Make-up man John Chambers was retained from the first *Apes* film to oversee the make-up. "Johnny came into the make-up department two or three different times. He was supervising the whole thing, after he had done the first one, of course, and won the Academy Award. He was the chief supervisor on the rest of the make-up and the masks. The designing was a collaboration of various people, but he had been made head of the department for those projects. He came down several times and patted us on the back and made sure everything was all right. It was really nice of him.

"Working with Heston and [James] Franciscus was interesting. I was mildly disappointed with Charlton Heston, but nothing big. I thought, here I'm going to be working with Moses, El Cid, I figured him to be a really warm, wonderful kind of outgoing kind of guy. But he's very shy and standoffish and very much to himself. He had told Twentieth, 'I'll only be in this second movie if you can shoot everything I have to be in, in one week, because I'm scheduled to go and do *Julius Caesar* in London, and that's very important to me. And I'll do it for free.' At least that's what I had heard. I don't know if they even paid him or not. I had a scene with him, and that was a thrill, working with Charlton Heston."

In Don's final scene, his character forces Heston and Franciscus into a mortal duel, then is crushed by the two actors between the spiked bars of a jail cell's wall and door. "It was choreographed like dance, so nobody gets hurt, and yet it plays like the real thing. And when it came time for me to be killed, crushed in the jail cell walls, I had planned on my character to be sympathetic. He was just protecting his little group of mutants. I've had so many people tell me over the years, 'You know, when I was ten years old and I saw you, you just scared the shit out of me!' Well, he was kind of a scary guy. That's how it was sold. And when he meets his demise, everybody could say, 'YAH! Kill the bastard!'

"[I thought] 'They're going to crush me in this wall and I've got this camera in my face. How am I going to die? Okay, I've got an idea.' So, when they crush me, I go, "Aaaaaaah!" and my eyes cross. You know, when you get crushed and your eyes cross and your tongue sticks out? So it looked really horrible and awful. And then I turn and fall on the floor, and turn over and peel off my face and say, 'I reveal my inmost self unto my goddddddddd!' The end. Yeah, yeah. I like that."

The film was directed by Ted Post, one of Clint Eastwood's pet directors. "Ted was like his name. He was like a big, old teddy bear. He knew exactly what he wanted, but he wasn't a distant director. He'd get down and dirty with you, and he'd tell you what he wanted and how he wanted you to approach it. He would joke with you. He was a warm, nice guy. We had some fun times, a lot of jokes and laughs. This was such a weird thing we were doing. And it could be as funny as hell, and we were trying to make it serious—Here, with everybody walking around with all this weird make-up and acting like apes and mutants. But he got out of us what he needed and the movie worked. And look what happened—thirty years later, who would have thought?

"There are not many projects that actors have a chance to say, 'We will be part of the historical balance of this industry from now until whenever.' There have only been a handful of films, *like Birth of a Nation, Gone With The Wind, Citizen Kane, Rebel Without a Cause,* and the *Planet of the Apes* series. It's very gratifying that we were in a project that is a historic milestone in the entertainment industry."

AIP's extremely successful *Black Caesar* (1973) was a gangster film starring Fred Williamson as Harlem gangster Tommy Gibbs, "The cat with the 45-calibre claws," as its ad copy went. Caesar was written and directed by outspoken B-movie kingpin Larry (*It's Alive!*) Cohen. The film reteamed Don, Williamson, and actor/director D'urville Martin from Paramount's 1972 hit, *The Legend of Nigger Charley.*

Ruefully, Don recalls that *Black Caesar* "was a black moment in my life [laughs]. Fred Williamson and I had done a movie together for Paramount that did really very well. In fact, I had to tutor Fred how to act. Fred was a pretty boy; that's all he was. I told him, 'You can't be a pretty boy. You have to be an actor, get down and dirty, and do the right thing.' So, later, now he's got a little prestige and power and he's producing these movies on the sly, and he asked me to be in this movie, called *Black Caesar*." Alas, Don also found D'urville Martin

impossible to work with: "He seemed to feel, since he started in New York, all else was beneath him!"

Nattily dressed in an all-white suit, Don (as "Crawdaddy") assists in the massacre of a Mafia picnic. "I did it as a favor, to be in the movie. I was there in physical presence, but, spiritually, I wasn't there. I didn't like doing the movie. The whole thing was working in the worst B-movie, like a B-horror film, or *Motorcycle Babes From Mars* or something. It was a horror. It was terrible. I saw a cut of it later, and went, 'Oh, the movie is so bad, it's embarrassing.' It's such a rank, amateur production. It's the worst production I've ever been associated with. Every actor in Hollywood has got one or two movies in their pockets that they really would rather forget, altogether."

That same year, Don appeared in a forgotten, little film, ***This is a Hijack***, whose title explains everything about it. The highlight of the film for Don was working with the late, great Neville Brand, a favorite character actor if there ever was one. Don wrote recently:

Neville Brand was one of my favorites, also! This movie was a total drag to work on, because the writer was also directing, and hoping to poke the lead actress, while pushing everyone else around, because he had no clue what he was doing. In the middle of one scene, Mr. Brand blew up over these shenanigans, threw his script in the air like confetti, and walked off the set with some well-placed expletives in this jerk's face. It took the producer several hours of pleading to get him to come back. But during that time, I had a chance to sit and talk with Mr. Brand about his life in the business.

Next up for Don at AIP was **_Sugar Hill_** (1974), and the plum role of voodoo overlord Baron Samedi. "Oh, yes," he says, with more than a pinch of distaste, "American International Pictures. The family of the Arkoffs! Sammy Z. [Arkoff] was about five foot-two inches tall. He smoked a cigar that was four inches in diameter. It was a huge cigar…He'd reach up and throw his arm around your waist.

"I'm supposed to be playing a voodoo god rising from the grave with an army of zombies. So, I said, 'Well, let me go back into my old theater bag of tricks here, and do what I'm supposed to do. Let me do a lot of research.' So, I got several books from the library. One was written by two anthropologists that had studied voodoo religions around the world. And another was written by a practitioner of voodoo from Haiti."

Don's research revealed that Samedi was based on an "all-powerful, omnipotent" Haitian deity, known as Papa Legre. "Throughout this voodoo culture, Papa Legre is the one single heavyweight dude. My character's name was Baron Samedi. It went through how the rituals of voodoo work. For those who believe in it, things can actually happen, good or bad…

"The two scientists related voodoo rituals to other rituals that take place in other religions such as the Catholic religion, the burning of the incense, the drinking of the blood, the wafer, the bread of God. These are rituals that are really taken right out of voodoo rituals. And relating the singing from the Baptist or Episcopalian or Presbyterian religions, even the Muslims and the Sikhs, all of the rituals all had a basis in the early African voodoo tribal religion that came west from the tribes of Africa when the slaves went abroad. So, I said, 'I've now got all this information. I'm going to make Baron Samedi scary. Boy, is he going to be scary.'"

Most of the film was shot in Houston, Texas. One "found" set, the mansion of voodoo priestess Mama Maitresse, was a house, Don says, "that looked like it had been abandoned for a hundred years. It even had an elevator in it. It had been abandoned for ten or fifteen years. The place was full of cobwebs and dust. It was really quite neat.

"The only thing I objected to is, here I am starring in this movie, and I'm being treated like a peon. Robert Quarry was under contract to Samuel Z. and AIP. He was working off the last bit of his contract, so he took all the salary. Here they are, paying me $750 a week and I'm starring in this bloody mess. Union law states that, when the performers travel, they travel first-class and they stay in a first-class hotel. And when they work on the set, they have a first-class dressing room.

"So, I get to Houston, finally—I didn't have any dressing room. It was like 95% humidity. It was 95 degrees, every day. They were talking about having me stand behind a car in the street to change clothes. Forget it! So, I went out and rented a forty-foot motor-home and I drove it to the set. And the producer went buggo, he went *off*: 'You can't do that! You can't drive that here! We have to pay the union drivers a thousand a week, and...' And I said, 'Wait a minute. Are you telling me that a driver of my motor-home makes more money a week than I do, and I'm starring in this piece of shit?' I said, 'I'm going to keep this until you provide me with a dressing room. And, in the meantime, I'm calling the union and letting them know exactly what you people are doing down here.' That's what they did at American International. They exploited everybody." However well *Sugar Hill* turned out, in terms of Don's performance, his dislike of Arkoff and AIP has not abated: "It as a sweatshop, for sure," he says.

The term "blaxploitation" (from "black exploitation," of course) strongly irks Don. "If I could get my hands on the reviewer who coined the phrase 'blaxploitation,'" he says, obviously frustrated, "I'd choke his ass until he turned blue, yellow, and green. He destroyed our entrance into the business as being *bona fide* filmmakers.

"The initial intention was an awareness that the stuff we were doing was a tiny bit exploitative, but [ethnic] America was looking

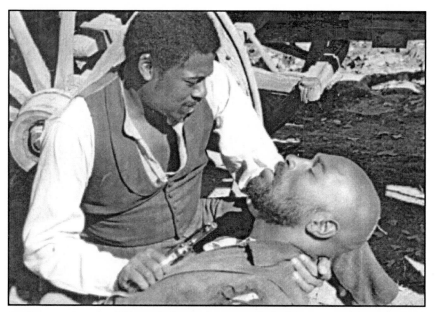

for its own heroes. Up until that point, we only had Caucasian heroes. It kind of excluded the whole other sixty or seventy percent of America: Asians, Mexicans, blacks. When we started our flow of films in the late '60s, early '70s, the theater chains were divided by 'A,' 'B,' and 'C' movies. 'A' movies play in the big houses downtown. 'B' movies play on the outskirts of downtown. 'C' and 'D' movies play in the neighborhoods, in almost every city, in the barrio, and in the ghetto, Asian Town, Korean Town. We were putting movies in these houses that had neighborhood heroes. They were making money hand-over-fist, and the 'A' and 'B' movies were falling on their face. They didn't know what to do, they didn't know how to do it. We were doing fine. It's easier for people to come out of these houses and go to their neighborhood movie houses, and not go all the way across town, and feel intimidated and have people stare at them. We were making money for everybody.

"There were some good ['70s black-oriented] movies: *Shaft,* and *Blacula* was fun, *Watermelon Man,* and *Cotton Comes to Harlem*. Good stuff. This reviewer said, 'Why are you exploiting these poor black people?' He was attempting to be on our side, but he drove a stake through everybody's heart. And by 1973, it was dead. We couldn't get any work. I was working every other week from '66 to '73." A major downward spiral in Hollywood began during the "energy crunch" of 1973, Don recalls: "They just quit making movies with our kind of characters. They started turning out *Texas Chainsaw Massacre* and *Chrome Pliers in the Night*—it was just terrible, awful junk—and putting them in 'A' and 'B' Houses. The 'C' and 'D' house had to close down, because they couldn't get product. They had lost their heroes. There were no longer any heroes."

The problems that arose weren't limited to ethnic performers, he explains: "On television shows, at that time, if you were a special guest star, your salary base was thirty-two hundred dollars a week." After the "energy crunch," though, he says, "special guests" were making around $700 less, per week. "They quit using big names. They didn't want to pay them. The whole business has just been on a downhill slide since then."

Don did a popular hitch as the terrifying "Sheriff Little" on tv's **The Dukes of Hazzard.** The actor's acquaintance with producer Leonard Kaufman, dating back to his **Daktari** days, helped win him the part: "Years later, I was called in by Leonard, now the line producer on **Dukes of Hazzard,** who said, 'I never forgot you from that day [that Don did the stunt for free]. We've got this Sheriff Little. Do you think you can pull it off?' I had a beard. I went home and put on my cowboy boots and a big, old ten-gallon Stetson. I went stomping in there to do my audition. Secretaries were falling off their chairs. I gave a wonderful reading." Sheriff Little's first appearance involved a panicky Sheriff Rosco P. Coltrane (James Best) and Boss Hogg (Sorrell Booke) attempting to sneak a van-load of "illegal hooch" past Don's character. Little proceeds to cock his shotgun in their faces, and blow the van to smithereens.

"They hired me on the spot," Don happily recalls. "I played him straight. He was a badass. It reminded me [of] way back when I was in high school, I had a chemistry teacher. Her name was Miss Herron. She looked like your old maid aunt, but she could chew nails and spit them out at you. She was scary. She would intimidate her students. Kids would end up crying if they didn't have an answer. Some kids would get really scared. I'd have to cover my mouth to keep

from giggling. But if she catches you laughing, you're next. This is the way I played Sheriff Little. 'Please don't let him see me!' It worked really well."

By 1999, Don's opinion of the New Hollywood had, understandably, soured badly: "My friends in this business around my age are all mystified as to what's going on. I was talking to a screenwriter and a script doctor. He had some really great credits; he just turned fifty. He tells me that they told him that he's too old.

"Money has so totally taken over the business. The mentality has a window that's ten minutes-old or ten minutes-new. If it's ten minutes-old, then it's discarded. We have all these blasted sitcom shows, they don't use any job-ins [when they hire outside people to be characters] anymore. They use the same six people over and over. If there is a job-in, the person comes in and delivers a telegram and walks out, unless it's an old comedian who plays a relative. Many films today are all computer-generated special effects, throw in some naked scenes, lots of gunfire, lots of bloodshed, car chases, airplane or ship explosions, and no story line. There are a hundred million great stories out there, but what do they do? They start making remakes of old cartoon shows or remakes of old classic movies."

Many chagrined, older actors have been appalled at the over-dependence on computer-generated effects in modern films. Don is no different: "They can computer-generate actors and actresses. They don't need us anymore. That's what it's coming to. Where's the story line? Young filmmakers that are just starting out are conscious of this. They want to tell stories." The actor has begun appearing in so-called "indies" in the last few years, including **The Hiding Place** (aka: **The Hollow Place**), a modern version of Poe's "The Tell-Tale Heart." "I play a policeman trying to investi-gate this horrible murder." The results deeply satisfied Don: "It's a wonderful little film."

"I just did a voice-over commercial for a plastic surgeon. I haven't had [almost any] work since 1995. I haven't had a day's work. I even took a voice-over class for animation. I went on an interview one day for a major project. This casting director asked, 'What have you done? Who have you worked with?' 'I worked with George Lucas.' Blank look. '*Star Wars*?' 'I thought Spielberg did those.' I started for the door. I said, 'One of us is in the wrong business here.' He said, 'What do you mean?' I said, 'Forget it, forget it. You don't know and I can't tell you.' He was screaming at me, 'Who do you think you are?!'"

Needless to say, Don became profoundly disillusioned with Hollywood, in general: "We used to pride ourselves on having the knowledge that came before us. The exciting things that made us want to be in this mess. Today, it's—bottom line—money. Who's got the money and who's on top, who's got the formula."

With work petering out for him—as has happened to *many* talented, journeyman actors once they reach fifty—Don finally retired from show business in 2000. He left Los Angeles permanently for his other home in Oregon. For Don, the shift from that ultra-seedy Gehenna to his native state "was like going from the stink of a skunk into the scent of night-blooming jasmine." He remains close friends with his fellow ***Daniel Boone*** alumnus and Oregonian, actor Dallas McKennon. Most recently, he has passed along some of his decades worth of experience by assisting with local collegiate theater, as he delights in his retirement.

THE FILMS OF DON PEDRO COLLEY

1969   *THX-1138*

1970   *Beneath the Planet of the Apes*

1971   *Vanished* (NBC tvm)
        The Cable Car Murders (aka: *Cross Current;* CBS tvm)
        Believe in Me

1972   *The Legend of Nigger Charley*

1973   *Black Caesar*
        The World's Greatest Athlete
        This is a Hijack

1974   *Sugar Hill* (aka: *The Zombies of Sugar Hill*)
        Herbie Rides Again

1975   *Death Scream* (aka: *The Woman Who Cried Murder*) (ABC tvm)

1980   *Casino* (ABC tvm)

1988   *The Blue Iguana*

1993   *Quest of the Delta Knights*

1994   *Cagney and Lacey: The Return* (tvm)

1995   *Piranha*

1998   *A Hollow Place* (aka: *The Hiding Place*)

TELEVISION

Don was a regular (as Gideon) on **Daniel Boone**. He was also on tv shows like **Daktari, The Wild, Wild West, The Virginian, Cimarron Strip, Here Come the Brides, Night Gallery, Nichols, Search, Little House on the Prairie, Adam 12,** and *Starsky and Hutch.*

ROYAL DANO

"Can you think of someplace where you can earn enough money to support a family and do as little as you have to do in this business? It's utterly amazing!"

The Tattered Man in *Red Badge of Courage* (1951).

For several decades, Royal Dano was a fixture in westerns. His lanky build, imposing height, expressive eyes, and slightly gravelly baritone made him instantly recognizable, no matter what he happened to be playing. He was cast, at one time or another, as a bandit, gambler, American Indian, a mute, and, in ***Tension at Table Rock*** (1956) as a printer, Royal's father's actual trade. With a little make-up and some ragged wardrobe, he looked like he had just stepped out of Antietam.

By the 1960s, Royal nearly specialized in playing great historical and literary figures. The role that brought him to early prominence was as Abraham Lincoln in a five-part series on ***Omnibus*** in 1952. The script was by the extraordinary James Agee, who also had a brief acting role in the series as Jack Kelso. In Nicholas Ray's ***King of Kings*** (1961), he was St. Peter, opposite Jeffrey Hunter's uncomfortable Christ. He was the voice of Marley's Ghost in the nominally literary, animated ***Mr. Magoo's Christmas Carol*** (1962). In ***The Skin Game*** (1971), he played John Brown under a landslide of fake, grey beard. Royal was cast in two productions

Royal Dano and James Agee.

of *Adventures of Huckleberry Finn*, one of which was directed by Michael Curtiz in 1960. The other was a 1975 television production, where he added Mark Twain to his roster of historical parts. He even played the infamous Hollywood censor, Will Hays, in his friend Larry Buchanan's *Hughes and Harlow: Angels in Hell* (1977).

But it was as Lincoln that he left the most indelible impact. Such an impact, in fact, that he was hired to voice Walt Disney's animatronic Lincoln automaton at the 1964 World's Fair. Afterwards, the figure was famously displayed at Disneyland. His marvelous voice could be heard there, at the Opera House attraction in Town Square, up until only recently. (It was replaced by a lame successor, who reportedly gave Lincoln a *southern* accent!) The lp record of his Disney Lincoln performance, *Great Moments With Mr. Lincoln*, sold a couple of million copies on Buena Vista Records. The album was narrated by voice-over great Paul Frees. At least Royal's brilliant original can still be enjoyed on vinyl. (Another lesser-known Dano role for Disney was in their *Old Yeller* sequel, *Savage Sam*, 1963.)

He also received a lion's share of horror film roles, beginning as an ornery townee in *Face of Fire* (1958). Some of his other *genre* credits include *Messiah of Evil* (1972); as a ghoulish mortician on *CHiPs*; as yet another monster-hunting villager in *Moon of the Wolf* (also '72, tv); as a seedy carny in *Ghoulies II* (1988); a comical revivified corpse in *House II* (1987); a gravedigger in *The Dark Half* (1994); and as a hapless old farmer, who fatally encounters the *Killer Klowns from Outer Space* (1988).

One of Royal's last truly outstanding performances was as Tom Fury, the appropriately weather-beaten lightning rod salesman, in Disney's *Something*

Wicked This Way Comes (1983). Actors occasionally come along who are born to play certain literary characters. Just as Clark Gable *was* Rhett Butler, and James Mason *was* Captain Nemo, Royal Dano was the only man who could play Tom Fury. (So what if that's a bit of an exaggeration?) An editor once told me that he could no longer read Bradbury's novel without picturing Fury as Royal. Many people give ***Something Wicked*** short shrift as a film, and it *is* a vastly scaled-down version of the novel. But Royal, like his co-stars Jonathan Pryce and Jason Robards, was one of the few film actors who ever seemed able to cope with delivering Bradbury's unique dialogue: "Hellfire storm's a-comin'! An electric storm, to clean your streets and wash away your troubles!" And Royal's amiable, memorable declaration, "Who tells 'ya? Tom Fury tells 'ya!"

(It should also be noted that Royal has been cast, again and again, as figures of doom…Mad, or apparently mad, prophets, whose pronouncements are, all too often, correct. These character include Tom Fury; Elijah in ***Moby Dick*** (1956), a character entirely invented by Ray Bradbury; and the Minister in ***The Right Stuff*** (1983), whose presence inevitably means the death of another astronaut.)

In ***Fangoria*** Magazine's "Pit and Pen of Alex Gordon" column, Gordon singled Royal out for a special profile in issue #55. His description of Royal's abilities could be applied to any of the finest character players: "A character actor like Royal Dano cannot simply put himself on display like a star can, assured that his radiance will attract every eye. He must be a wily mendicant for the audience's attention, making up in craft what he lacks in glamour. He doesn't just play a scene, he caresses it…he steals it." (One of the finest examples of Royal's overwhelming ability to do precisely that is his remarkable cameo, as a maimed Confederate soldier, confronting John Wayne during the opening of ***The Undefeated*** (1969).)

I first contacted Royal for an interview about George Pal's 7 **Faces of Dr. Lao** (1964). Royal's **Undefeated** co-star and friend, John Agar, gave me his number. I called Royal up, and immediately started asking him the kinds of damn fool things that only a rank amateur can come up with. "Did you keep any of those lightning rods that you carried in **Something Wicked This Way Comes**?" I recall asking him. "Oh, no," Royal patiently answered to this total stranger, "They were big, heavy things." Throughout the period that I was acquainted with him, his patience and personal grace never faltered.

I was given an astonishing glimpse of Royal's profound professionalism when I conducted this interview in late February, 1994. He was on oxygen at the time, but still went ahead with the interview as if nothing extraordinary was going on. About halfway through the questions, though, he dropped a bombshell on me: his oldest son, Royal, Jr., had died the previous day. I was flabbergasted. Royal paused somberly, reflected for a moment, and, without further ado, continued answering questions, trouper that he was. Perhaps he knew that that was his last chance to tell his stories properly.

I only spoke with Royal once more after this interview. He was cheery and glad to talk; we discussed either **Welcome to Hard Times** or **Day of the Evil Gun**. A few weeks after that conversation, on May 15, 1994, Royal was gone. Michael Weldon called me with the news not long afterwards. I still feel a deep, lingering debt to Royal for his outstanding kindness to me.

Some other esoteric Dano appearances: he was interviewed extensively for Lawrence Grobel's **The Hustons**, but Grobel's use of a particularly off-color Dano quote rankled him. (I will not quote Royal's opinion of Grobel and his editors, for reasons of taste.) In Lillian Ross' 1952 account of the making of **Red Badge of Courage, Picture,** Royal is quoted and mentioned several times. Some heated dialogue between Robert Blake and Royal can be heard on the soundtrack lp to the underrated **Electra Glide in Blue** (1975). He also cropped up in pen-and-ink form in Marvel Comics' **House II** movie edition comic book.

Royal Dano was born November 16, 1922 in New York City. His father, he explained, was "Caleb Edward Dano, a printer for the New York papers, for many of the newspapers. A journey printer, back in the days when that was sometimes all you had. He worked on big papers, like the San Francisco *Chronicle* and the Chicago *Tribune*. And he would take trips on ships, and he worked for the *Times* in New York [and] the New York *Daily Mirror*. He wound up working the last twenty-seven years for the New York *Daily News*." Royal's mother "was an Irish immigrant by the name of Mary Josephine O'Connor."

As a boy, Royal was quite a movie buff. His favorite stars included, he said, "Gene Tierney, Laraine Day, and Sonja Henie…especially as a young pubescent. When she came skating into the picture, crotch-first, it was tremendous…Boy, did they put a lot of those shots in the pictures."

As a boy, Royal "went to the public schools in New York and Catholic school—I started out with the nuns and the brothers, the monks. Then when we went out on Long Island, the first school I went to had a pot-bellied stove to keep them warm. That was in Jackson Heights. Then, finally, the put up new buildings. We went there. I went to Hallon High in New York."

Royal's college career was "Just NYU, briefly," he said. "I was taking a nighttime course during the day because at that time, I belonged to the state guard. I was working on the Daily *News* and I belonged to a kids' military organization called the Junior Naval Militia. Between all of these things, I would try to squeeze in a little bit of sleep. I'd also try to get laid, every once in awhile. Made life kinda difficult; there isn't much time in the day left over."

His career with the military began early: "Well, I was platoon sergeant with the 17th Regiment, New York Guard, and my responsibility was to clear the Borough Bridge." The New York *Tugenbund*—radical German sympathizers—were a major threat during the early years of World War II. The military commanders feared that the Bundists would isolate Manhattan. Said Royal, "If they took over the bridge, it would isolate the military training camp on the island from the ships that were sailing out of the Manhattan docks, you see. My job was to, at the slightest provocation, to assemble the men in my platoon and head for the Queens borough and defend it."

It was only when he "went into the regular army," Royal said, that he began acting: "I had an appointment to the US Maritime Academy in King's Point, New York. And I waited and I waited and they were trying to turn them out right and left. All the courses had been cut to three years, even at Annapolis and there just wasn't that much room. They were trying to get the guys through and get 'em out to sea at the Merchant Marine Academy. And I was held up, too—

He graduated high school in February, 1942, he said, "and they stalled me most of the year and I had this naval deferment. And then all of my buddies were leaving, everybody I knew was on their way out, including some of the guys who I had gone up with to join. I put in applications with the Royal Air Force and when the papers came to my home, my dad opened 'em and he started yelling like hell. He was not in favor of supporting Britain in anything—they burned the White House, you know. And then my mother just hated them for occupying Ireland. "So, anyway, I just went to the naval headquarters downtown and asked them when I was going. They said I wouldn't go till July and, meanwhile, the landings had started in North Africa. I figured, 'Shit, the Americans are there. The war'll be over in a couple of months.' And, so, on the way home, I got off the train and went to the draft board office and said, 'How do I waive my deferment?' And they said, 'We'll waive it for 'ya!' They were so desperate for fill-in soldiers. They said, 'When do you want to leave?' You usually got seven days. I said, 'Tomorrow.' I knew my dad would have a fit. And I left and eventually got assigned to a truck regiment sent to India. The truck regiment's mission was to open the Burma Road, which wasn't in existence.

"And while I doing that...I think the first job I had after high school was working for the New York *Daily News,* and the guys had a newspaper where they printed dirty jokes, a little risqué material, and I got this thing and I'd tell these jokes to the guys. And one day I was telling a joke and the airborne major said, 'Hey, sergeant, you gonna do a show for us?' And I said, 'I can't do a show. I don't know how to do it.' The only others I had done were high school shows, y'know. And he just more or less ordered me to do a show and I did [one] with a burlesque comic.

"I was in doing my regular job at the time, a section sergeant with a truck outfit. Did that [show], then he wanted me to do another one. So I was put together with a singer, who is still a good friend of mine and whom always wanted to write songs and he did write one good hit, 'Sixteen Reasons Why I Love You.'" The singer's name was William Post, who later settled in Kansas.

"Well, it was after the first tour of the show we had put together, which was called **Over and Back**. And we took it up to the top of the Burma Road and then down. And we played places like Manipore, which is where the British had held out. When they were relieved, we got in there. That was in India."

Royal met his wife "Well, after this first tour down into Burma and back out, we were supposed to get to China. So, the place we were supposed to go to China at fell to the Japanese, who were counter-attacked and retook it. And so we were sitting there at the mission hall at Burma Airport waiting for the plane to pick us up and take us to China, the little group of guys in **Over and Back**." A superior officer told them the base in China had been lost, "and so they shipped us around and sent us back into places like Delhi, and to Caracci, on the other side of India. And [then] to Bombay, into Ceylon, to play [General George S.] Patton's headquarters. And then they did a survey. This was the first time I'd ever heard of these kinds of things. Advertising people used to do 'em all the time to see how ads were affecting people. They wanted to know how the show did, so they contacted all the bases. And one of the biggest bitches was that they didn't have live women. They had all guys dressed as broads, y'know?

"And that got addressed. So they sent out a call to the British Friends and the Royal Indian Army WACs and the American WACs, the Red Cross. And Peg [Dano's wife], was over there with the Red Cross and she had been in the Barter Theater [in Virginia], back in the days when Greg Peck was there." When Royal first met Peggy, "She was up serving coffee to the guys who were flying at an airbase up in Via Sam, where the guys flew up over the hump. And we were put together in a show called **Brother Rat**, which the fellows took and turned into a musical. The Colonel sang a song like [sings], 'Oh, I'm the Colonel/ So come to attention./ Listen carefully to every little word I mention.' Everybody had a number to do and the general parts of the show stayed the same. She played the little ingenue in there. And I played the taxi cab driver that was running around hocking everything everybody wanted to hock. And we met on that, and, here we are, getting towards fifty years later."

When the subject of Hollywood's supposedly turbulent marriages came up, Royal quickly debunked the media's distorted notions on the subject: "Everybody's got the wrong idea. A reporter once jumped into a car when we were getting ready to leave the location [of *Tribute to a Bad Man*]. It was Steve McNally, Jim Cagney, and myself. And this guy jumped into the limo—practically unasked—and said that he was reporting the thing and he wanted to know about about the Hollywood [gossip]. We were up in Montrose, Colorado, I think. And he said, 'Do you guys get a lot of women when you got these big Hollywood parties?' And Jim says, 'No, my wife would probably kill me if I got into one of those!' And he said, 'How long have you been married?' And Jim, at that time, said, 'Oh, thirty years,' something like that. And of course I had been married since '46, because we couldn't get married overseas. I was an enlisted man and they didn't give us that privilege, not that the others had any more goddam sense than we did. And so, now, I had been married ten years by that time, and so I'd had a couple of kids. And I said, 'Nope, I haven't been to any either.' And then he turned to McNally and McNally said, 'Well, I don't have much time for Hollywood parties. I've got eight kids!' And [this reporter's] whole thing was looking for some big scandal that he could write about of the BIG Hollywood deals. Actually, I've found that small towns are wilder than this town, it's just that we get a lot of publicity.

"The other guys were REALLY professionals in that little entertainment unit I was put in," Royal explained. "And, by the way, the Commanding Officer was Melvyn Douglas. He started in as a private. What had occurred was that we were doing a second show. I was pulled off the lines with Malaria and I was put into a bad, little hospital. And this guy, Bill Post, that I told you about, phoned me and he says, 'I heard Melvyn Douglas was coming through and I took him our script.' I said, '*Our* script?' Our script was a bunch of jokes that we'd put together, y'know? And Douglas was given an assignment to get entertainment down the Burma Road, 'cause the morale was lousy in Northern Burma. And not only on the Burma Road, but to the outlying areas where they were holding lines.

"And to get to the guys and give 'em entertainment one night, we played the [foreign] 38th Division. They didn't understand a word, but they had interpreters. And, boy, did that screw up the laughter. You'd tell one joke, the interpreter would interpret it, and the laugh would come in the middle of the next joke…We'd pull into a place like Toledo, and they had some kind of a set-up for a stage they'd built for us or something. And then we'd go around and play all the non-ambulatory wards. So everybody had singles, plus their show. So you came in and played even the locked wards." One of Dano's male cohorts, who did a Carmen Miranda act in drag, was attacked by an over-amorous psychiatric patient.

After the war, Royal returned to New York City. His father had died, and his mother had become ill and been taken to a hospital, Royal said, "And we were struggling along." Shortly afterwards, Peggy returned to America, the two were married, and had their first son, Royal, Jr.

"I was staying at the Hotel Times Square, on 8th Avenue and 43rd Street," Royal said. "It was run by a friend of the family, and we paid something enormous [for rent], like thirteen bucks a week. The guys I had been with were professionals and been pros before the war. They called me up and said, 'We're going out to look for a job. You want to come?' I went with them and wound up getting a job.

"It was a play called *Barnaby and Mr. O'Malley*. It closed out of town and, very fortunately, they fired me the day before they closed. So I got two weeks extra salary, which I wouldn't have gotten if they hadn't fired me the day before they closed! And then, shortly afterwards, I picked up *Finian's Rainbow.* That ran for two years." In those salad days, Royal recalled, "I worked with very talented people. Guys like Lee Tracy—Glenda Farrell, wonderful talent."

"I did a play with George Abbott in '49. It was a hell of a part and I got sensational reviews. There was a headline in bold type: 'Abbott Discovers New Comedian.' You know, Abbott was so famed for comedy. That was in '49. The show only lasted a couple of performances, but I kept going around looking for jobs. I ended up in an audition for the original *South Pacific*. And I went into the audition scared to death because I was gonna have to sing. I had my music under my arm, but I was so dumb because I didn't bring my own pianist. I was gonna have to use their guy, who really doesn't give a shit what you do. He pounds away at the piano, and you get up there and sing with no protection.

"I went up. I was in my [Government Issue] raincoat still. A lot of the guys would take their uniforms and dye 'em black and turn 'em into suits. I hadn't quite done that, but the raincoat was still pretty good. And [director] Josh Logan says to me from the audience, 'Can you sing?' I said, 'That's what I'm here to find out.' Smart ass, right? He said, 'Thank you very much. We'll call you if we need you.' But while I'd been waiting, a guy was taking pictures. He said, 'Get out of the way, kid! Hey, move out of the way!' He had been standing me up to get a picture that he wanted without saying a damn word to me. And the first thing I know, about a month later I got a call from *Life* Magazine asking me questions. And then this thing appeared in *Life*. It was a page-and-a-third and it was featuring this portrait. [laughs] You can see the fear in my eyes, going up to audition. And there was a photo essay on Broadway. It turned out that a fella by the name of Gene Smith, who was a famous photographer, had done the essay. And I went up to his apartment and he gave me the picture. And I had a hundred copies of it made and sent them out all over the place: the studios, tv stations, casting people and whatnot, and didn't hear anything from it. I also sent out the original, like a jerk. I later found out that that original would have brought over a thousand bucks, to have an original Gene Smith.

"A year later, they were putting together a picture and the director was going over the photos in the files at Universal in California. The director was Teddy Tetzlaff and he was looking at the pictures and he pulled mine out and he said, 'That's an interesting face. Can it act?' So they called up the New York office and spoke to one of the men and, thank heaven, he had seen the show that Abbott had produced. So he said, 'Yeah, he's a good kid.' So we're sitting there and we owed everybody and his Chinese uncle: the grocery store, the cleaner, the telephone company, the gas company. And this guy calles me up and says, 'Would you accept $600 a week?' This was nineteen-hundred-and-fifty. The last real job I had was for twenty dollars a week, working for the *Daily News*. That was roughly a thousand bucks a year and here was a guy offering me more than that for two weeks work. I almost came apart at the seams! [Drolly] I had a hard time saying 'Yes,' because I started to stutter. That movie was ***Under the Gun.***"

It wasn't until 1951 that Dano landed a truly notable film role: The Tattered Man in John Huston's ***The Red Badge of Courage*** at MGM. In a casting coup, Audie Murphy played the lead, author Stephen Crane's cowardly young soldier. The supporting cast of Civil War soldiers included William Schallert, Whit Bissell, and cartoonist/author Bill Mauldin. The film was brutally trimmed by MGM, who then burned the excised footage.

"They had a general audition in New York City," Royal said, of his being cast, "and I went up to the MGM office to audition along with five thousand other people. And when I got in there, they just asked me to read and I did. I was very nervous, and this voice came out and it said [imitating Huston], 'Well, kid, this is a helluva thing to ask anybody to do at this time of the morning.'"

Royal affectionately recalled working with the prolific character actor, John Dierkes, then a neophyte: "John had worked for the Treasury Department. Prior to that, he'd been a Red Cross rep and he'd also married a Red Cross rep, Cynthia, but he was stationed in England. He was a very personable guy, big craggy-faced son-of-a-gun. And John [Huston] didn't want to look at him because Orson Welles had met him and put him ***Macbeth*** (1948), no background, no experience, no nothing. By the time I came into the business, I had probably put away something like a thousand shows."

The Tattered Man's show-stopping death scene was cut, as Royal explained: "They built a long, long dolly track and tracked [the two characters] down the hill. And the moral questions were when the Tattered Man asks [Murphy's character], 'Where were you hit, son? Where were you hit?' Somebody might find out that he wasn't really wounded. So he runs from the Tattered Man and leaves him."

In the classic, operatic ***Johnny Guitar*** (1954), Royal played a tubercular bandit, one of The Dancing Kid's (Scott Brady) gang. Joan Crawford and Sterling Hayden starred. "I became great friends with [Ernest] Borgnine and Ben Cooper and Scott [Brady], who just died here, a while ago. See, we had our own little group going, the four bank robbers. [Borgnine] played Bart Lonergan. Ernie and I are both Masons. It's a great organization. When I go to places like South America, I'll stop in [to a Masonic Lodge] and, all of a sudden, I have a lot friends." Royal had nothing but praise for ***Guitar***'s even-tempered director Nicholas Ray: "Oh, Nick was wonderful. He never blew."

In Alfred Hitchcock's black comedy, *The Trouble With Harry* (1955), Royal played the sheriff of the film's tiny hamlet. The excellent cast included John Forsythe, Shirley Maclaine, Edmund Gwenn, and Mildred Dunnock as the Sheriff's mother, who are all trying to deal with or dispose of Harry, a corpse. Hitchcock allegedly treated actors like "cattle," something that Royal adamantly refuted: "All that stuff that said he was terrible to actors was all bullshit. He was very considerate of them. Some *bad* ones—rather than insult them or tell them to take up another profession, as some directors do—he'd just remove them from the spotlight and put them where they couldn't be seen [laughs]. I played the sheriff. I just thought [Hitchcock] was great. It was Shirley [Maclaine's] first picture. She married a friend of mine. She married him, and that made her an adult, so she was certainly becoming independent.

"There's a sequence where the camera is in the room while the [dead] body is in the bathtub. And John Forsythe is there and Shirley is there, and John is painting a picture. And I come in and I want to look at the picture because I'm investigating. And I'm at such an angle that I don't see the body in the bathtub. But the audience does and they're waiting for me to discover it. But, somehow or other, I get turned a different direction each time, so I don't see it. And I went up to Hitchcock after we had shot the sequence and said, 'Gee, Hitch, these two lines should be juxtaposed and they should be reversed. It'll work better.' And he said [imitating Hitchcock], 'I can't very well do that, Royal. You see, when you say that, it's my cue to cut to Shirley. Then the next word out of you brings me over to John...' And he gave me the whole sequence of cuts, all worked out beforehand, everything laid-out to a 'T.' And I tried to ruin 'em by reversing the lines. It would have destroyed the tension in the audience. And I just stood back there, and my mouth just went agape. But everything was so planned in his mind, that he had lined this thing up prior to shooting. But he was always pleasant about rejecting. And then he always sat underneath the camera lens. He would pan right with his head, pan left, and he would see what the camera was seeing. It was a very interesting experience."

Huston's *Moby Dick* was filmed around the same time: "*Moby Dick* was really in '54, because when we completed *Trouble With Harry*, which was really a British story which we shot in Vermont, they asked me to do *Moby Dick*, which was an American story we were shooting in Europe. It was supposed to be New Bedford [Connecticut] fishing village." Not only did Huston specifically request Royal as Elijah, Royal recalled, "He had a fight for me to be in it." The British union regulations would only allow for four Americans on the film, "And they were a bunch of bastards about that," Royal added. "They already had Huston, Orson Welles, and Gregory Peck...*And* Ray Bradbury, so they were loaded to the gun'alls with Americans, and four was the maximum. When they came to casting Elijah, he saw a bunch of people he didn't like. They said, 'Will you be using an English actor?' And [Huston] said, 'You haven't got any to fit this character.' And they finally gave in and I shot the sequence in Ireland, outside of Cork. It was always a pleasure to shoot with him because he was just so good with his actors. He was just the best of 'em."

Universal's **Man in the Shadow** (1957) was a suspenseful, black-and-white modern western. Royal played Sheriff Jeff Chandler's deputy. Jack (**Creature From the Black Lagoon**) Arnold directed, Royal said, "And he had Orson [Welles] in the cast. We were walking up to the set one day and I said to him, 'Jack, how do you feel about directing Orson Welles?' He said, 'That's no problem whatsoever. I'm just gonna let him do whatever the hell he wants to do.' Jack was a very bright man.

"I remember we had a scene in there where Jeff Chandler and I go up…They brought in some dogs for Orson Welles. They went out and they got these dogs that were real monsters. [laughs] Welles was supposed to walk down [some stairs] with the dogs, one on each side of him. Of course, his girth was growing all the time. Then, when we got down there, he told us to get the hell off his land and we have a fight. And I was Jeff's assistant and I go charging up there and a guy throws a knife and hits me in the heart, and down I go. That type of thing. While they were getting ready for the shot, the stand-ins were working and one of these goddam dogs leaps out and grabs an electrician with his teeth by the hand and just shreds part of his hand. And Orson Welles said, 'Well, that solved that one. I'm not gonna be out there with those goddam dogs.' So they took Terry Wilson, the stuntman, who had been on **Red Badge** and I had known for many years by then, and he had to pad up to look like Orson. Well, Orson—when he pulled in his tummy, his chest would swell out to a laughable point. Terry got padded to look like Orson and Orson looked at him and said, 'My God! What are you doing to me? You're making me look like an utter grotesque!' [laughs] He couldn't see himself, really.

"When they came to where the guy threw the knife at me, Jack wanted to do it on the run. That meant putting a plate on yourself that's got a cork front to it and a steel plate in the back of it. And they strap it around you under the shirt. They run piano wire from where you are to where the property man is. And, normally, if you were standing still, they would hold the piano wire absolutely straight, then with a slingshot, they would shoot the knife at you. In this case, they were running backwards and the guy couldn't keep his balance, and when they fired the knife, the knife went wandering all over the goddam place and came within a half-inch of the edge of the plate, which really scared the shit out of me, I'll tell you!

In 1959, Royal traveled to Sweden to shoot **Face of Fire**, a seldom-seen variation, of sorts, on **The Phantom of the Opera**, starring James Whitmore and Cameron Mitchell. Whitmore's character is hideously scarred while saving a boy from a burning house. "We had a number of things we had to do," Royal recalled, "like burn the house down where the man gets burned." Svenska Films, Royal explained, was not prepared to deal with such a massive blaze safely. "They put a lot of liquids around, and it went off prematurely. The guy doubling

[James] Whitmore came running out of that goddam place carrying the kid, and the blanket was on fire. And the fire started getting out of control and they had a hand-pumper out there with four men on each side. It began to get so hot that they had to leave the damn thing, one at a time. So finally it got so that there was only one guy left trying to pump it with one hand and not catch fire. The guys had to leave the camera apparel, the heat became so heavy. Our cameraman, shooting handheld, stared rushing in trying to save what he could because we were losing the whole set. Then the main studio started smoking. They had to call the Stockholm Fire Department [laughs]. We almost burned down Svenska Films!"

Don Siegel's ***Hound Dog Man*** (1959) was an attempt to cash-in on Elvis' popularity, by casting teen idol Fabian in a similar vehicle. Royal appeared, along with L. Q. Jones, Jane Darwell, and Arthur O'Connell. Of O'Connell, Royal said, "We were buddies. My mother was an O'Connor, and his name was O'Connell, and I grew up in the Irish district. We did pretty well together, except he was a bachelor and I was a married man, so there were points there where we had to separate." The two later appeared together in ***7 Faces of Dr. Lao***, as a villain and his thug, respectively.

Royal called Fabian "A damn nice young man, a very nice young man, who was just a kid at the time. They gave him a bad time, the press did. We were out on location and he had to take a leak. So he went off to the side to pee in a bush. And a guy came up trying to take a picture of him, so Fabian decked him.

"The difficult thing [about making the film]," Royal noted, "was learning to play the violin left-handed. But I learned it and I always have felt that you've got to get all the finger-work done so that nobody catches you making a mistake, when an actor has to play an instrument in a movie."

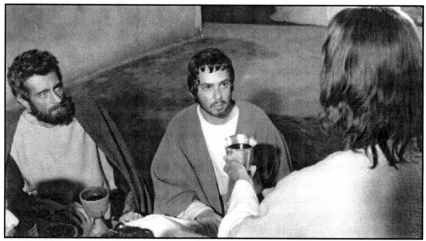

Amid the rest of the astonishing cast of Nicholas Ray's biblical epic, ***King of Kings*** (1962), Royal played St. Peter, under one of his many false beards. The hopelessly miscast Jeffrey Hunter played Christ, Siobhan McKenna, Mary, and

Rip Torn well-cast as Judas. Royal remembered having to get to the set of this Samuel Bronston production in a tearing hurry: "We took off, the plane was forced back. It had engine trouble. It had to dump its fuel and land, and the engine had to be replaced. It was one of those new 707s at the time. And it finally got there, and, when it landed, we were surrounded by the fire department. Scared the hell out of most of the passengers. Some of them didn't continue. The rest of us had a couple of free drinks off of the steward. Then we reported back to the airport and got ready to take off in the evening and we were headed for Montreal, or something like that, then up and over to Paris. The steward and I had become buddies and about, oh, an hour before the end of the flight, he said, 'Think I ought to wake everybody and tell them we're not going to Montreal?' One of the *other* engines was giving out and the only place we could get one was New York. We flew into New York and had another four-hour wait. Now, some more people started leaving, especially when the saw the *crew* leaving. The crew *had* to leave because they were only allowed so many hours on duty; with all the delays we had had, they had used them up, so they had to put a new crew on. *That* drove about seven or eight other people not to fly in the airplane. We went to Paris and landed, right in the middle of a French strike.

"So they put us up in a hotel and set us up with a Spanish airline to fly us into Madrid. When we got to Madrid, it looked like half the Spanish police force was waiting for me to land. I went tearing up to the Hilton Hotel and when I got there, Samuel Bronston was there. He threw his arms around me—I didn't even know him! It's just that he was losing money every day that I wasn't there. But to the people that were scattered around the hotel, it looked as if I was his bosom buddy. No sooner had I finished that, then I must have had about six offers of screenplays from all over the place. They must have thought I was bankable and a terribly important American! [laughs]"

In George Pal's unique fantasy/western, ***7 Faces of Dr. Lao*** (1964), Royal played one of Arthur O'Connell's thugs, and was paired with another familiar western face, John Doucette. Royal was only slightly familiar with Pal's movies when he was cast: "I had seen ***The Time Machine*** and some [of his] other pictures. I went in to see him for a lesser part, and then I got in there, and we were talking. The make-up man was present, Bill Tuttle. He said, 'Oh, hi! Hello, Royal.' And Tuttle said, 'Dano's one hell of an actor,' and George just changed his mind, and gave me another part."

During the film's final major scene, Royal and Doucette attempt to kill, then are terrorized by, the Loch Ness Monster, a stop-motion puppet. Like so many other actors confronted with invisible co-stars, Royal did the obvious thing when it came time to shoot the scenes: "You just have to imagine. George pointed out where we should look. Then you let imagination take over." Royal said that he "got a big kick" out of making Dr. Lao, "especially when I saw those little models of myself and John. They were pretty damn good, little, life-like things."

Royal Dano and Dr. Lao.

One of Royal's most bizarre roles—if it can be called that—was in the "Gravy Train" dog food commercials. For many years, they featured a tiny, stop-motion chuck wagon and western driver, being chased around by a dog. One of the animators on *Dr. Lao* related that it was the film's "little, life-like" Dano model that was used as the wagon's driver. When he was told this, Royal exclaimed, "I'll ask for residuals!"

When the subject of character great Elisha Cook, Jr. was broached, Royal lit up: "Oh, Cookie? I've known Cookie for years. He has the greatest metabolism. He can drink the biggest drinkers under the table, drink for drink. They'd pass out, he'd still be up, get up, go to the can, come back, and be ready to start again."

Royal recalled Cook warmly as a friend, "full of stories about the old days," he said. "He would get to drinking sometime, and he would just put it away, one after the other. He would say, 'See you tomorrow, Royal!' Next thing I know, I got a phone call at the bar over from Universal—We were working on some picture over there. I said, 'Hi, Cookie. I was looking for you,' He said, 'Oh! Oh, was I supposed to meet you there?' I said, 'Yeah, you left the bar about two a.m.' He goes, 'OH, that's where I was!' And I said, 'Where the hell are you now?' And he said, 'Tijuana.' I said, 'How did you get there?' And he said, 'I don't know. Somebody dropped me off down there.' Apparently, somebody was going to Mexico and they drove him down to Tijuana and dropped him." Royal found the film's lead, Henry Fonda to be far less personable: "Henry kept to himself, pretty much."

On several occasions, Royal worked with Lon (*Of Mice and Men*) Chaney, Jr. Chaney began his career in westerns, rose to prominence in horror films, and, by the end of his life, was appearing mainly in westerns again. "I liked Lon," Royal said, "and we got along pretty good. Towards the end, on that later picture, he was having a terrible time. You know, alcohol is one hell of an addiction. He was a talented man and he just got into a battle with that and couldn't win it." On *Day of the Evil Gun* (1968), Royal recalled that Chaney's alcoholism was so bad, he had to be replaced: "Yeah, they gave it to Paul Fix. They tried to shoot [Chaney], but they couldn't get anything."

Many western actors were prone to hit the bottle, not just Cook. Of *Welcome to Hard Times'* cast, Royal related, "Aboard that picture, we had some pretty heavy drinkers. We had Aldo Ray, John Anderson, Keenan Wynn. You know, we never really had a drink on that picture at all. We used to go to the studio, and work, and go back and go home. The bartender at the studio, who ran a bar nearby, thought it was gonna be a field day when he saw the cast on this thing. Turned out that everybody on it was afraid to start."

When asked if he enjoyed filming *If He Hollers...Let Him Go!* (1968), Royal replied, "I've enjoyed doing nearly all of my pictures. I've always thought it was a hell of a way to earn a living...."

In the film, Royal played a particularly vile bigot. An incident during its shoot gave Royal an unforgettable memory: "I do remember, one day, I had to do this seduction of this young girl. She was a very bosomy youngster. She had to take off her bra and all that stuff. All the crew members were standing around watching and she got nervous about it, spoke to the director, and they asked everybody to leave. And, so, in the sequence of events that followed, I'm holding onto her. I strip her down, then lay her down on the couch. Her eyes popped, and I kind of rolled over and looked up, and there were all these gray-headed crewmembers. They had left the visible part of the set and gone up into the rafters. They had also invited all the guys from the neighboring sets, because she had a great set of boobs on her. [laughs] I was so hysterical with laughter, it took me about fifteen minutes to quiet down. Of course, immediately after I rolled off of her, she started to cover herself, but they were a little bigger than she could cover with her hands!"

The luridly-titled *Machismo: 40 Graves for 40 Guns* (1970) was a mystery for Royal: "I'm trying to remember. Some of these titles get changed around and I can't remember the picture from the title. Some of these movies have come up and I don't even remember making them. One turned out to be a picture where they took **The Virginian** and combined it with that Texas Rangers thing that Neville Brand did. And people were asking me about that movie, and I would say, '*What* movie?'"

One of Royal's most interesting '70s credits was the genuinely eerie **Messiah of Evil** (1972), written and directed by Gloria Katz and Willard Huyck (**American Graffiti**). Elisha Cook and Charles Dierkop co-starred. In spite of its tiny budget and drive-in horror plot, the film succeeds on a number of levels. Royal plays a reclusive painter, living in a seaside town, and is mainly heard in narration. His daughter (Marianna Hill) comes looking for him, only to discover that the town has been overwhelmed by satanic forces, and its very drab residents transformed into cannibalistic zombies (Royal's character included). "They had a little gal on there [Hill] who had to stab me with a pair of scissors. She said she couldn't do it, just couldn't do it. She said, 'Say something dirty to me.' I said, 'What do you mean? All you've got to do is just raise your hand press down against my chest, that's all.' She said, 'I can't do it! I can't do it! Some something dirty or filthy to me!' So I said, 'Fuck you.' 'No! More! More!' I finally started using a lot of foul language and she finally got all worked up. I looked, she nodded at me, I came in, and she stabbed me. She was one of the damnedest people I ever met in my life. I did a few other things to get her going, but they're not publishable."

In the stylish United Artists cult favorite, **Electra Glide in Blue** (1975), Royal played an Arizona coroner. Robert Blake starred as Wintergreen, a motorcycle cop, and Elisha Cook appeared as a deranged desert rat. "The original director had been fired," Royal recalled, "and the young producer [James William Guercio] took over." Guercio managed the pop group Chicago, at the time, and they appear on the film's soundtrack. "We had all gotten together the night before, had some cocktails, and had a rehearsal session. We went over the script and went through it and I figured out a few things I would do. A fella by the name of Samson—*apropos*—was a regular cop down there," in the film's location, Arizona. "He had to come in and I said, 'Get rid of him' [Robert Blake's character]. So, he took Blake by the arm, and he just took him out the door.

"I knew something about Samson. He's had some pretty good street brawls. At one point, he was in a diner, and there were two guys with knives. And he couldn't handle them in there. So he belted one of them, grabbed the other one, threw him through a plate-glass window, got him outside, and beat the bejeezus out of him. I'd heard about that, so I said, 'When I tell you to take him about this time, TAKE HIM OUT. You remember what you did in the diner?' He said, 'What about Blake?' I said, 'He won't mind.' I said, 'Remember when you took the guy out of the diner? Well, take [Blake] out the same way in the shot, which is a 50/50 shot between the two of us.' And *in* comes the cop and *out goes Blake*— I mean, he just...POOF!"

In Phil Kaufman's fascinating revisionist western, **The Great Northfield, Minnesota Raid** (1974), Royal played mad Norwegian, "Crazy Gus" Gustafson.

Kaufman, Royal said, "originally gave it to me in English and he said, 'Translate this into Norwegian.' So we had a friend of his come up and read it to me in Norwegian and that was the last time I heard anything on it. So I was stuck. I called up Bill Warren's secretary, Linda, who later married him. She came over here with her mother—we went to dinner, Peggy [Royal's wife] and Linda and her mom, 'cause she's a Swede—and between the two of them, we put it together in Swedish…phonically. And I learned it phonically. And then I went to Phil Kaufman and I said, 'Y'know, Phil, back in those days, the Norwegians were dominated, so were the Danes, by the Swedish kingdom and Swedish was really the language.' [laughs] So he's always kidded me about the routine I gave him to justify speaking Swedish instead of Norwegian." (For more on this film, refer to the R. G. Armstrong chapter of this book.) Royal later appeared in Kaufman's *The Right Stuff* (1983).

In 1974, Royal played a minister in Steve Carver's ***Big Bad Mama***, a Roger Corman production, starring Angie Dickinson as a Depression-era outlaw. "I had a hell of a lot of fun with that," Royal said. "My son [Richard] played the bellboy," Royal recalled. Royal's younger son, Richard "Rick" Dano, appeared in three films with his father, and continues to act. He can be seen in films like ***Big Wednesday*** (1978), and on tv in shows like ***Happy Days*** and several episodes of ***Laverne and Shirley***. He resembles a slightly shorter, more muscular version of his old man, with the same piercing blue eyes.

There was a screw-up during the taping of this interview. Some priceless anecdotes Royal told about his work on, among other things, ***Drum*** (1976), ***The Outlaw Josey Wales*** (1976), and ***Something Wicked This Way Comes*** (1983) were lost. Fortunately, memory has served those stories well. In ***Drum***, the cut-rate sequel to the infamous ***Mandingo*** (1975), Royal played a scurrilous slave-catcher, who drops by Warren Oates' mansion with a herd of captured runaways. The slaves later revolt, and storm Royal's bedroom, armed with scythes. When the actors and stuntmen playing the slaves burst in, Royal was supposed to fire two pistols loaded with blanks that he had concealed in bed, under the blankets. When he fired them, the loads didn't pass through the sheets, they set them on fire. As if that weren't enough, the scene called for the slaves to hack Royal to death. Royal described the stuntmen as being very muscular, and he said that they got a little over-enthusiastic with their whacking. Their scythes' blades were harmless rubber, but they had very solid, metal frames, and Royal ended up black-and-blue.

Royal recalled a scene in ***The Outlaw Josey Wales*** where Clint Eastwood makes his entrance before the townsfolk, who are huddled around tables in a saloon. The shots with Royal and the other supporting players were shot in an interior saloon set, but the footage of Eastwood entering the swinging saloon doorway was shot on a set that was wide open to the chilly outdoor air. When the footage was screened—and I don't know whether it made it to the finished film or not—the filmmakers noticed that, unlike the others in the scene,

Eastwood's exhaled breath was highly visible. It unintentionally made him look, as Royal put it, "like a dragon."

For **Something Wicked**, Royal read for the part of Tom Fury, the itinerant lightning rod salesman, for the film's director, Jack Clayton. Clayton was so thrilled by Royal's audition that he got up, walked over to him, embraced him, and said, "You're my Tom Fury!"

When it came time for Royal to destroy Pam Grier's character, The Dust Witch, by stabbing her with one of his lightning rods, Royal tersely said, "Oh, I was looking forward to that. Very famous cleavage…" Inevitably, Royal's association with Ray Bradbury came up. The two had an association spanning forty years; Bradbury had scripted **Something Wicked** from his own novel, and had gone

Herman Melville one better by inventing Royal's character, Elijah, for his adaptation of *Moby Dick*. "That cheap bastard!" Royal said of the writer, with mock indignation. "Every time he writes a part for me, he dresses me like a reject from the Salvation Army!" His opinion of Bradbury as a person was very warm, though: "Oh, he's a great guy." (It should be duly noted that Bradbury also contributed Orson Welles' narration for *King of Kings*.)

In his final film role, Royal was a gravedigger in horror director George A. Romero's *The Dark Half* (1994), based on Stephen King's novel. Royal watched over the false burial of Tim Hutton's literary alter ego. "I remember that it was cold as hell," said Royal. "And they had a little wardrobe girl, who was kind of cute and very bright. She strung some wire and hooked up a hair dryer gun and she stuck that down in the top of my bib overalls, turned it on, and it was very warm. Then she stuck it in the side, where it buttons at the waist, and she turned it on there, and that was really welcome." Of Romero, Royal enthused, "I loved working with him. He made that happen. It doesn't happen often enough. Very down-to-earth, and he knows what he wants. He doesn't confuse the issue when you're shooting. And his lady's a pretty damn nice lady, too [Christine Forrest Romero]."

Royal was never signed to any studios. As far as his favorite western roles, Royal had, he said, "A couple of 'em. *Man of the West*, because I don't say anything through the whole show: I'm a mute. And another one would be *Saddle the Wind*," which was directed by Robert Parrish, and starred John Cassavettes and Robert Taylor. Of his directors, Royal's favorite was John Huston. His favorite actor to work with was Gary Cooper.

As an older man, he was more satisfied with his work than ever: "I'm offered far more money today then I was ever offered as a kid." Had he enjoyed his career? "Oh, my God, YES! Can you think of someplace where you can earn enough money to support a family and do as little as you have to do in this business? It's utterly amazing!"

THE FILMS OF ROYAL DANO

1950   *Under the Gun*
      Undercover Girl

1951   *The Red Badge of Courage*
      Flame of Araby

1952   *The Bend of the River*
      Carrie
      Abraham Lincoln: The Early Years (**Omnibus** five-part series)

1954   *Johnny Guitar*

1955   *The Far Country*
      The Trouble With Harry

1956   *Tension at Table Rock*
      Moby Dick
      Tribute to a Bad Man
      Santiago

1957   *Crime of Passion*
      All Mine to Give
      Man in the Shadow
      Trooper Hook

1958   *Saddle the Wind*
      Man of the West
      Handle With Care

1959   *Never Steal Anything Small*
      Face of Fire
      These Thousand Miles
      Hound Dog Man
      The Boy and the Bridge

1960   *The Adventures of Huckleberry Finn*
      Cimarron

1961   *King of Kings*
      Posse From Hell

1963   *Savage Sam*

1964   *7 Faces of Dr. Lao*

1966   *Gunpoint*
      The Dangerous Days of Kiowa Jones (tv pilot feature)

1967   *The Last Challenge*
      Welcome to Hard Times

1968	*The Day of the Evil Gun* *If He Hollers, Let Him Go! (aka: Dead Right)* *The Manhunter*
1969	*Death of a Gunfighter* *The Undefeated* *Backtrack* (Theatrical release of the 1965 pilot for **Laredo**.)
1970	*Machismo–40 Graves for 40 Guns* *Savage Sun/ Run, Simon, Run* (tv pilot)
1971	*The Skin Game*
1972	*Messiah of Evil* (aka: *Dead People*) *The Great Northfield, Minnesota Raid* *The Culpepper Cattle Company* *Moon of the Wolf* (ABC tv movie) *Howzer*
1973	*Cahill, U. S. Marshall* *Electra Glide in Blue* *Ace Eli and Roger of the Skies*
1974	*Big Bad Mama*
1975	*The Wild Party* *Capone* *Huckleberry Finn*
1976	*Drum* *The Outlaw Josey Wales* *The Killer Inside Me* *How the West Was Won* (ABC miniseries)
1977	*Bad Georgia Road* *One Man Jury* *Hughes and Harlow: Angels in Hell* *Murder in Peyton Place* (ABC pilot)
1978	*Crash* *Donner Pass: The Road to Survival*
1979	*In Search of Historic Jesus* *Last Ride of the Dalton Gang* (NBC tv movie)
1981	*Take This Job and Shove It*
1982	*Hammett*
1983	*Something Wicked This Way Comes* *The Right Stuff* *Will There Really be a Morning?* (CBS tv movie) *Murder 1, Dancer 0* (NBC tv movie)

1984	*Teachers*
	The Red-Headed Stranger
1986	*Cocaine Wars*
1987	*LBJ: The Early Years*
	House II: The Second Story
1988	*Texas Guns* (aka: *Once Upon a Texas Train*)
	Killer Klowns from Outer Space
	Ghoulies II
1990	*Spaced Invaders*
1993	*The Dark Half*

TELEVISION

Only a few of Dano's tv credits were: an endless variety of westerns, *Alfred Hitchcock Presents, Hondo, Lost in Space, The Rifleman, Night Gallery, Kung Fu, Planet of the Apes,* and two appearances on *Amazing Stories.* The 1983 tvm *Murder 1, Dancer 0* was a pilot for an intended cop series, to star Robert Blake as Joe Dancer. It never came to be, but Blake intended to use Royal as a regular, had the show been picked up.

The *Killer Klowns from Outer Space* dvd includes several behind-the-scenes photos of Royal, as well as deleted out-takes of him.

Royal was supposedly in *Chandler* (1971), which would mean his scenes were cut.

Scott Skelton, the author of *Night Gallery: An After-Hours Tour,* relates that Royal made an uncredited appearance, of sorts, after his initial *Night Gallery* role. In his (credited) *NG* episode, "I'll Never Leave You—Ever," Royal plays a cuckold, whose wife burns a wooden effigy of him. Royal's character roasts, and his howls of agony were so convincing and unsettling, they were reused during *NG*'s next season to overdub screams for Cornel Wilde.

A closing Dano anecdote: Royal always liked Bette Davis because of a kindness she did him, in the '50s. He saw Davis at a party, surrounded by people, and walked over to introduce himself. But when he reached her, he was so stunned by her, he drew a total blank. She leaned over, cupped her hands around her mouth, and whispered, "*Bette Davis.*" She did it in such a friendly way, Royal always spoke well of her.

JONATHAN HAZE

"Any time you put me in wardrobe and put a lot of make-up on me,
I was a happy camper."

By 1960, it looked like Jonathan Haze was doomed to endless supporting roles in Roger Corman's films. For Corman, he had already played Mexicans several times, along with cowboys, assorted thugs and gangsters, a very blonde Viking, and a weaselly bartender, among other roles. His unimposing height and olive complexion—the latter of which pegged him for roles as foreigners—probably didn't help. (He looked something like a better-looking Nick Cravat.) But it was to be his single starring role in a Corman film that would become his signature performance.

Roger Corman and Charles B. Griffith's gruesome comedy, ***The Little Shop of Horrors*** (1960), has had a popular life-span nearly as astonishing as the inferior ***Rocky Horror Picture Show*** (1975). As many who read this probably know, the original Little Shop has become one of the most perennially popular "B"-movies—and *el cheapo* video releases—of all time. Not only that, but it spawned a stage musical, had a major Hollywood remake in 1986, and was even the basis for a short-lived kid's cartoon series, ***Little Shop***. And, just as Tim Curry will never be able to dissociate himself from ***Rocky Horror***, Jonathan Haze is inextricably linked to having originated the part of ***Little Shop***'s central character, the dopey, luckless Seymour Krelboined.

With its pitifully low budget and plentiful (and extremely funny) ethnic humor, the original ***Little Shop*** wouldn't have a chance of getting made today in touchy, over-priced Hollywood. There are eerie night sequences in Los Angeles' Skid Row, ca. 1959, that no modern big-budget snoozer could touch for ambiance. The scenes of Jonathan confusedly walking around those desolate streets at night strike a very odd chord—You pity the poor *schlmiel.*

After acting in high school and summer stock theater, he migrated to Hollywood. There he began his career as part of Roger Corman's stock company of actors, whose other members included Ed Nelson, Beverly Garland, Barboura Morris, Mel Welles, and Bruno Ve Sota. Just as L. Q. Jones was regularly partnered with Strother Martin, Jonathan wound up paired with another Corman staple, Dick Miller. Besides ***Little Shop of Horrors***, the two appeared together in Corman films like ***Naked Paradise*** (1957); they battled "Beulah," the upside-down ice cream cone alien, in ***It Conquered the World*** (1956); Jonathan was stick-up man Russell Johnson's accomplice in ***Rock All Night*** (1957); and the two made the grave error of heckling the unhecklable, Don Rickles, in ***X–The Man With the X-Ray Eyes*** (1963).

In the mid-sixties, Jonathan was forced out of acting into working on the opposite side of the camera in a variety of capacities. His acting has mostly been confined to working in commercials. But, in 1999, the American Movie Classics Network ran a serialized monster movie, ***The Phantom Eye***, which reunited Jonathan and Roger Corman as actor and director for the first time in nearly forty years. After all those decades—and becoming a grandfather—Jonathan is still as fit as ever, his enthusiasm undimmed.

Jonathan was the cover boy of issue #5 of ***Filmfax***, which included a feature interview with him. Other comments that he made about his work with Corman are interspersed into the director's autobiography, ***How I Made a Hundred Movies in Hollywood and Never Lost a Dime***; likewise, with Mark McGee's Corman survey, ***The Best of the Cheap Acts.***

Jonathan Haze was born in 1929 in Pittsburgh, Pennsylvania, the son of a jeweler, Harry Schacter, and his wife, Betty . He was a movie buff, and frequented the neighborhood theater, which served, he recalls, as a babysitter for many parents. "It was a big event," he recalls, of his glorious childhood Saturday matinees. Their cost of admission included a free candy bar, and entry in a sweepstakes.

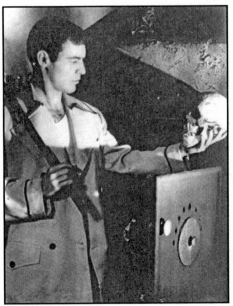

The actor explains that he was more interested in sports as a high-schooler than acting, and he fell into it almost accidentally. "There was a playhouse group called The Pittsburgh Playhouse," Jonathan says. "And, at one point, a friend was doing a play there and he says, 'Why don't you come over and try to do this play?' I said, 'That sounds like fun.' And I did the play, which was *The Long Goodbye.* Then I did several other plays, and that got me interested in it.

"I was interested in not just the theater at that point either, 'cause Buddy Rich was my cousin. He had a band, and he played with a lot of big bands, and they used to come to Pittsburgh. I used to go and hang out with Buddy backstage, and it was very glamorous. All the girls waiting at the stage door, autographs, and all that jazz, and it kind of blew my mind, you know? [laughs]

"Buddy was brilliant—genius talent. He could do everything. Aside from playing drums, he was a fantastic singer and a great dancer. He always wanted to be a song-and-dance man. His parents had been in vaudeville. He would tour with his parents' act from the time he was born. He never went to school in his life. He had been a drummer since he was four. As a matter of fact, he led Woodrow Wilson's inaugural parade with a drum, and he was called 'Traps, The Boy Wonder.'" Miles actually became his *parents'* mainstay. "A lot of times, these child-labor people used to come backstage, and they would pop a cigar in his mouth and act like he was a midget. [laughs]

"Buddy was a big influence on my life. When I got old enough to leave home, I stayed with Buddy and his wife at the time in New York. We got to be real close. And when my acting career wasn't exactly moving, he offered me a job to go on tour with him and one of his bands. As I traveled the country, I guess I must have been nineteen, eighteen years old, I was on top of the world.

"At one point, when I was on tour with Buddy, he was booked into the Strand Theater in New York with Josephine Baker, who none of us had heard of. And it was a big deal, because Baker had been this gigantic star all over the world. This nightclub owner from Miami brought her to his club in Havana. She was a big smash and everybody loved her. He offered her a United States tour that he promoted and produced. His name was Ned Schuyler.

At Miles' "two-week booking" at the Strand, Jonathan recalls, "We had lines around the block. We were doing seven or eight shows a day, with a movie in-between, and she was just the toast of New York. Then she was booked in Philadelphia at the Earl Theater and Buddy, with a small group, was booked into the High Hat Club, which was a jazz club in the black neighborhood of Philadelphia. And, strangely enough, we were opening on the same day.

"We set up the instruments and decided to go and see how Baker was doing. She was in tears, and her manager was running up and down, worrying and nervous. Apparently, the first show had been pretty awful. I mean, she was spoiled, she had been working in a theater in New York that was geared for stage performances and had an established pit band, that they then augmented with Buddy Rich's band, and she had that music in her head. And the Strand had lighting designers and people to make her look great. She got to Philadelphia and to a theater that didn't have regular stage shows, and a pick-up band in the pit, and no Buddy Rich.

"So Buddy made a deal with Ned Schuyler [to play], and then Schuyler was complaining about all the technical things that were wrong, and she was really upset. So I said to them, "I can fix that." I mean, I was just a punk kid. I didn't know my ass from my elbow. I quickly got together a lighting plot and worked with the lighting guys and got everything organized. And he hired me at that point to stage-manage the show. So I was running the show, I was giving all the cues, I was getting the props, and I was doing all that stuff, and we went on tour."

The experience had an even greater impact on Jonathan than his tenure with Miles. "It was incredible to be around those people, and the types of people who came to see the show, and would come backstage. I was meeting the elite of the country. I was meeting Joe Louis, Sugar Ray Robinson. It was amazing how she appealed to such a broad-based audience." After a "total tour" of America, Jonathan says, Schuyler arranged a second tour. Miles left, and Jonathan stayed. "It was a wonderful time to be around show business...It was incredible."

Haze's second tour with Baker concluded in Los Angeles, but Jonathan didn't root himself there, quite yet. "I went back to New York and tried to act there. It was really difficult to break into it, and I went home to Pittsburgh for a summer and I worked as stage manager for the Pittsburgh Civic Light Opera Company." One of Jonathan's fellow actors "was driving to California," he says. So he rode with him to San Francisco, and hitchhiked to Los Angeles.

"I got here with twenty bucks in my pocket," Jonathan says, of the auspicious beginning of his acting career. "I had an aunt that agreed to put me up, and I didn't have any rent, for the time being."

Like Paul Koslo, Jonathan worked as a gas station attendant. While working at Tide Oil Company on Santa Monica Boulevard, a regular customer, Wyatt "Barney" Ordung," used to chat Jonathan up: "He told me he was a writer, gonna be a big director, blah, blah, blah. It was fun to talk to people, so I would talk to him. One day, he said he had gotten a deal to make a picture and did I want to act in it? He took me to meet Roger Corman. It was Roger's first movie. It was called **Monster From the Ocean Floor** (1954). Roger hired me to play a Mexican deep-sea diver. In those days, you didn't hire Mexicans to play Mexicans, you hired somebody that looked like one. [laughs] I grew a moustache and got a good suntan, and I got fired from the gas station for having the moustache. I did that movie, and Roger and I got friendly...It seems like I worked in probably his first twenty-five or thirty movies."

For Corman, Jonathan worked on many of the earliest ARC (American Releasing Corporation)/AIP (American International Productions) films. One of the very first was **The Fast and The Furious** (also '54), a racing film starring John Ireland and Dorothy Malone, which was later remade. "It was a sports car-racing picture. At the time, racing cars were gonna be big in movies, with a lot of big studio movies about car racing. And Roger managed to get together this little old car-racing film with John Ireland. I think he got John by promising him he could direct. We went and borrowed sports cars from our friends, and used-car dealers and stuff, and took 'em out, took the windshields off, and put numbers on them and shot racing scenes.

"In those days, it would have been impossible to go out and buy or rent those cars, so we borrowed them. There was a lot of that kind of stuff going on, To save money, we would do these things. So, that was really the second picture."

After that, Jonathan was in probably his most major credit, but from which most of his part was excised, Elia Kazan's **East of Eden** (1955), which needs no introduction. Jonathan was cast, he explains, "Because I looked like an old actor named Mario Siletti, who was an Italian character actor who played an Italian farmer in the film. They needed somebody to play his son. There was a big subplot that dealt with Mario and his son. Mario was growing lettuce and vegetables for the war effort, and Ray Massey's son was just hanging around doing nothing. And I was getting drafted and he wasn't. Raymond Massey was the president of the draft board. There was this scene where, just before the birthday party scene, my father and I approach him on the street. And Mario Siletti's begging Massey not to draft me. Massey doesn't listen, he walks to this party. That scene has been cut down to where I have one line and I think Mario has one line.

"And the months and months of work I did in the lettuce fields of Salinas, and all that stuff, was just not in the movie. And I got paid for all of that. It was great to be on a big movie, and I met James Dean, and we got to be good friends. He was a fabulous kind of raw talent. I don't know what it is he had, but, boy, it was strong. And Dick Davalos, who played his brother in the movie, never went anywhere. Dean just skyrocketed."

ARC's **Five Guns West** featured Jonathan as William Candy, an escaped convict and Confederate mercenary. It was the first of five films that Corman directed in 1955 *alone*, as well as his directorial debut. Jonathan echoes several other Corman regulars in saying that Corman had a "hands-off" approach to directing, letting his actors do much of the work. "Roger never seemed too nervous about anything," he says. "He was nervous about money, which is the only thing

I can remember him being too nervous about. As far as directing, it was an expediancy. Directors were expensive, so Roger said, 'Whoa, if that guy can do it, I can do it. I'll direct myself.'

"And that was his first time. He didn't know much about how actors worked or prepared or anything. But he did have a wonderful sense of what movies would sell and what movies wouldn't. He was very good getting on some kind of a run, if he heard some big studio was doing a certain movie, he would do it quicker. In other words, he'd get on the same milieu and do a movie that would come out before the big one would come out. He did that a lot."

Early in his career, Jonathan's outlook on acting was very blunt: "It was all guts. I never worried about anything. It was fun and games, and I was enjoying it and I never felt any trepidation about it. I always tried to take any part that I

Five Guns West.

could get and give it something that I could give it, something special. I never tried to play myself, I always tried to play a character. And I enjoyed it. I was having a wonderful time.

"It was like going to college, for an actor to be working with professional actors and in good roles. The roles I did in Corman movies were incredible roles and, a lot of times, were roles that I was not absolutely right for. And it was wonderful to get those kinds of roles and have to stretch myself and have to do things I'd never done before. It was fabulous. It was better than any acting school I could possibly have gone to."

Corman's *The Day The World Ended* (1956), a post-nuclear science fiction film, featured Haze in a tiny part as a disfigured radiation victim. "Anytime you put me in wardrobe and put a lot of make-up on me, I was a happy camper. [laughs] I had a great time. I was around the picture all the time. That was really a teeny little part. I don't even think I said one line. I remember falling down a hill with this make-up on."

The monster in *Day The World Ended*, "Marty the Mutant," was designed, built, and worn by the extraordinary Paul Blaisdell, creator of AIP's most famous foam-rubber beasts. "I used to go out to Paul's house in Topanga Canyon when he was building monsters and doing stuff. We used to hang out together. He was quite a character. He was very creative and did wonderful things for no money.

We were all forerunners of what was to come [in science fiction movies]."

Despite the absurdly hectic shooting schedules and miniscule budgets that he faced, Jonathan respected Corman, and remembers their work together rather fondly. In those days of slack Union control, Corman's rep. company was encouraged, Jonathan explains, to "wear many hats": "I once told Roger, 'Let me stage the fight scenes in your movies. I used to be a boxer, I know about action, I know about the fighting, let me do the fight scenes.' He said, 'Go ahead!' For several movies, many movies, I put together the fights and the action. He took me to New Orleans for *Swamp Women* (1955) to teach the women how to fight. I mean, he would let you do things. If somebody came in and said they could write a script, he's day go ahead and write it, he'd let them do it. If somebody said they were a director, he'd help them get started as director. So he was very good on that level.

"And he'd let you act! If you came in with some outrageous character, he'd let you play it. So Roger was excellent at those things; he was not a great director of acting, where he would go to scenes where he would give you things. You played what you yourself came in with, most of the time. Of course, you adjusted it, based on what the other actors did, but, basically, you got to work out the prep on your own characters."

Cell 2455, Death Row (1955) was an adaptation of the popular, non-fiction account of convicted killer Caryl Chessman's life; Corman regular William Campbell starred, with Buck Kartalian in support. "That was directed by Fred Sears for Columbia, with Bill Campbell playing Caryl Chessman. Bill Campbell was one of the guys I knew from Schwab's Drugstore, whose brother Bob [R. Wright Campbell] was a good friend of mine, that I had gotten started with Roger as a writer. He wrote *Five Guns West*. I got him that job and then he wrote a part for me in *Five Guns West,* and also one for himself, and we played brothers. I had met Fred Sears at Schwab's, as well, and he got me on the call for one of the gangsters. That was my first real movie that I worked in, aside from Corman. It was fun. I got to hold up some liquor stores and shoot people and do all the things that I as a kid had always wanted to do. I was so indoctrinated from seeing all these movies as a kid that I had always dreamed about being in films. I wanted to be a deep-sea diver, like I eventually got to be in *Monster From The Ocean Floor,* and I wanted to be a cowboy, which I got the chance to do. I was this wild kid from off the streets, and here I was, acting in movies, playing cowboys and Indians. It wasn't the serious kind of business that it is today."

In *Gunslinger* (1956), Jonathan played a bartender, the toady of '50s B-movies' ultimate dream girl, the drop-dead gorgeous Allison Hayes. "Allison was gorgeous, beautiful, wonderful, sweet, charming, sexy, voluptuous…and talented. And she had the most fetching personality of any woman I think I had met in the business, up till then. She was just a delight, and a wonderful woman."

It *Conquered the World* (1956), an infamous Corman low-budget quickie, has become a bona fide cult classic. Jonathan and Dick Miller played a couple of comic relief soldiers, confronted with the film's klunky, marvelous monster, Paul Blaisdell's Venusian. "I think it's a hell of a little picture," Jonathan states, "considering that it was made with very little money, and considering that the monsters, the little flying goodies, were not really very sophisticated. They flew them on fish poles. [laughs] They had like twenty-five extras; they did big mob scenes with twenty-five extras. It was all shot locally and I thought it was damn good…

"That was the first film that Dick Miller and I kind of did a comedy duo together, and it was effective and everybody loved it. If we had done it later on, after television had gotten really hot, we could have been a really good comedy team for television. I knew Dick from New York. We both used to hang out at a restaurant called the Bird in Hand on Broadway, where a lot of actors used to hang out. We used to be friends and we used to go to movies together. [The Bird in Hand] was like a poor man's Lindy's, famous for its strawberry cheesecake.

Corman's *Not of This Earth* (1956) starred Paul Birch, a staple of, among other genres, '50s science fiction cinema, as a nefarious alien vampire, visiting Earth under the unconvincing pseudonym "Mr. Johnson." Jonathan played ex-con Jeremy Perrin, Johnson's chauffeur. "Paul Birch was, of course, a professional character man who'd been around for many years and he was very good. He was a terrific journeyman actor."

The film satisfied Jonathan, especially Charles Griffith's script. In 1995, Jonathan commented, "That picture had a great cast. Dick Miller's thing [as a comic vacuum cleaner salesman] in that was absolutely brilliant. Dick is a very talented kid, and deserves to be doing better than he's doing. Having worked

with Roger on a lot of pictures kind of puts the kiss of death on you as far as doing much in big movies. And thank God for television. That's where you were really able to get something going."

Rock All Night (1957), which was mainly a series of rock numbers by various pop groups, starred Dick Miller as "Shorty," a defensive tough who suffers from a bad case of "short man's syndrome." Russell Johnson and Jonathan played stick-up men on the run, holding the patrons of a nightclub hostage. Shorty saves the day. "That was taken from a television show," Jonathan explains, "Dane Clark had played that little tough guy that comes into a bar that's being held-up by these two crazies. It was a very successful television show. Roger bought the rights to it and remade it as a feature with music...

"We had a wonderful time. I think we shot on existing sets. Roger would take existing sets and use them by writing a story around them. Chuck would knock off a story in a couple of weeks and we'd go in and do it. We were having a good time. We were making some money working at our craft and we never too ourselves really seriously."

Haze worked briefly on Bruno Ve Sota's surreal *Daughter of Horror,* aka: *Dementia* (1953; released '56). It was Haze's first actual, unbilled film role, shot silent and in black and white. Ed McMahon provided uncredited narration! "That's the one that Bruno Ve Sota directed. I was around and I might have acted in it, but I just can't remember what I did there." Clips and posters from *Daughter of Horror* later appeared in *The Blob* (1958).

Carnival Rock (1957) was another Corman rock 'n' roll movie, starring another of the director's regulars, the late Susan Cabot. "I had maybe three or four scenes in the whole movie," says Jonathan. "It was really interesting, because Roger had brought out this hotshot actor from New York, David Stewart, who was a real character. He was straight out of the Actor's Studio and he was a total method actor. I remember one scene where we were working on the midway at the carnival and he gets bad news. And I was standing next to him, and he said to me, 'Listen, would you do me a favor? When we get to this point in the scene, when he tells me this, will you stick me in the ass with this dart?' I'm standing there next to him and he says the line, and I JAB this thing in him and he does this incredible reaction. And I said, 'Jesus, is this what acting is?!' [laughs]"

On occasion, Jonathan attended acting classes. "I studied in a group out here that was run by Jeffrey Hayden, who was Eva Marie Saint's husband and had been at the Actor's Studio for years. Anthony Quinn put this group together. It was wonderful. We were able to do incredible scenes and really work ourselves out."

United Artists' *Bayou* (1957), aka: *Poor White Trash* (1961), became one of the most lucrative, well-known drive-in movies of all time. It played in theaters well into the '70s, on the basis of its exceedingly lurid title. "It was originally called *Bayou*, with Timothy Carey." Haze played Carey's silent crony in the film. "It was made by a guy from Mobile, Alabama who owned drive-in theaters, named Mike Ripps. They hired Roger and I to come down and do it. Ripps had been a visitor on the set of *Swamp Women*. He was a friend of the Woolner Brothers, who made *Swamp Women*. He decided he loved it, and was going to make his movie, too. After *Bayou* flopped, Ripps added some footage and retitled it *Poor White Trash*, and it was embarrassingly successful."

Three lowlifes find an enormous stash of heroin in the very obscure *Stakeout on Dope Street* (1958), one of whom was played by Jonathan: "It was a film that Andy Fenady and Irvin Kershner put together, and I think Roger had money in the film. Roger wanted Dick [Miller] and I to play two of the kids. It was about three kids who find a quarter of a million dollars worth of heroin. They were gonna hire somebody to play the lead kid who they thought was a leading man enough for the role.

"And, somehow, [cinematographer] Haskell Wexler got involved in the film and he agreed to shoot it if they hired his brother Yale to play that part. For some reason, Dick wasn't happy with the script, and they hired a guy that was a friend of Yale Wexler's in New York, named Moe Miller. He changed his name after the movie to Stephen Marlowe, and I don't think he ever had much of a career.

"But it was a hell of a film. Fenady and Kershner had worked on Paul Coates' *Confidential File*, a television show that did things like these *Hard Copy* shows do, today." The show ran features, like a visit to death row, or an intimate view of a "junkie kicking a habit," Jonathan explains. "They decided to take that and blow it up into a feature. It was incredible, it was a good movie." Wexler shot the non-union film, but could not receive credit because he was "a union cameraman." Wexler's credit reads "Mark Jeffrey," his sons' names, combined.

Director Kershner graduated upwards to vastly more successful fare, like *The Eyes of Laura Mars* (1978) and *The Empire Strikes Back* (1983). *Dope Street* was shot on the pitiful budget of around "$38,000, in black and white," Jonathan recollects. "The schedule was for three or four weeks, which was a long time for me, because Corman was doing six-day pictures. Once they switched to a five-day week and the sixth was overtime, he switched to ten-day pictures, which was two weeks. So this film was longer, but they ran out of money so I got a piece of the picture for my last week or two on the film. The film was sold to Warner Brothers for something like $250,000 or $200,000. My two-percent of the movie was paid based on the sale, not on the gross receipts. But that was the only film that I had a percentage of, that made me money.

"Chuck Griffith, who had been a writer with Roger on many, many films up until that point, was in a steam room at the 'Y' or at some sports club. And he met a movie attorney, and, somehow, the attorney got convinced that Chuck was a big part of why Roger was so successful. He offered to present Chuck to Columbia Pictures as a writer/director/producer. They were convinced that Chuck was going to be another Sam Katzman for them. Chuck wrote two films to be shot in Hawaii. One was *Ghost of the China Sea,* and the other was *Forbidden Island*. He gave me parts in both pictures, 'cause I had gotten his career as a writer started. As a matter of fact, I introduced Roger to just tons of people who eventually worked for him, and helped Roger cast a lot of his pictures. I introduced him to Mel Welles, Bruno Ve Sota, Dick Miller, Bob Campbell, and all these people. So Chuck hired me and off to Hawaii we went to do these two movies."

Haze's first and last starring role is also his most famous performance: the mother-dominated Seymour Krelboined in the original *Little Shop of Horrors* (1960). On the verge of being fired, Seymour begs his boss, Skid Row florist

Gravis Mushnik, to look at his newest find, a bizarre Venus Fly Trap-like, potted planet Seymour has dubbed "Audrey, Jr." The sickly plant, it turns out, feeds on blood. And when Seymour provides it with a steady diet of fresh human carcasses, it blossoms (along with Mushnik's revenues). "Roger had already done *A Bucket of Blood* (1959)," relates Jonathan. "From that being reasonably successful, Roger decided to make a film in the same milieu. And there were some sets at the Chaplin Studio that he might be able to use. He made a deal with whoever had these sets that he would pay the cost of striking the sets, if he could use them for a few days. So, right away, he got Chuck Griffith working on another *Bucket of Blood*."

Dick Miller was offered the part of Seymour, but he refused because he thought it was too similar to Walter Paisley, his role in *Bucket of Blood*. "It was a smart move, because had Dick played it, it would have been," Jonathan says. "Because it was the same character, and Dick played things differently than I did. I played things more outrageously than he did." Instead, Miller appears in a supporting role in the film: Fouch, a flower-eating customer.

The film's breakneck shoot was an intense experience for young Haze: "I got the part a week before we were ready to start the shooting and I had to learn the entire script, because we did all the dialogue scenes in two days on those sets. And it was the first time I had ever heard of anybody using multiple cameras on a shoot. Roger had two cameras, and he would have one camera in a wide shot, and one camera in a close-up, and he'd get two shots out of each run-through."

"It was not easy to build a character, because, to begin with, he killed people and I was supposed to be funny. The only way I could do it was to play the guy kind of nerdy, and kind of naïve, and vulnerable. I knew, working with Roger, particularly on a film that was going to be principally shot in two days, that I had to come there with whatever I was gonna do prepared, know the lines, know what I wanted to do, because, rarely, did you get more than one take. The sets were funny and sleazy. It was great fun. It was almost like doing a stage play or a live television show. You had to come in with a completely evolved character.

"Then we did three days of second unit, all the exteriors, the chases, and the Skid Row stuff. The original two days, we had a union crew, and then we went on the streets. Roger wasn't even there. Chuck [Griffith] and Mel Welles kind of set it up and directed it. We shot three nights [in] downtown Los Angeles all night long. We were exhausted. Actually, the movie was a week, we spent a week shooting. It was like a lifetime. I think the movie took over our lives. I slept in the wardrobe."

Jonathan is as amazed as anyone by the film's uncanny lasting power: "Nobody thought we were doing something that would have such a lasting impact on the business. I still get a hundred fan letters a year. I still go to conventions, horror film conventions and stuff, everybody wants my autograph. It's strange to be a celebrity for something I did almost forty years ago for two days, a week, actually. Nobody remembers any other film that was made that year. Everybody knows that film. Every film student that comes out of college knows it by heart. The people that love it that I've talked to have seen it over and over again.

"Jack Nicholson did one scene or two scenes in *Little Shop of Horrors*. That was really fun. It was hysterical. And I knew Jack from around town. Jack and I were sort of friends. Jack certainly has gone a long way from there. I mean, when I look at *Little Shop of Horrors*, I wonder, 'How come he did it and I didn't?' [laughs] When Nicholson's big break arrived, says Jonathan, "I was already working in production at that point. I was offered a production job on *Easy Rider*, turned it down to do *Medium Cool*."

The *Little Shop* stage musical is to Jonathan's liking: "The songs were very clever, I thought it was really well done. I thought the plant was incredible. But I think it lost a lot. I think that it lost the sleaze factor. It wasn't sleazy. And I thought that the other thing that they lost out was having somebody play Mushnik that wasn't ethnic. I mean, Mushnik was a cheap, greedy Jew! [laughs] And there was a lot of hostility from the Anti-Defamation League, that we played this Jewish character who was only interested in money, which is stupid. I think they [racial jokes] are valid, if done in good taste.

"In 1962, my acting career had gone to hell. I was real disappointed. I had an agent while I was doing *Little Shop of Horrors* who saw that picture, and thought it was terrible, and who thought that I was rotten in it. He wasn't doing anything for me and I got very disillusioned. I was being offered crap to do. I had just carried a movie, starred in a movie. Yes, it was a small movie, but I thought what I had done in it was quite successful, and quite funny. I thought it was gonna open doors for me. Instead, it almost killed me in the business.

"I was no longer in tight with Roger. Roger had gone on to bigger and better things." Without the "insurance" of working for Corman, Jonathan explains, his career went into the doldrums. "And I couldn't take the rejection," he says. "I was tremendously egotistical at that point in my life. I decided I couldn't take it anymore and decided not to act." Thanks to his friend Gene Walker, Jonathan got steady work for "a couple of years," he says, sailing a recreational boat for producer Harold Hecht, Burt Lancaster's partner, along with Hecht's wife and friends. "We'd live on the boat," Jonathan recalls, "and take the boat out when nobody else wanted to go out. I learned about sailing boats, and about knots and splicing.

"I heard in 1962 that they were getting ready to do *Mutiny on the Bounty,* and they were having trouble finding ship-riggers. So I called MGM, and told them that I was a sailor who knew about square-rigged boats. They put me to work as a prop-maker. They had three boats on Lot 3, two in miniatures, one was a twenty-eight-foot miniature, one was a thirty-eight-foot miniature, one was a ship that was tied up at a dock, and they needed all the proper rigging. And they were really particular about doing all that rigging authentically.

"So I had a wonderful job. I would go to MGM, go into Lot 3, climb into the rigging of these boats, and I'd be tying knots and splicing, and doing all kinds of nautical stuff. It was fantastic. And, one day, MGM decided, or someone decided, that I had to get into the union. And the union wouldn't take me as a prop-maker, because I wasn't really a prop-maker, so how could the union take me as a prop-maker? So they suggested I be laid-off the movie! That was my association with **Mutiny on the Bounty**! It was fun, I had a great time, they had me operating the boats and the tanks, and they had me doing all kinds of stuff and I really enjoyed it. I was really hurt when they had to let me go."

The only film Jonathan ever wrote was AIP's infamous **Invasion of the Star Creatures** (1962), a slapdash science fiction comedy featuring two pneumatic aliens, and a pair of abominable comedians. Its script was originally titled **Monsters From Nicholson Mesa**, and all of the characters were named after people associated with American International Pictures. (The "Nicholson" of the title was AIP co-founder, James H. Nicholson, *not* Jack!) It was directed by Jonathan's friend and co-worker, the bulky actor/director, Bruno Ve Sota. "At that point, Roger was paying $1,500 for a script," says Jonathan, "which we thought was a lot of money. Dick [Miller] and I sat down a couple of times and tried to work a couple of things out and it just seemed we weren't getting together.

"So I started to write, and in a week, wrote that picture. I turned it in to Roger, and he showed it to Dick, and Dick said, 'I'm not going to be in it because I didn't write it.' Later, Mel Welles had formed a film company and I sold it to him. When Mel's company finally crashed, he sold it to AIP. They decided to go real cheap, they had comics play the roles. I guess Dick and I, at that time, may have been on bad terms over the script." About the names of the film's two comely aliens, Poona and Tanga, Jonathan just giggled and said, "That was one of W. C. Fields' favorite words, 'Poontang.'"

Haze played Gustaf, a mute servant, in **The Terror** (1963), a horror film Corman hastily cobbled together on sets left over from **The Raven**. "I had a few scenes with Boris Karloff, but most of my scenes were with the old witch. And that movie was shot over quite a period of time with several directors. I think Roger had done another movie someplace in Europe, and had done a lot of background shots. I don't remember if Boris Karloff was in the other movie or not, but he had all these shots he wanted to make a new movie with.

"He had several directors: I can remember Francis Coppola was one of them, and Jack Hill was one of them, and Danny Haller was one." Another was USC grad, Monte Hellman. "The movie was shot really sketchy," explains Jonathan. "It was shot like you didn't know where the hell you were, you wanted to know where it was related to the rest of the movie. It was kind of a hodge-podge, hard to deal with because you never really knew how the character got to where it was, or where it was going from there. As a matter of fact, I was a deaf-mute through most of the movie, and then, finally, because they couldn't figure an ending to the movie, I spoke. It was fun."

Co-director Monte Hellman, relates an unforgettable episode, centering on Jonathan. "At one point," Hellman says, "Jonathan got paid I think more than anybody else for the work we did on *The Terror*. We had just unbelievable schedules then—we shot everything in five days. We had some horses; instead of getting trained movie horses, which we couldn't afford, we just rented some horses from Griffith Park stables. And we took it down, we didn't have a wrangler, we had one horse in a trailer. And we shot the scene, and we couldn't get the horse back in the trailer to move on to the next location, where we needed the horse again.

"Jonathan comes to me and says, 'How much will you pay me to get the horse in the trailer?' And I said, 'Fifty dollars.' And he goes over to the horse, whispers in its ear, and the horse goes right in the trailer. I said, 'Jonathan, what did you say to the horse?' And he said, 'I told him if he didn't get in the fucking trailer, I'd beat the shit out of him!'")

Eventually, Miller and Haze settled their differences, and appeared together once again in Corman's *X–The Man With The X-Ray Eyes* (1963), starring Ray Milland as Dr. Xavier. "Ray Milland is a gentleman. Total gentleman and wonderful actor, and I thoroughly enjoyed being around him. The reason that Dick Miller and I were on the movie is because it was Don Rickles' first movie, and Roger felt that Don was a terrific comedic ad-libber. So he hired Dick and I to sit in one of the performances with Ray Milland and Don Rickles, where they read people's minds. Roger wanted Dick and I to heckle Don Rickles and get him going, so he would throw some of those wonderful fast lines that he threw in his nightclub act.

"What happened was the first time that Dick and I started to heckle him, Don got mad and said, 'Wait a minute, this isn't in the script.' He didn't want to have anything to do with ad-lib. He wanted to play the character. So Dick and I sat there and did a few lines, and that was it. It wasn't one of our better performances or better roles, to say the least. You know something: That's the only picture that I get residuals on. All of the other films were made before residuals were in the SAG contract, so that's the only picture. Every once in a while, I still get twenty-five cents or a dollar-and-a-half or something, residuals on someone's screening of *The Man With The X-Ray Eyes*."

In a left-handed way, Jonathan actually worked on Tony Richardson's *The Loved One* (1965). "I did research," Jonathan says, "In other words, Haskell Wexler owned that book, contract, he wanted to do it himself. He wanted to direct the movie and produce it and make it himself. And he hired me to do a lot of research on the undertaking business. And I would go to the mortuaries, talk to undertakers, and go to Forest Lawn and try to get a job, and take me on a tour. I would call various places and try to find what the ongoing attitude was, and what their pitch was, and all that stuff, and I recorded all these phone calls. And I would call and talk like a Mexican, and see if I could get buried at Forest Lawn; it was an all-white cemetery, and they would give me this runaround. It was very funny.

"And Haskell had promised me if he got the film going I would be an associate producer or have some kind of production job on it. And then what happened was [producers] Marty Ransohoff and John Calley formed a production company, and they bought out Haskell's rights and hired him as the co-producer and the cameraman. And I was left out. Another big disappointment, another big rejection in my life. It's a hell of a movie…I was real disappointed not to be around that movie, and not to get to know the people that were involved in it."

As he began phasing out his acting work, Jonathan worked on an obscure John Derek film, *Confessions of Tom Harris* in 1966. "I was production manager, assistant to the director," reveals Jonathan. "That was an interesting movie, because Don Murray had met a group of farmers in Orange County that were religious types, New-born Christians or whatever, and he promoted them into putting up the money for this film, based on the fact he told them he was going to do a religious film. And then he did the movie about this boxer that rapes this woman under the Santa Monica pier. It was a true story. We had the boxer and his wife on the set with us."

Actors John Derek and David "*Ozzie and Harriet*" Nelson directed. "John is brilliant," Jonathan enthuses. "John's photographer is in-fucking-credible. But the movie somehow really doesn't make it. Linda Evans was John's girlfriend at the time, and she played the girl, and she was just gorgeous. And it had a lot of great characters in it, and a lot of beautiful stuff in it, but somehow it just didn't make it. I don't know, it should have made it, 'cause it had all the elements." The film was re-released several times, beginning in 1972, under the more exploitative titles *Childish Things* and *Tale of the Cock*.

Also working in production, Jonathan was involved with the first "Billy Jack" movie, *Born Losers* (1967). The film followed the *basic* "Billy Jack" movie template: the kung-fu hero defends an oppressed group (in this case, a small town's womenfolk) from heavies (lustful, scuzzy bikers, this time, played by biker movie regulars like Jeremy Slate and Bob Tessier). "I met a guy, through Haskell, as a matter of fact, that was a partner with Tom Laughlin on putting together *The Born Losers*. They hired me as producer/assistant director, and it was very interesting...

"They had a whole group of real Hell's Angels in this movie, who were just wild, uncontrollable people. And here I was: this little guy, supposed to be assistant director, pushing these people around, telling them where to go. There was a lot of heat, back and forth...

"Laughlin was a wild man. He would go crazy, scream and yell, and stomp around, and all that. We would go into places, and we would get thrown out of towns. We were shooting in Seal Beach, California, which is a little beach community, and I didn't tell 'em what we were gonna do. And we show up with these Hell's Angels and motorcycles, and we closed down the main street of Seal Beach, and we had these guys doing wheelies, up and down the street. Finally, the city manager showed up, and shut us down.

"At one point, we did a scene where these Hell's Angels steal a police car. Somebody saw these guys driving this police car and called the police. Pretty soon, there were about ten police cars there, and guys with guns, and they thought the Hell's Angels had stolen the police car, but we were just makin' this movie. So we had a lot of problems on that movie, as far as bringing these types into these places. But it was great fun. I always enjoyed working. I don't think I ever was on a film that I disliked."

Haskell Wexler once again recruited his friend, Jonathan, for the counter-cultural, semi-documentary, *Medium Cool* (1969). The actor states that Wexler "was responsible, on a lot of levels, for me doing a lot of things in my career. I was working as executive producer with a commercial company called Dove Films that was a partnership between Haskell and Cal Bernstein. And Haskell had wanted to do a film so badly. And, finally, he had this idea about going to Chicago, which is his hometown, and doing this film during the Democratic Convention in 1968. The film was loosely scripted—Haskell had written it. We could go where things that were happening actually happened. And we would take actors and actresses and put them in the middle of riots and in the Convention, all *during* the Convention.

"And I think the picture holds up beautifully, it's a historical representation of what was happening at the time, with several fictional stories going on, during all this real stuff that was going on around it. There was a life: go to Chicago, get involved in the hippies' movement, Jesse Jackson's 'Operation Bread Basket,' the hillbillies that had come up from the south, the [dispossessed] coal miners...We were around all of these real people, so it was quite exciting. I actually line-produced that film, and I thought, again, it was going to open doors for me, and it didn't!

"Basically, I got involved in the production side of the business. I became an assistant director, production manager, associate producer, producer, executive producer, and, basically, that's what I was doing. A lot in the commercial business, but also some films. I co-produced a film with Tommy Smothers, called *Another Nice Mess* [1972]—that was a mess." The latter was an attempt at a parody of the Nixon administration, starring impersonator Rich Little as Nixon.

"Basically, I did very well, working in production, and I was executive producer with a lot of commercial companies, a lot of them involving Haskell. We had a company called Wexler-Hall, which was Wexler and [cinematographer] Conrad Hall; we made commercials. I was executive producer with them. I was executive producer with Haskell at Lucasfilm Commercial Production. Haskell and I were partners, at that point. We had our own unit with various commercial companies. We made very good money and I did it, and I went a lot of places, and it was a lot of fun and all that. And I always wanted to be an actor [laughs], so it was kind of a weird thing.

"I worked with John Wayne. I did two series of commercials for Great Western Savings out here, and it was the last two jobs that John Wayne did in his life. He was amazing! He was quite a human being. He was indeed bigger than life. We went up to Oregon, Northern California to film these commercials, and people would come out of the walls. Women would come to the hotel bringing him cookies they had. It was like traveling with Jesus. And he was funny, he was quite a guy. He would wait outside my room at the hotel up there in Oregon with a bottle of tequila, said, 'Come in from work. Let's sit down and have a talk.' He poured two water glasses of tequila, which he traveled with cases of. And we'd sit there and drink and talk. Of course, I was very left-wing, and he was very right-wing, and we would have these wonderful arguments. Not hostile, but just for fun, and it was great. He was a wild man and very outspoken, and we would just go at each other. He called me a little mafia bastard. He hated the fact that we had two women camera assistants on the job. And that was the first time he'd ever seen women crew people. He couldn't believe it. 'That goddamn Wexler,' he says. 'I bet he takes a shower with those two.' He'd see the girls lugging camera equipment, he'd say, 'Goddamn, look at that. Is that better than having somebody that can do the work?'"

For nearly eighty days, Jonathan shot three early interactive films for a Japanese theme park on locations around the world—"In Europe, Africa, South America, Central America, and did a lot of effects shots," he says. The film was shot in Show-Scan, a process that involves 70mm film unspooling at 60 frames-per-second, which is projected on a gargantuan screen. "And because of the size of the negatives," says Jonathan, "the size of the film, actually, and because of the speed that it's shot at, there's absolutely no flicker, and the world is in focus. It's incredible…It was probably the best job that I've had in recent years.

"And then, after that, I went back to being an executive producer with Haskell, filmed at a commercial company, which eventually went broke." Wexler tired of commercials, and quit them. Jonathan did "a few freelance jobs with commercial companies," he says, "And I wasn't happy, because, with Haskell, I was the big boss and I made all the decisions, and I did the budgets, and I ran it. And then I go work for another company, and some twenty-four-year-old girl is telling me how to do my job. I was working through other people's budgets, I had to answer to somebody about everything, and I just didn't like it.

"When that ended, I just decided not to do anything for a while, and just sit back, and look at myself, and decide what I want to do with the rest of my life." During that period, Jonathan began doing memorabilia shows, and has been amazed ever since that so many people want his autograph. "It's good for my ego," he admits.

"I've been trying to jumpstart an acting career," Jonathan said in 1995, "Which is very difficult, because I'm from the old school, and I'm not used to the way it all functions these days. You need a manager, you need an agent, you need all these fucking people that are going to get your money, and they don't do anything for you. [laughs] People are afraid to take a chance, so I'm still trying to get something going. Basically, all my life, I've looked for heightened experiences and adventures, and all that stuff.

"I've hated my life over the last couple of years because I don't have that going, and I'm trying at this point to get it going again. That's where I'm at. I'm not at

the point where I need any money. I mean, I managed to make money while I was doing commercials and stuff, and invested money, and I'm fine, and I need the stimulation. I need problems to solve. I'm so used to solving everybody's problem and now that I don't have that, I'm too busy looking at my own problems.

In 1996, Jonathan and Dick Miller bumped into each other at an audition and discovered that they were up for the same part. "I'm still very active. I work out every day of my life, am in good shape. I feel good. I think that I still have the talent that I had— Certainly it has to be adjusted! I gotta play people that are older than I ever played in my life. I just wanna do it for the fun...I wanna come back and do something where I can show what I can do."

THE FILMS OF JONATHAN HAZE

1953	*Daughter of Horror* (aka: *Dementia*)
1954	*Monster From the Ocean Floor*
	The Fast and the Furious
1955	*East of Eden* (uncredited)
	Cell 2455, Death Row (uncredited)
	Five Guns West
	Oklahoma Woman
	Apache Woman
	Beast With a Million Eyes
	Swamp Women (aka: *Swamp Diamonds*)
1956	*The Bold and the Brave*
	The Day the World Ended
	It Conquered the World
	Not of This Earth
	Attack of the Crab Monsters
	Gunslinger
1957	*Rock All Night*
	Carnival Rock
	Bayou (re-released as *Poor White Trash* in 1961)
	Naked Paradise (aka: *Thunder Over Hawaii*)
	Viking Women and the Sea Serpent
1958	*Stakeout on Dope Street*
	Teenage Caveman
	The Ghost of the China Sea
1959	*Forbidden Island*
1960	*The Little Shop of Horrors*
1962	*The Premature Burial*
	Mutiny on the Bounty (Boat rigger)
	Tales of Terror (production assistant—uncredited)
1963	*Invasion of the Star Creatures* (screenplay)
	The Terror
	X–The Man With the X-Ray Eyes
1965	*The Loved One* (Uncredited research)
1966	*Confessions of Tom Harris* (aka: *Childish Things, Tale of the Cock*)
	Track of the Vampire (aka: *Blood Bath*)
1967	*The Born Losers* (assistant director)
1969	*Medium Cool* (associate producer)

1972	*Another Nice Mess* (co-producer)
1979	*11th Victim* (CBS, associate producer)
1981	*Vice Squad*
1982	*Heart Like a Wheel*
1999	*The Phantom Eye* (AMC tvm)

Contrary to rumors, Jonathan was in no way involved with Corman's *The St. Valentine's Day Massacre* (1967). *Gunslinger* and *It Conquered the World* were both shown in debased versions on *Mystery Science Theater 3000*.

TELEVISION

Dragnet, 77 Sunset Strip, others.

Bo Hopkins

"Acting is a gift, if you've got it. Some people don't have to study as hard as others, but I think it's all a gift, and it's what you do with it. If you can survive in this business, then you've won. If you just hang on and survive."

Few actors are granted opening scenes as intense as Bo Hopkins was in Sam Peckinpah's *The Wild Bunch* (1969). As one of the film's many genuine psychotics, Hopkins played Clarence Lee "Crazy Lee" Sykes, a lowly outlaw left to guard three hostages as the titular gang makes their getaway during the film's opening shootout. (Screenwriter Alan Sharp once said that the film begins with a climax.) In one of *The Wild Bunch*'s most absurdly violent and operatic sequences—and that's really saying something—Crazy Lee first shotguns his off-camera prisoners, and is then himself gunned down by three bounty hunters. Not one to be upstaged, he manages to sputter, "How'd you like to kiss my sister's black cat's ass," before he wipes out all three of them. Then, Albert Dekker finishes Hopkins off by filling him with two final slugs. Then, the movie really starts.

But what did Bo do for an encore?

Hopkins went on to appear in two other Peckinpah films: the director's adaptation of Jim Thompson's *The Getaway* (1971) and *The Killer Elite* (1975), cast as yet another frightening sociopath (but one hell of a shot). He played a duck-tailed member of Sam the Sham and the Pharoahs, the gang that memorably initiates Richard Dreyfuss in George Lucas' *American Graffiti*

(1973). (He was reunited with his *Graffiti* co-star, Candy Clark, for a cameo in Lucas' *The Radioland Murders* (1994).) He was also in a slue of '70s westerns, action movies, and the occasional studio drama, like John Schlesinger's supremely dark *Day of the Locust* (1975), in almost a parody of his cowboy roles. This is not to mention Alan Parker's *Midnight Express* (1978). He was often cast as unsavory rednecks, in films like *The Fifth Floor* (1978). He worked several times with Burt Reynolds, in, among others, the quintessentially southern *White Lightning* (1973).

Like his Peckinpah cohorts, L. Q. Jones and R. G. Armstrong, Hopkins is continually cast as sheriffs, in everything from *A Small Town in Texas* (1976) to the fun, low-budget *Mutant* (1984).

From the time I spent talking with him, I gathered that the years have left Hopkins an utterly affable, mellow man. He still acts regularly in films like Oliver Stone's *U-Turn* (1997), and Richard Linklater's *The Newton Boys* (1998). For quite a while, he was even getting television airtime as a pitchman for anti-smoking products.

Like Dick Bakalyan, Hopkins had a very troubled youth. His slightly high-pitched drawl marks him as a native Southerner. He was born in 1942 in Greenwood, South Carolina. "My dad died when I was nine, and then we moved in with my grandmother. And I run away from home a lot, and got put in a lot of homes."

When Hopkins was thirteen, he discovered that he had been adopted. He dropped out the eighth grade, and spent time in a reform school (a tomato ranch). At sixteen, he was arrested for being a lookout during a robbery. Thanks to an uncle, who happened to be a district attorney, he was given the option of adding on two years to his age and joining the Army. Hopkins served his time in Korea. "And then I got out of the service, and I wanted to finish school…I got married, and then we were married just nine months, and got a daughter, named Jane.

"Then I got into a little theater play, and I got me a scholarship, in Danville, Kentucky. From there, they pulled me out of school, and put me on stage with actors from New York. I got the lead in three plays, went back to South Carolina, then went to New York, didn't like it much, went back to South Carolina. And from there, I came to California. I got a scholarship to a couple of schools— Desilu was one of them." His first professional acting assignments were on shows like *The Mod Squad* and *Gunsmoke*.

In Hollywood, Hopkins attended the Actors' Studio. "Mostly, I would go and sit in on a class, and listen to Lee [Strasberg] critique scenes. And then Martin Landau, I went to some of his classes, and just observed, and participated in a few things. That was about it. I did a movie called *Thousand Plane Raid* [1969], and then, right after that, I got into *The Wild Bunch*. I'd technically say *The Wild Bunch* was my first movie, but the first one I did was *Thousand Plane Raid*. I did three pictures for Sam Peckinpah, and he was very good to me. I

The Wild Bunch.

loved working for him…He was a very good director, and I had fun on all his movies. And he was a good man. He had faults, but who doesn't?

"Working with Bill Holden, and Robert Ryan, and Ernest Borgnine, and L. Q. Jones, and Dub Taylor, and Ben Johnson—All those guys were my friends. And they continued to be my friends. Bill Holden bought my girlfriend a poncho.

"[Holden] had to pull out back to talk to David Wolper about a documentary he was doing in Africa, and he told Wolper about me. [Then Wolper did] *The Bridge At Remagen* (also '69) and I got the part. And he got me in another movie later. Robert Ryan did my first interview, because I didn't know what interviews were. And that's the kind of people they were, just great people to work with. I love Robert Ryan. I thought he was a gentleman, and Bill Holden was the same way. They took their craft seriously, but they didn't take the shit outside of there. They were men's men, I would say. By that, I mean they did their work. At [the proper] time, they were professional. Beyond that, their life away from the camera, they didn't really care about that. They just cared about their work."

During the opening shootout, Peckinpah called on Hopkins to improvise a piece of business with one of the extra players. "Well, in the beginning, the girl that was a school teacher there, [that] they had hired as an extra. I was supposed to kiss her on the ear. And she wasn't reacting right. So Sam said, 'Look, uh, when you go up to her this time, just stick your tongue in her ear.' And I did, and I got a big reaction, and he printed it.

"I did *Macho Callahan* (1970) after that, with Jean Seberg, and David Janssen. They were real great people to work with. David was very fun, fun-loving, and loved to play golf. Jean, I kinda had a little crush on her, 'cause I was playing a kid who did, anyway. And she was the sweetest woman. And I don't know what happened later. She had a tough time, [after she] did her first movie, [as] Joan of Arc [*Saint Joan* (1957)], and the critics killed her. And I think she showed a lot of guts by staying in the business, and she proved them wrong, because she could act."

One of the steady stream of western roles Hopkins took was as one of Lee Marvin and Jack Palance's fellow ranch hands in William Fraker's underrated *Monte Walsh* (1970). It was cinematographer Fraker's directorial debut, and was severely truncated by its studio. "Lee Marvin and I were good friends after the movie was over," relates Hopkins, "and I'd go down to see him and Pam, his wife. And I love Lee. Not only his acting, but I love him as a screen persona, and he was just a great guy, once you got to know him. He was hard to get to know—he's like a lot of people. But once you got to know him, he was just...he insists you come by the house and see him. And, you know, it was just a big thrill, to have him as a friend."

THE FIRST KILLING WAS AN ACCIDENT...
BUT WHAT HAPPENED NEXT WAS NOT!

FOR THREE DESPERATE PEOPLE IT WAS

The Only Way Home

In Peckinpah's *The Getaway* (1972), Hopkins played bank robber Al Lettieri's partner, [character name]. Steve McQueen starred as Doc McCoy, their leader. "I loved working with Steve. We became friends on the movie, and, of course, I was a big fan of his, anyway. I miss him. I wish he was still here. I wish a lot of 'em was still here. And I guess we kind of had something in common, if he let you get to know him. I had a lot of fun with him. He had a tough time, too [growing up]. You know, I just miss him an awful lot. He died too young.

"Sam told me to comb my hair in a scene, when Steve was giving us a map on what we were going to be doing. And he didn't tell Steve. After the scene started, you know. Steve said, 'Okay, we're going to start over here, hit a bank here, then we're going to go over here.' And then I started combing my hair. He said, 'Whoa, whoa, whoa. Why is he combing his hair?' [Peckinpah said] 'Because I told him to.' 'Oh, okay.' Steve, he had to know everything that was going on. Sam just laughed.

"And one day, I'm riding a motorcycle, it wasn't a big one, it was one of the dirt bikes. And Steve says, 'Well, how come he rides and I don't get to ride?' Sam says, "Cause if he gets killed, who gives a shit. But if you get killed, we lose a lot of money.'"

Hopkins struck up a friendship with Al Lettieri during production. "I loved Al. He and I were real good friends. He took me to see *The Godfather*. I didn't know what it was about. Of course, when I saw it, I was just flabbergasted. It was such a great movie, and he was great in it. And, you know, he was just getting his career started. And he was just a great guy to know…I had a lot of fun with him."

That same year, Hopkins played an employee of *The Culpepper Cattle Company*, yet another early cowpoke role: "I think *Culpepper* was a movie we did that was really realistic. [Director] Dick Richards made sure of that. Jerry Bruckheimer was the producer. *The Wild Bunch* and that one are a lot of the stunt guys' favorite westerns, because of the reality in it. And I really enjoyed doin' it. I loved the character [I played] in it."

In George Lucas' first big hit, *American Graffiti* (1973), Hopkins played the leader of the Pharoahs, who intimidate Richard Dreyfuss, then initiate him into their ranks: "I loved working with George [Lucas]. He's very quiet and unassuming. I like directors that way. He didn't have an ego problem with an actor, and he loved to listen to ideas. In fact, Candy Clark and I did a little cameo in *Radioland Murders*; he directed it—First time he directed since *American Graffiti* [actually, since *Star Wars*]. He directed our scenes, and I always thought a lot of George. Very proud of him.

"I call Paul [Le Mat] every now and then. In fact, I gotta call him again. I like Richard [Dreyfuss], always have. We all had the same trailer. We all dressed in it. Richard was a great guy, a conversationalist. We loved to talk about politics and things like that, and Harrison Ford was the same way." It also afforded Hopkins the opportunity of reuniting with Ron Howard, whom he had first worked with on *The Andy Griffith Show*—the job that got Hopkins his SAG card.

The majority of the movie was shot at night in Modesto, California. "Well, it was something you had to get used to. You go in at six [p.m.] and you got off at six [a.m.]. And if you're getting paid, you kind of try not to think about it. But I don't really like night shooting, never have. But, you know, if I'm getting paid, I have to do it."

Hopkins was in two Burt Reynolds films, back to back: *White Lightning* (1973), also featuring R. G. Armstrong; and *The Man Who Loved Cat Dancing* (also '73). "Well, I just finished *American Graffiti*. And I'd fly down to rehearse with Burt on the weekends. And then I'd go to, after I'd finished three weeks of night shooting, I flew down to Little Rock, and we started a movie. And I still had to sleep during the day. But I had a lot of fun on that movie."

Then came *Cat Dancing*. "I did *White Lightning* before that, and my agent had to me in to meet [director] Dick Sarafian. So I got that part, because Dick wanted me for it, and, of course, it was great to work with Burt again, and Dinah Shore, and Sarah Miles. And, you know, I just love working with Burt—We'd do imitations, and he's a great friend."

In '73, Hopkins went to Spain to act in Sam Fuller's *The Deadly Trackers*, but Fuller was replaced as director by Barry Shear midway through filming it. "I worked with Sam Fuller in Spain. Well, it was great working with Sam and Richard [Harris] both. I was still a kid, and I enjoyed working with them, and it was a good script."

Hopkins was a hired gunman in Peckinpah's *The Killer Elite* (1975), starring Robert Duvall and James Caan. "Peckinpah just sent me a script, and told me to do something with it. And I came up with the idea of wearing the [sun] glasses, and they were my own. I had them made, tinted blue, and I tried to make the character cool, you know? I love working with Jimmy [Caan]. He knew what he was doing. He was very good in martial arts, 'cause he'd been studyin'. Of course, he loved sports, so we played basketball. And I had a great time with Jimmy. We shot most of it in [San Francisco's] Chinatown. And the boat, the ghost boat or whatever, it was docked."

He also appeared as a sleazy sheriff in Jack Starrett's *A Small Town in Texas* (1976), co-starring Tim Bottoms and Susan George. "I love working with Jack. He directed me in two things, one with Johnny Cash, *Thaddeus, Rose, and Eddie* (1978). He was a good actor's director, because he would let you improvise if the scene wasn't working, and I like that. I remember it was a small town in Texas where we shot it, because we did *The Getaway there*. A place called San Marcos, and I had a great time, 'cause I had been there before."

Hopkins played "Tex" in Alan Parker's *Midnight Express* (1978), the infamous, brutal story of an American drug smuggler serving time in a hellish Turkish prison for smuggling hashish. "They had been shooting two weeks before I got there. So when we got there, they were well into the movie. They were shooting, like, the beginning.

"It was a very tough film because it was so damn...*down*. You had to get your own sense of humor about it. So that's the main thing I remember. And, of course, I was always scared when I was at the airport, that somebody'd plant something on me. I thought it was a good movie."

In 1979, Hopkins was in Bill W. L. Norton's *More American Graffiti*, playing the same character as in the original. "Well, I didn't like it as much as the first one, because it's hard to do a sequel, very few succeed. I think what happened with that one was they tried the split-screen things, and it didn't work. And I think that the story was there, but the split-screen thing I don't think worked for the audience. I think if they'd—of course, it's my opinion—if they shot it like they did *American Graffiti*, it would have done a lot better. Candy's now a good friend, and Paul Le Mat."

Hopkins was a regular on ABC's *Dynasty*, but quit because of differences with the network. In a 1981 interview, he said, "I never walked on any show before. I've never been drunk on a set, never caused trouble, never been fired. But I have my pride. They can take away my house, my Mercedes, my pool. Just leave, me and my dog, and I'll be alright. I don't care if I never work again. I can walk out of this town with my head held high, leaving half of the s.o.b.s kissing behinds as they've always done."

It proved to be far from the end of his career. He was even brought back for a *Dynasty* special. "Right after that, I did a thing called *Sweet Sixteen* (1983). And then I did a lot of movies, in between, and went to South Africa to do a movie, and then shot some here. And then, I came back and did another special, two-hour *Dynasty*, and I did four, five other films. Hell, I even forgot some of them."

Hopkins acted in *Bounty Hunter* (1989), starring exploitation favorite Robert Ginty. "I loved Bob...That's the reason I did the movie. He's directing now, which is good, because he's a good actor's director. I think I've seen it once and...that was a long time ago...You know, I could never comment on something I do, but I enjoyed working with Bobby."

The cast of *The Legend of Wolf Mountain* (1991) included Mickey Rooney. "I had a great time doing that, because [Rooney] told stories all day. And I got to listen to a lot of 'in' stuff that I didn't know. We shot it in Utah, and up in the mountains. And every time we would take a break or something, Mickey would tell stories, and that was what was fun.

In 1992, he was in *Inside Monkey Zetterland.* "I did that because it was sort of an artsy-fartsy...or an artsy-*artsy* movie. The kid, Steve [Antin], played my son in *Sweet Sixteen*, so I got to play his father again."

Hopkins was reunited with Lucas and Candy Clark in *The Radioland Murders* (1994). "Well, I went and did it in Georgia. Fred Rouse called and wanted Candy and I to go down and do a cameo in it, [to] play the mother and father. So that's the reason I did it, because of George Lucas. They cut a lot of our stuff out, too, so we weren't in it that much.

"I did a rodeo movie with Dwight Yoakam, called *Rodeo Clown*, and then I did a family movie with puppets, called *Lunker Lake*. When I got back from that, I went to work for Oliver Stone, with Sean Penn, and Nick Nolte, and Powers Booth in *U-Turn* in Arizona. And that was a big thrill, working with Oliver. I really enjoyed working with him. He reminds me a lot of Peckinpah," Hopkins laughs, "in a way. He's got that sense of humor, and we'd tease each other a lot. I mean, he'd tease me more than I teased him.

"And it was great working with Sean Penn and Powers Booth, who is a friend of mine. And Sean Penn, who's just a great actor, just love working with him. Hope to do something else with him.

"In the last three years, I guess, the parts I get are what I like. I can pick and choose. I don't have to do anything, unless I want to.

"I think I've been very lucky. I've had a good career. I hope it gets better now, because I think I've matured a lot more, and, also, I want to open up some new creative juices. And I have an eighteen-month-old boy," Hopkins laughs. "I think I've been lucky to work with some of the greatest actors of all time, and I've been lucky to have come along at sort of the end of another era. I've been very fortunate in my career with the people I've met, and the movies that I've done. Some of them that will always be here, so my son can see 'em.

"Acting is a gift, if you've got it. Some people don't have to study as hard as others, but I think it's all a gift, and it's what you do with it. If you can survive in this business, then you've won. If you just hang on and survive."

THE FILMS OF BO HOPKINS

1969	*The Thousand Plane Raid*
	The Wild Bunch
	The Bridge at Remagen
1970	*Monte Walsh*
	Macho Callahan
	The Moonshine War

1971	The Only Way Home
	Cat Ballou (NBC pilot)
1972	The Getaway
	The Culpepper Cattle Company
1973	American Graffiti
	The Man Who Loved Cat Dancing
	White Lightning
	The Deadly Trackers
1974	The Nickel Ride
	Doc Elliot (ABC series)
1975	The Day of the Locust
	The Killer Elite
	Posse
	The Kansas City Massacre
	Runaway Barge
1976	A Small Town in Texas
	Charlie's Angels (NBC feature pilot)
	Dawn: Portrait of a Teenage Runaway (NBC tvm)
	The Invasion of Johnson County (NBC tvm)
1977	Tentacles
	Aspen (NBC mini-series)
1978	Midnight Express
	The Court Martial of Lt. William Calley (tvm)
	Thaddeus Rose and Eddie (CBS tvm)
	Crisis in Sun Valley (NBC tvm)
	The Busters (pilot)
1979	More American Graffiti
	Last Ride of the Dalton Gang
	The Innocent and the Damned (NBC mini-series)
	Beggerman, Thief (NBC tvm)
1980	The Fifth Floor
	The Plutonium Incident (CBS tvm)
	Casino
1983	Sweet Sixteen
	Ghost Dancing (ABC tvm)
1984	Mutant
1985	What Comes Around
	Dark Horse (tvm)
1986	Nightmare at Noon
	Houston: The Legend of Texas (CBS tvm)

1986 *(cont.)*	*A Smoky Mountain Christmas* (ABC tvm)
1987	*Trapper County War* *Down the Long Hills* (ABC tvm) *Sex Appeal*
1989	*Bounty Hunter* *Big Bad John* *President's Target* *Stalker* (aka: *Man From Nowhere*)
1990	*The Final Alliance* *Mark of the Beast*
1991	*Blood Ties* *The Legend of Wolf Mountain*
1992	*Inside Monkey Zetterland* *Center of the Web* *Black Creek Under Surveillance* *Terror of Manhattan*
1993	*The Ballad of Little Jo* *Return to Wolf Mountain*
1994	*Radioland Murders* *Cheyenne Warrior* *Texas Payback* *Wyatt Earp: Return to Tombstone* (tvm) *The Feminine Touch*
1995	*Painted Hero* *Riders of the Storm* *The November Conspiracy* *Carmen-R.I.O.T.* (aka: *R.I.O.T–The Movie*) *Half a Dog's Life* *OP Center* (tvm)
1996	*Demon Kid* *Fever Lake* (Direct-to-video)
1997	*Uncle Sam* *U-Turn* *Rodeo Clown* *Lunker Lake*
1998	*The Newton Boys* *Phantoms*
1999	*From Dusk Till Dawn 2: Texas Blood Money* (Direct-to-video) *Getting to Know You* *Time Served*

2000	*South of Heaven, West of Hell*
	Big Brother Trouble
	Vice
	The Thundering 8th
	A Crack in the Floor
2001	*Cowboy Up*
	Choosing Matthias
2002	*Don't Let Go*
	City of Ghosts
	Mending Fences
2003	*Shade*
	The Road Home

TELEVISION

Hopkins's tv work includes: *The Andy Griffith Show, The Virginian, Gunsmoke, The Mod Squad, Wild, Wild, West, Bonanza, Nichols, Supertrain,* and regular spots on *The Rockford Files* and *Dynasty.*

L. Q. JONES

"Aren't you getting tired here, yet? We've been at this an hour-and-a-half. I charge by the minute! God, I hope I don't have to make it all the way from '61 to '94!"

Lanky, bushy-haired, and the perpetual center of attention, L. Q. Jones is the Roger Miller of character actors. He is as hysterical and enjoyable to watch as Miller's off-kilter songs are to hear. If it ever seems like L. Q. should have been a stand-up comedian instead of one of the cinema's preeminent western scumbags, there is a definite reason. He *was* a stand-up comedian, years before he let himself go unshorn, begrimed himself, and set foot in front of a camera, Colt revolver in hand.

A perfect example of L. Q.'s bizarre sense of humor comes courtesy of William Tuttle, MGM's former make-up department chief. Tuttle, L. Q. and several crewmen were making their way through barren desert to get to a location, sometime during the '60s. Surrounding them was nothing but flat desert sands. L. Q. gazed out at this wilderness, and said, "I remember when all of this was nothing but apartment houses."

His unique name has a fascinating history. He was born Justice Ellis McQueen in Beaumont, Texas on August 19, 1927. "L. Q. Jones" was the name of the very first character that McQueen ever played on film, in Raoul Walsh's excellent adaptation of Leon Uris' **Battle Cry** (1955). Some of United Artists' publicity material for **Men in War** (1957) mistakenly listed him as "Al Q. Jones." If you ask L. Q. what his initials stand for, he will probably reply "Little Queer." His co-stars used to call him "Loquacious Jones," probably because of how free he is with his mouth.

(Speaking of which, L. Q. talked back to his tyrannical friend, Sam Peckinpah, on the director's own sets. In that regard, he is unique. "Sam and I always got along," L. Q. explains. "I told him he didn't have enough talent to direct me to the men's room, but that's the only way you can handle Sam." And while we're on the subject of indifference towards the irascible, L. Q. was famous, at one point, for calling up writer Harlan Ellison and requesting his presence on the line by inquiring, "Is Numbnuts there?")

L. Q.'s first scene in **Battle Cry** should have warned Hollywood about what they were in for the next fifty years, but the fools just kept right on hiring him, anyway. He first pops up in an early scene, among a group of disparate Army recruits, being shipped out to boot camp by train. The narrator introduces each recruit, in turn: the young Texan, strumming his guitar; the pride of the Navajo; the bookworm; the Ivy League preppie; et al. Then, abruptly, the narrator's voice drops to the scornful tone of a tenth grade math teacher doling out detention: "There's one in every group," he tells us, as we see L. Q. mischievously giving one of the other soldiers-to-be a hotfoot. There could have been no more perfect beginning to L. Q. Jones' career in the movies. The word that best sums up his consistent screen persona is "hellion." He is one of the screen's outstanding one-percenters.

The Hunting Party.

That was only the beginning. Memorable moments abound among L. Q.'s performances, even in thin material like *The Hunting Party* (1971). The film is a lame western that cribbed as many elements from Peckinpah movies as it did from spaghetti westerns—and only from the explicit parts. In it, L. Q. plays Hog Warren, a member of Oliver Reed's cutthroat band. These amiable degenerates kidnap Candice Bergen, and L. Q.'s character cordially introduces himself by attempting to rape her. Cliché noble outlaw Reed kicks L. Q. in the face to cool his affections. Later, though, Reed apologizes to L. Q. for the rough treatment he had dished out. "Aw, hell," L. Q. says, almost shyly, "I like being kicked."

(It should be duly noted that, along with Elisha Cook, L. Q. has one of cinema's highest mortality rates. He is an actor, as Lee Marvin would say, whose characters seem destined for a cheap funeral. For starters, he was shot by James Coburn in *Pat Garrett and Billy the Kid* (1973), stabbed by Clint Eastwood in *Hang 'Em High* (1968), and had his neck snapped under David Carradine's foot in *Long Wolf McQuade* (1983). But, in a movie as littered with corpses as the most vicious of L. Q.'s westerns, *Casino* (1995), L. Q. escaped unscathed. Has he become—God help us—respectable?!)

L. Q. and Strother Martin often made a memorable pair, especially as the lead "gutter trash" bounty hunters in Peckinpah's *The Wild Bunch* (1969). They are unforgettable, exulting over the bullet-riddled corpses of the slain outlaws after the film's climactic "Battle of Bloody Porch." Or, a few moments later, as Robert Ryan numbly walks away from his fallen former comrades, L. Q.'s orders his scurvy partner, Strother, to hand him his knife, since "this here boy's got some gold in his teeth!" Peckinpah made a visual metaphor for their viciousness by cutting from images of vultures descending on the apparently endless slaughtered bodies, directly to a scene of the verminous L. Q. and Strother doing likewise.

This dingy duo also set the off-kilter, theatrical tone for the underrated *Ballad of Cable Hogue* (1970) with their pivotal appearance early in the film. They start the film's action rolling by not simply abandoning Hogue (Jason Robards) to die in the desert wastes, but by leaving him with a mocking little duet. After L. Q. had started his own production company, LQJaf (L. Q. Jones and Friends), he gave Strother the plum role of the leader of a modern satanic cult in California in his *The Brotherhood of Satan* (1971). "Strother and I have been friends for a hundred years," L. Q. says. "We always have fun."

In Philippe Mora's berserk monster movie, *The Beast Within* (1982), L. Q. plays the sheriff of the kind of small southern town that only exists in drive-in movies. The camera cuts to him at one point, deep in an earnest phone conversation. "Oral sodomy?" he says to the anonymous, hapless soul on the other end. "Well, that's why this is a small town," he stoically explains. (L. Q. was "typed" playing sheriffs for a while, a not especially unpleasant fate that also befell Bo Hopkins and R. G. Armstrong.)

What many people seem to have never realized about L. Q. is that, beneath his Texas wildman façade, there lurks a very shrewd, well-read businessman. Among other accomplishments, he was able to create an extremely inventive science fiction movie, *A Boy and His Dog* (1975), on a middling budget. He then nurtured it into a hit over two theatrical releases. (Not to mention its extremely successful video run.) How can L. Q.'s directorial credentials be in doubt when, in *Boy*, the only film he ever officially directed, he was able to coax a good performance out of his young lead, *Don Johnson*? (At certain points in *Boy*, it sounds like

Johnson is half-imitating L. Q.'s voice.) But the cherry atop all of this is that the film's canine lead, "Tiger," who gives one of the finest animal performances on film. The urbane, telepathic "Blood," Tiger's character, has been referred to as "George Sanders in a fur coat," and won the PATSY Award (Performing Animal Trained Star of the Year). (The late Tim McIntyre provided Blood's orotund voice.)

Aside from being unique as an actor and director, L. Q. is also a unique conversationalist. He punctuates his statements with little asides, like "Oh, diddle," or, in a plummy, British accent, "Right-o." He almost inevitably will call you "Baby." He phoned me after this interview originally ran, and opened our conversation with "Ya got ten minutes to get out of town." He can always be counted on to come up with some new anecdote, no matter how many yarns he might have bored you to tears with already.

Other interviews with L. Q. can be found in the documentaries *Sam Peckinpah: Man of Iron* (1992) (He is none-too-subtly wearing a *Boy and His Dog* t-shirt), *The Wild Bunch: A Portrait in Montage* (1996), and in Mike Siegel's upcoming *Passion and Poetry: The Journey of Sam Peckinpah*. He also provided extensive—and extremely funny—commentary for the laserdisc and dvd releases of *A Boy and His Dog* (1975). In print, he was interviewed in Garner Simmons' and David Weddle's biographies of Peckinpah.

Justice Ellis McQueen was born August 19, 1927 in Beaumont, Texas. "I lived more times with a guardian than I did with my parents," L. Q. recalls, "because my mother and I were in a wreck when I was four and she was killed. And my dad was not of a bent to take care of a four-year-old hellion. And so they brought in my grandmother to take care of me, and an aunt to take care of me, and I drove everybody insane. So, finally, a lady, named Anita McBurnett, who was nearly a twin of my mother, even though they were not related, decided she was going to take me on. So she had just gotten married and took me to live with them, and I stayed with them the rest of the time.

"We lived in town. My guardian owned a hardware store. But my grandparents had a place in town, and a house out in the country. And, so, on weekends a lot of times, I'd go out with my grandfather, and work the stock with him, plow a little bit, get in his way." As a young man, L. Q.'s education "went up through college. I'm a few hours short of three different degrees, but I have none." He attended the University of Texas, as well as a smaller, junior college. He also served in the Navy "for a short period." Afterwards, he worked as stand-up comedian, and as a rancher in, of all places, Nicaragua.

His movie career began with 1955's *Battle Cry*. ("This is a *career?*" L. Q. inquired.) It was one of America's finest action directors, Raoul Walsh, who gave L. Q. his break into pictures. "Well, Raoul was a rounder—a roue, if you will," says L. Q. "A wild man...Actually, he started in pictures, I believe, in New York, and then ended up coming out here, where he was helping organize pictures, working in 'em as an extra. Then he became a big star himself as an actor, and was working in 'em as an actor, starring in pictures. Then he had the accident that removed an eye. He decided not to [go on acting], and started directing, and Raoul probably single-handedly kept Warner Brothers afloat during the short times. He made some of the biggest, some of the best pictures...

"I have very fond memories of Raoul. I walked in from Nicaragua, and Fess Parker drew me a map—Fess and I had been rooommates in college. He was being considered, I think for a part in *Battle Cry*, which he eventually got. Anyway, he drew a map on the back of a shirt front stuffing, how to get out to Warner Brothers. So I walked out.

"At that particular time at Warner Brothers, they had a double gate with one guard, so that you walked up to the guard if you had an appointment, he buzzed the gate open, and you went in. When you were coming out on the other side, they were keepin' a pretty tight check, so he buzzed and you could go out. Well, just as I was walking up, and I had no reason to be there other than the fact that I wanted to talk to somebody about *Battle Cry*, a little blonde with the tightest sweater you've ever seen in your life was coming out, so he swung his attention to her, of course, not me. [The gate] buzzed, I walked in, walked down the hall, went in to Hoyt Bowers' office, who I knew was casting. Now, Cathy, his secretary, would throw King Kong out if he didn't have an appointment, but she was down the hall picking up some coffee. Oh, boy. The door to his office was open; he was on the phone. So, I said, What the hell. I walked in, sat down, put my feet up on his desk, and waited till he got through. Then I told him how lucky he was that I was there to play the part of L. Q. Jones.

"He promptly called Cathy, and the both of 'em threw me out. He listened to me for a few minutes, and then he said, 'You've got no experience,' you know, 'Buzz off.' So, I came back and I was tellin' Fess what happened. And he said, 'Well, you gave up too easy. Go back out and talk with him again.' And I said, 'I won't be able to get in.' So, he gave me the phone number. I called up and talked to Hoyt. And he said, 'Look, leave me alone. You don't have any experience. You don't know what you're doin'.' So, he said, 'Wait a minute. I'll tell you what. Call me at three o'clock today.' 'Okay.' So, I went back and talked to Fess, and he said, 'Well, you're gonna call?' And I said, 'No, I'm not gonna call.' 'Well, why not?' 'Well, it's just when you're talking to some guy, the easiest thing to do is just say, 'Call me at a later date,' and then he won't take the call.' And he said, 'Look, if he didn't want you to call, he'd tell you to shove off.' 'Oh, okay.' So, I called, and he said, 'Look, you just don't have the experience.' And I didn't. And I kept talking. And he said, 'Tell you what—come out tomorrow morning and you can talk to Solly Baiano.' Solly was head of casting at Warner Brothers.

"So, I showed up the next morning. And he took me over, and he said, 'Look, this is gonna be very short, 'cause Solly's gonna throw you out on your ass. But you've talked your way this far. See what the heck you can do.' I sat down and talked to Solly for about two, three minutes, and he was about to throw me out, when the phone rang. Turns out it was Raoul Walsh and he was talking to Solly about something for the picture in the way of casting. And, somehow, Solly mentioned the fact I was there, and he couldn't get rid of me and I could hear [Walsh] on the phone. And he said, 'Bring him up and I'll throw his ass out.'

"So, I went up with Solly. Solly went into the office, stayed there for two or three minutes. The door popped open, he says, 'Come in.' I walked in and stood there, and there sits Raoul and he didn't have his patch in. 'Cause a lot of times when he was tired, when he got a little chapped, he would take the patch off, and put a little handkerchief in the hole. And that's where he was sitting. He stared at me, and I stared at him. Neither one of us said a thing for about five minutes. Finally, he said, 'Can you learn lots of lines.' And he said, 'How tall are you?' Remembering the part from the book, which I read, L. Q. was about 5' 7", weighed probably 180, 185 pounds. So, I said, 'I'm 5' 7".' He said, 'You're a goddamn liar, you're six feet tall. Can you learn lots of words?' 'Oh, yeah, oh, yeah.' So, he said, 'Okay,' turned us out, and said 'Give him a test.' Well, I didn't know it at that point in time, but, for the part of L. Q. Jones, they had tested over 250 people, almost all of 'em professionals. Well, I went in, did the test, which I saw later, and Raoul had a lot more guts than I did.

"Anyway, they had the casting meeting, I think, probably a couple of days later, and they were talking about who was going to do what, and who had been signed for what, and they came to the part of L. Q. Jones. And Raoul says, 'I want this kid,' mentioning me. And Solly and the heads of the studio—[Jack] Warner was, of course, but Steve Trilling was the man running it. He said, 'Raoul, for Christ's sake, be reasonable. You're going to Villegas, it's five thousand miles away. If you get down there, and he can't even repeat his name, you're screwed and so are we!' He said, 'Be reasonable. Just take one of the other people we know can do the part. When you get back in town, you can hire this guy and use him. Just do that!' And Raoul said, 'Let me tell you somethin'. Either he does the picture, or I don't.' That was the end of that. So, he went to bat for me, and I've been ever thankful."

In Elvis Presley's first feature film, the post-Civil War, semi-western **Love Me Tender** (1955), L. Q. played one of ex-Confederate Neville Brand's lackies. L. Q. and the King "became fairly good friends," L. Q. remembers. "A bit strange with Elvis, of course, because he was a huge hit. I was basically in the picture because of the man who was producing it, named [Dave] Weisbart, who I had done a picture for at Warner Brothers. This was at Twentieth [Century-Fox]. And, so, I didn't know Elvis, didn't know any of the people over at Twentieth. This was my first time to work over there. But everybody was prepared to absolutely hate him. Even the crew, which was very unusual. They were really ticked that somebody was coming in to do this. Elvis showed up two days later—everybody in the world loved him. But we became really good friends, did eventually three pictures together."

L. Q. measurably warmed up to the subject of another co-star from the film, the imposing Neville Brand. "Ah!" he exclaimed, imitating Brand's gravelly voice,

"*Neville Brand*? Neville tried to kill me on the picture. But that's okay, he didn't do it on purpose. We'd been shootin' for two or three weeks. Neville was known to visit the bottle frequently. And we showed up for a fight, saber fight one morning, and all of us were there, except Neville. Who can remember this late?—but, we probably were due to start shooting around eight-thirty or nine. It's now ten, he hadn't shown up. Eleven, he hadn't shown up.

"Finally, here he comes and he is totally hung-over. So, they managed to get him cleaned up, into his uniform, and horseback. And it turned out the director said, 'Look, L. Q., you know what you're doing with this.' I didn't know anything about sabers, but he said, 'Look, get in there and do the fight with Neville.' And I put on another wardrobe and whipped in to do the fight with him. And, of course, he was so gassed, he took a swipe with the saber, damn near took my head off. I just managed to stop it before it got there, promptly fell off his horse, and that was the end of that shot. As a matter of fact, I'm sitting here with a book that Neville gave me. Because they were going to do this picture, and Neville was goin' to be in it, he thought I ought to talk to him [about this] picture of a book called **Andersonville.** It's a tremendous study of that [Civil War prison] camp and the prisoners, Andersonville, in the South…Good man."

On Richard Fleischer's World War II drama, **Between Heaven and Hell** (1956), L. Q. co-starred as a tenant farmer, forced into serving in combat alongside a wealthy landowner (Robert Wagner). "But I was very lucky, because I did a lot of work with Bob Wagner, and Bart [Burns], and two or three others. Because if you look at the picture, the central theme of what the picture is about actually is represented with the relationship between Wagner and ourselves. He's the wealthy [land] owner and we're the bottom of the rung [his employees]. And it was because of the stupidity of an officer that we got killed, which is what made him attack the officer, which he ended up in the brig for." Some of the supporting cast's roles "didn't make the screen," as L. Q. recollects. "Most of it did, because Harvey Lembeck was very good at what he was doing, which is comedy relief. Wagner was playing it straight. I worked in the middle. Bart Burns kind of floated hither, thither, and yon. We had a good piece, and Richard [Fleischer is] a good man, fun to work with."

In Anthony Mann's excellent **Men in War** (1957), L. Q. was one of the main soldiers, serving under Robert Ryan. It was their first of several films together. L. Q.'s **Battle Cry** co-star, Aldo Ray, also memorably appeared. But L. Q. remembers it more vividly for other reasons: "It's the only picture that I've ever made, and I use pictures both as pictures and television; so it'd be a combination—I understand, people have told me somewhere around 800. It is the only picture that we ever shot, that I ever shot, *in sequence.* Yep, we started off with the first shot that was called for in the script, and went straight through.

"Bob [Ryan] was super. I enjoyed Bob very much. To me, at least, one of my favorite pros. Never was a huge star, or the phrase that's used in the business, 'a star of greater magnitude.' But he had that comfortable niche just below that, where he was a leading man, but he played a character lead. I guess it kind of attracted me, because, basically, most people consider me a character man. Most of my stuff is actually character *leads*, once I got started. When you first get started, you take anything you can get. I'm like somebody like, say, Strother [Martin], who played just straight, character pieces, and played 'em gorgeously. I was allowed to do leads, and, then, I began to bleed the two together, both characters and leads, to try to do somethin' a little bit different with some of 'em."

Unfortunately, one of the most intriguing opportunities L. Q. had to work with Ryan never came to fruition. Ryan "paid me a great compliment," L. Q. says, "when we did *The Wild Bunch* (1969)." The cast was staying near the *Bunch*'s location. In one house, were Ben Johnson, Warren Oates, and L. Q., among others. "Bob had a house to himself," L. Q. explains. "As it turned out, I spent a lot of time, since we worked in the same group with Bob, just he and I—We started jogging together, walking together, got into poker games, fights, and we became really good friends. And, at that point in time, he was going to play Lew in *A Boy and His Dog* for me, until he got ill." Lew Craddock was the part Jason Robards eventually played in *Boy*. "He also asked me…Bob Ryan, Jimmy Stewart, Henry Fonda, and I forgot who the fourth one was had a company that went out when they were available in the summertime to do plays. They had a very close company, just those four, and they would do 'em, and give all the money to a charity associated with the Screen Actor's Guild. And Bob invited me to join the group, and I'd've sold my seat in hell to do it, except I couldn't afford to take three months off, and not make any money. So, I had to pass, but I would have thoroughly enjoyed it."

As for *Men in War* itself, L. Q. relates, "If you look at it, it's not really a good picture. It's close. It's a strange picture. I ended up doing another two or three for the guy [Philip Yordan] who wrote it. And, as a matter of a fact, he wanted to buy *A Boy and His Dog* once I had done it, but I hadn't seen him in years. He was over in Spain, working. I would've liked to have worked with Bob in *God's Little Acre* [1958, also directed by Mann]. It was done by the same group, and I was going to accept, then I got another job just before that, and I was gone when they started shooting, so I was screwed."

One of *Men in War*'s green supporting players provided his co-stars with much unintentional amusement: Vic Morrow. "Vic was a brick," L. Q. said, laughing. "He was very funny. Let me see, when we did *Men in War*, I had probably done, not a whole bunch, but I had probably done twenty, thirty pictures and television. Vic came in along with four or five people from New York with Vic: Jimmy Edwards, the black, there were two or three others, and they had never done a picture. They had worked on the stage. They may have done a picture where they stood in the background or walked through, but never where they had anything to do. So, I remember Vic, because Bob and I were lying there one day, giggling and laughing about something, and we heard a line of dialogue. Very short line, it was like, '*What did he say?*' And we weren't paying attention. Then, 'What did *he* say?' '*What* did he say?' 'What did he *say*?' And we glanced around and there was Vic and Jimmy Edwards rehearsing Vic's line. They rehearsed that line for thirty minutes. *At least* thirty minutes. We got ready to shoot, and Bob and I were giggling around, just damn near collapsing in laughter. And we had, in the meantime, talked with the director. And we got all ready to go, got it all laid out, did a rehearsal. And just before we started shooting, the director said, 'Uh, listen, Vic, that line you've got'—which was the only line he had at the time—'just forget about it. We don't need that here. And we'll press right on.' We tried to do the scene and Vic was so flustered, he fucked everything up, totally. We all collapsed in laughter, went back, got it straight, and did his line, and everything was okay. But that's the most I remember about Vic from the picture [laughs]. Strange."

By 1957, L. Q. was beginning to be typed in war movies, a trend that was to change permanently, very soon afterwards. Later that year, he made his first war/comedy, **Operation Mad Ball**. The immortal Ernie Kovacs led its extraordinary cast. Being sandwiched between so much comedic talent kept L. Q. on his toes, throughout the shoot: "When you step in with Jack Lemmon, in comedy, and Arthur O'Connell, you gotta hustle. And Mickey Rooney [laughs], who was also in the piece. But Ernie and the rest of us became great friends. Now, Ernie smoked cigars, and he smoked cigars incessantly. You got the feeling that he smoked cigars asleep. He was never without a cigar. And we drove him insane, because he'd light up a cigar, the director would call, and they'd have to run off, so he'd put his cigar down. As soon as he put it down—we kept 'em around—we took a hammer and nails and nailed his cigar down. Now, he would come back, still jabbering with Lemmon or O'Connell, and not thinking, he'd pick up his cigar. Of course, it broke in two, where we had driven the nail in it. We must have cost him $1,000 by fucking up his cigars. But he was such a nice person, he went along with it. We had a ball, the whole bunch of us. I mean, truly a ball."

The next year, L. Q. was re-teamed with Raoul Walsh on Walsh's adaptation of Norman Mailer's epic World War II bestseller, **The Naked and the Dead**. It co-starred the popular stripper, Lili St. Cyr. L. Q. remembers her as a "Gorgeous lady. Just totally gorgeous. As a matter of fact, when we got through with the picture, she invited my wife and I over. And we went and had dinner with her— probably one of the few people to do it, 'cause she was extraordinarily shy. Just was totally nervous around people.

"**The Naked and The Dead** was probably the most definitive novel of World War II, far more than **Battle Cry. The Naked and The Dead** was just one of those things that put it that everything is a loser when you fight a war, which is true. It's a very downbeat picture. I'll give you something that very few people know. Do you have any idea who wrote the original screenplay for **The Naked and The Dead**? Norman Mailer wrote the book, but who wrote the screenplay? You could win a small fortune with this one, 'cause no one will ever know. Charles Laughton. And do you know what the normal length of a script is? Do you have any idea? We were shooting shorter pictures then. The script would be anything from ninety to one hundred pages. A very busy script or a talking script would be one hundred-and-ten. An extraordinarily talky picture—we made a lot of those—would be one hundred-and-forty. Do you have any idea how long the original was? Six hundred-and-some odd pages!

"So, they dismissed Charlie, and brought in Raoul. He was not the first choice. I don't know why he wasn't, but they had put a couple on to write the screenplay, and it was the Dawsons, I believe, but I've forgotten their names. And we went to Panama to shoot it. And we shot the first two weeks, and we didn't have page one of the script. Raoul was good at that. He always had been. Every morning, we'd meet in his tent at, let's say, eight o'clock. And we'd sit there with Cliff [Robertson], Raymond Massey, Aldo [Ray], Joey Bishop, Richard Jaeckel, Jerry Paris, a bunch of us. And we'd sit around and Raoul would say, "Hey, I tell you what. Right here, Cliff, you say...I'll move you over...and you say...Raymond, why don't you think about this..." And then he'd turn to Joey and I, and he'd say, "Look, we need something funny that I'm gonna do today. See what you two can come up with." And then we'd all go to work, get ready, get out to the location, and we'd just pretty much build the scene as we went along. But it wasn't that unusual. Raoul did a number of his pictures that way, far better than the script we finally ended up shooting.... when it finally got there!"

One golden age director L. Q. also worked with repeatedly was Edward (*Crossfire*) Dmytryk. "Oh, I loved Eddie," L. Q. says. "I loved Eddie and Jeannie, his wife. I first did **The Young Lions** with him, and then I was supposed to do something else." That "something else" turned out to be a western, **Warlock** (1959). The filming of **Young Lions** began in Paris, and it was there, L. Q. says, "Eddie and I became very good friends, as did Jean. By the way, don't ever play cards with her: she'll lift your scalp."

"I talked with him not more than two or three weeks ago, because he's teaching here at USC. He's an extraordinarily talented man. They really screwed him over with that communism bullshit. They screwed him up, and there were years when he couldn't do any work, because he had done some monumentally good pictures with, God, Dick Powell, Robert Ryan, did a whole bunch of 'em. And there's a big hole where he was not allowed to work. Actually, I think **The Young Lions** was the first picture that he was able to do once he came off the suspension list."

It would be impossible for L. Q. have walked away from making two films with Audie Murphy—**Showdown** (1963) and **Apache Rifles** (1964)—with nothing to say about the war hero. Because, as L. Q. slyly put it, "Everybody has something to say about Audie. A basket case, a banana. Yet I thoroughly enjoyed him, he was a hard worker. He and I became friends.

"The thing that made him the hero of World War II [was that] his elevator didn't go all the way to the top. He was a strange man. Slightly dangerous, carried a gun a lot of the times, not on the set. But, we were on location and

L. Q. and Audie Murphy.

almost everything he and I did—I think I did three pictures with him, altogether, I'm not sure—but we'd spent a lot of time on location. When you get on location, you get in with a strange group of people occasionally, and Audie was just stranger than they were strange. So, [laughs] the thing to do was stay away from Audie a little bit, unless you wanted to get into real trouble.

"And, yet, when he was not drinking—just one of the nicest people in the world, very soft-spoken, close to being shy. I worked with the three most decorated soldiers in World War II. Audie Murphy was the first; Neville [Brand] was the most decorated Marine; and I worked with Chesty Puller, who was the most decorated officer in World War II. Chesty was the advisor on, I think it was *The Naked and The Dead*. One of the toughest human beings that ever walked." Puller distinguished himself at, among other battles, the hellish Iwo Jima.

Inevitably, the subject of how L. Q. became associated with Sam Peckinpah arises. "One never becomes associated with Peckinpah," L. Q. began, cryptically. "I bumped into Sam the first time, on a picture that Don Siegel directed, called *An Annapolis Story*. It had been released under, I think, *Navy Blue and Gold*, with John Derek. But Sam was the dialogue coach working for Don Siegel. And Sam and I became pretty good friends, and I was helping with the dialogue of some of the other actors. How the hell he was presupposing I do that, I don't know, but I was. And then I lost touch with him, didn't see him. Got a call, the agent did, from Peckinpah, and he wanted me to do *Ride the High Country.* So, then we got together on, I think, from that point, eight or nine pictures."

Along with Walsh and Peckinpah, L. Q. became a regular in the films of Don Siegel, another master "action" director. "Don was like Eddie Dmytryk in one regard," L. Q. explains, "or Eddie was like Don, it was hard to tell. Don could take a very mediocre script and do good things with it. He had a feel for action. He liked people, although he was rather standoffish, but he still liked people. And so we took [the script] *Navy Blue and Gold*, which is a piece of shit, and he turned it into a reasonable picture [*An Annapolis Story*]. And we got to be good friends, 'cause I was motor-mouthing one day about what a good ping-pong player I was, on the set. And I was a good ping-pong player: I had been taught by a state champion and I, if I had taken the time to pursue it, probably could've been one of the champions. Somehow or other, Don got around to it, and said, 'What are you doing for lunch? Listen, why don't we go play some ping pong?' And, at that point in time, there were a couple places in town you could go in and pay for a table and use it, you could rent it for thirty minutes, an hour, whatever you wanted. We rented one for an hour, and he beat the bejesus out of me. He was an extraordinary ping-pong player. And from that time on, we just got to be good friends." One of L. Q.'s co-stars in Siegel's *An Annapolis Story* (1955), Alvy Moore, became a close friend, and, later, L. Q.'s producing partner.

Youth sensation Fabian starred in Don Siegel's *Hound Dog Man* (1959), an attempt to cash-in on Elvis' string of hit movies, particularly *Love Me Tender*. The young non-star was rather out to sea among the film's seasoned cast. "Fabian's a very nice person. That's just it—he's very nice," says L. Q. "I didn't care for the songs he did. That's okay, because he didn't care for a lot of the stuff I did. He did 'em well. He was not that talented as an actor, but worked hard at it and was just a nice person. Again, we had some fun, but the people he was with, though, it's kind of hard [to keep up] when you're working with that group…You know, Christ almighty, you got Royal Dano, Jane Darwell. Jane Darwell's, you know, the best thing going! Stu [Whitman], who was very good. Carol Lynley, very good, and a whole bunch of people through it. And when you do that, you gotta really hustle.

"But the good thing about our business is, if you step into a scene with [Spencer] Tracy, you were in real trouble to begin with. The main thing about our business, almost everyone, especially the big people, the really big people and the really big stars, and the really good people, will do anything in the world to help you, as long as, a) you have a modicum of talent, and b) you're trying to do it right. And Fabian would have been up the creek if he stepped in with a bunch of people who were just mediocre in what they did. His singing would have been fine…you know, it wouldn't have interfered with his music. When you take somebody like Don Siegel , who understands how to shape and help, and then put him in a group of people, then they pull his act up. And he did, I think, a very commendable job."

In 1960, Elvis Presley made a bid for more respectable roles with Don Siegel's *Flaming Star*. He starred as the half-breed son of Indian Delores Del Rio and a white father. It marked L. Q.'s second appearance in an Elvis western. "Elvis was Elvis," L. Q. simply states. "Again, Elvis was a rather introverted personality. If you happen to watch him on stage in the wings, he was having hissy fits, he was so nervous. The instant he stepped out into the light, he changed into an entirely different person. And he was having trouble, again, making the move to overcome his natural shyness. He was not a good actor, he could have become one, and he wanted to become one, but the prices that they were paying for him then were so high, that they expected him to come in, do his thing, and leave. Well, Don was helping him quite a bit. And look at the people he was surrounding him with: John McIntyre, not a finer actor in the history of our business. Dolores Del Rio, gorgeous lady from Mexico. A huge star, huge. And, God, she must have been in her late fifties, early sixties—*still* just a totally gorgeous female. Such a nice person. But all really good people mixed in with him. Again, then Don was helping, Dave Weisbart was also producing that one. A nicer sweeter, more helpful person never existed than Dave Weisbart. And so they helped Elvis put everything together.

"Elvis pulled one of his tricks that he loved to do. He and I were always at each other. But he pulled one on Siegel and Dave Weisbart. Everything was going along swimmingly, but, also, it was all dependent on Elvis, 'cause he did a lot more in *Flaming Star* than he had done in *Love Me Tender*. It was at that point in time that Elvis was heavily into his karate stuff. He was breaking bags, and punching this, and doing flips, and they were always afraid something' goin' to happen to him. So, we finished shooting on a Saturday morning, 'cause we were on a semi-location. He took off for another couple of lessons. We came back Monday morning, ready to go to work. Everybody gets to the place, we're all made-up, reasonably in place. Elvis had a slightly later call than the rest of us. And just as we're getting ready to shoot, here comes the limo with Elvis, and the door opens up, Tony gets out and Sonny gets out, and they're arguing, you can hear 'em. And here comes Elvis, and his arm is wrapped in a cast from his fingers all the way up to his shoulder. Well, Siegel almost passed water, for Christ's sake. Dave Weisbart blanched, and we thought he was gonna faint. They went rushing over to Elvis. 'Good God, what are we going to do!' And, just before they got there, of course, Elvis let it drop and ran to his make-up room, because it was all a phony, he just put the thing together! [laughs] But I thought David Weisbart was gonna have a heart attack. It's not real hard to imagine; I think he probably had $3 or $4 million at stake, and here's the star of it, crippled!" The final film L. Q. and Elvis made together was *Stay Away, Joe* (1968), starring the two as American Indian rodeo riders! Though it was genuinely ridiculous, the film afforded L. Q. a tremendous amount of screen time.

L. Q. can only be spotted briefly in Don Siegel's bleak World War II classic, *Hell is For Heroes* (1963). In support were L. Q.'s old roomie, Fess Parker, James Coburn, and Nick Adams. The cast was headed up by Steve McQueen in an unforgettable star turn as a borderline psychotic soldier. Since L. Q.'s actual name is McQueen, the inevitable question arises: is he related to Steve? "Good God, no!" L. Q. is quick to point out. "I worked with Steve a couple of times. Steve was his own man, and nothin' wrong with that. He just worked a little bit different. But he was a nice person, a tough person. Loved to race. Had a good time. Was very lucky, the way things unfolded for him. 'Cause Steve's not much of an actor, but he's a good personality, he's a good person, good presence. And, so, he was careful at picking the stuff that he did—did a gorgeous job of it, and worked very well. I was basically through with *Hell is For Heroes* before he came on.

"I had an accident. I was supposed to go further into the picture, but I had an accident coming to work—my neck was about the size of my head from whiplash, and stayed that way for 'bout three or four weeks. Sometimes, as a matter of fact, the scene I did with Bobby Darin, the scene outside in the truck, just happened to notice, I think I'm wearing something around my neck, because it had already started swelling. I had the wreck that morning, and still managed to get to work. They danced around me till I got there and I thought we were gonna be able to go on. But it started swelling up really bad, and I wrapped something around my neck so we could go ahead and do the piece. We finished that. I just told Don I didn't think I could go any further unless it came down, but it didn't, and it stayed that size for at least two weeks. So, I was out of it from that point on. Then Steve then came on and started his work."

Like his fellow Peckinpah vet, R. G. Armstrong, L. Q. rhapsodizes over the late, great Warren Oates: "One of a kind. Hell of an actor. Very nice person. Warren and I became extraordinarily good friends—probably ended up doing seven, eight, nine shows together."

In Peckinpah's elegiac western masterpiece, **Ride The High Country** (1962), L. Q. played one of the trashy, hillbilly Hammond clan, Sylvus. "They sent us up to the Tetons to do the shooting," L. Q. remembers, "and the snow was, God, six feet deep, eight feet deep. We were living in chalets, and having to scrub around to shoot, and we were falling behind. So, the company, since this was the second picture Sam had ever done, without consulting with Peckinpah, they pulled the plug, cancelled the shoot, and put everybody on the busses and sent us back here. Because they were losing money, they were going to shoot it on the lot, as opposed to where Sam wanted it. Well, they hadn't bothered to tell Sam. And when he found out, it took three of us to restrain him, 'cause he was going insane.

"Now, they had the car for him, to bring him back. But he said, 'Screw you. I'm gonna go back with my friends.' So, he came on the bus with us. As will often happen, and I knew better than this, but we got into a poker game. Sam and I were kneeling on a seat, playing over the back. We had no place to put the money, so I used my hat. Now, I probably won $1,000 while we were playing. When we got to L. A., they're wasn't a penny in the plate! Sam, that idiot had taken all of the money, and spent it, and lost it. But do you think he was going to pay me back? No way.

"We got here, he was so ticked that I was gonna call and have 'em pick me up, but his car was in the garage that he had rented by MGM. So I said, 'Come on with me.' So, we popped in his car, damn near scared me to death driving home, 'cause he was so mad. Then when we got home, he said, 'Screw it. Take the car,' which was a Corvette, 'and get it back to me when you can.' I think I kept it a month before I gave it back. But he got so mad that when we finally got back to shooting, we were shooting in Bronson Canyon, a place where a lot of people shoot here. Yeah, I must have shot twenty pictures in Bronson. Uh, he was so furious, that he made 'em snow the machines for the entire canyon! We were up to our kazoo in soapsuds. And, of course, soapsuds are okay, but they burst and collapse so quickly. And, so, when you do it with soapsuds, your crew is constantly busy snowing, and he drove 'em insane. But he got what he wanted, and that was the last time they ever pulled a plug on Sam.

"When they released the picture, they put it out with another picture that MGM had made. I will not favor you with a title, because there's no need to mention it. It went out second on the bill. The other picture was a total dog. And they were about to pull both of 'em, when somebody said, 'Wait a minute,' and started checking the records, then made some phone calls and found out, to the best of their ability, that people were coming to the show—by this time, it was already in the drive-ins—to see *Ride The High Country* and not even stay for the other picture. So, for the first time I've ever seen them show any brains, a major studio pulled the picture, held it for a little while, and then put it back out by itself as a single, and it took off. Sam won all sorts of awards for it."

What could have been Peckinpah's finest, most mature film, **Major Dundee** (1965) was eviscerated. Around forty minutes were cut from the post-Civil War epic before it was released. "They just butchered the picture, [producer Jerry] Bresler did," L. Q. relates. "There are sequences from that picture that never made the screen, that any one of which is an award-winner. But, he just cut 'em up so badly, changed it around so much, that it totally destroyed it. It's not a bad picture; it's not a good picture. It's not that coherent. Sam's version of it, I think, was too lengthy [160 minutes], but Bresler's [134, then 120 minutes] was too stupid. Matter of fact, they had the preview for it, and Bresler was with [Harry] Cohn, the head of the studio. And from people I know that know Cohn very well, [they] said when the preview was over, the limo picked up both of 'em to take 'em back to the studio. And once they got in it and got away from the preview, Cohn told him he was a complete, utter, talentless ass, threw him out of the limo, and drove on without him. And then they tried to put it back, but, unfortunately, they had already cut the negative, so it was impossible to do some of the work they wanted to do." Like most of Peckinpah's westerns, the film had a character actor cast for the ages: L. Q., Warren Oates, Dub Taylor, Ben Johnson, Brock Peters, John Chandler, R. G. Armstrong, and many others. Charlton Heston starred as Amos Dundee, and Richard Harris and James Coburn co-starred.

LQJaf (L. Q. Jones and Friends) remains, to this day, L. Q.'s production company. He began it, he says, "way back, not under that name, when we did a picture called **The Devil's Bedroom**." Did he direct it? "If anybody could be accused of it, yes, I did." L. Q. also produced and acted (under his real name) in the film, which was shot as **Fury of Vengeance**. "**The Devil's Bedroom**, oddly enough, they play in porno houses," because of its lascivious-sounding title. L. Q. roared with laughter: "I love to go watch the faces of the people in overcoats as they try to figure out why this picture is in a porno house, 'cause you could show it at a church; it wouldn't make any difference.

"It was a true story about a guy in Texas, and it works off of a quirky law that is still on the books in Texas, and that's that said you can be committed to an insane asylum by members of your family. And the story caught my eye because here was a guy that was—the part was eventually played by John Lupton—who was a loner…[Lupton and L. Q.] started out in *Battle Cry* together. Anyway, that's the kind of a character he was. They were 'land poor'—They had plenty of land, they just didn't have any money. And his brother ends up marrying the town tramp, and then it's discovered there's oil on the property. And she wants it, but she cannot sign the papers for it. The land actually was in the name of the character that John played. And they couldn't convince him to sell it or lease it for the oil. And so she vamped and set it up so that it looked like he was guilty of murder. He was not, and she gets his brother to go along—they're married, of course. She seduces him into committing him to the asylum. And, then, he escapes from the asylum, and then there are a couple of murders, and they think he's committed 'em. He did not. They were accidents. And they eventually ended up holing him up in a place called the Devil's Bedroom, which is a big cave. And in trying to get him to come out of the cave, which he will not do, they poured kerosene in, the idiots, and set fire to it, and they set fire to him and killed him. Sort of a comedy. So, we decided to do that for $13 or something. It's one of the worst pictures ever made."

In 1969, L. Q. was executive producer of *The Witchmaker*, a low-budget horror film shot in Marksville, Louisiana. It was the first official project of LQJaf, and co-starred his old friend and partner, Alvy Moore, who was also an associate producer. A number of Playboy Playmates (including Sue Bernard and Diane Webber) were in the cast. With all of these sexpots floating around, were any nude scenes cut to get an "M" rating, as opposed to an "R"? "Oh, no. No, no. It's just a story based on witchcraft. We used ladies that are gorgeous, but they are all clothed. In those days, even today, I wouldn't make a nudie, especially from my company. We just used 'em. And they were used as seductresses, as witches. It's a strange little picture. It's not real good, but for its time and its genre, it is very good. We ended up on a whole bunch of ten best-of-the-year lists with the picture. Alvy and I went out with it to start it off, and we set records for about two or three weeks. And, then, Columbia, who we'd made a deal with, said, 'Look, we know how to handle this from this point on,' and they did. And it went *straight down the tube!* But it did okay. What the heck."

The next feature L. Q. made with Peckinpah was not one of the actor's favorites: Warner Brothers' perennially controversial *The Wild Bunch* (1969). The director called in L. Q. to play possibly the most degenerate role of his career: T. C., one of the thoroughly repulsive bounty hunters under the command of Thornton (Robert Ryan). "Sam and I were in contact with each other all the time," L. Q. recalls, "and I knew he had a project, didn't know what it was, 'cause he didn't talk about it till he was ready. And whenever he was ready, he just sent us a script, and said, 'This is what I want you to do.' There were about ten of us in the group—his stock company, as it were. So, he had Strother, Warren, R. G. Armstrong, Dub Taylor, John Davis Chandler, Ben Johnson. And Sam would either call you and say, 'I want you to do something,' or he'd send you a script and say, 'This is what I want you to play.' And you'd read the script and there'd be two lines in it about your character. But you knew better. You knew what he was going to do, so you just made your deal, and went on about your business. Because once we got there, he started changing things around. Because he knew us, he was comfortable with us, we could carry this stuff to his satisfaction in how he wanted it done. And, so, what you started out with didn't really make any difference, because it was gonna be changed so much."

Having worked so closely with Peckinpah for so long, L. Q. became aware of some of the director's subtlest—and strongest—skills. Among the director's other gifts, "He's very much into wardrobe. But so am I—that's okay. As a matter of fact, he had me helping with wardrobe, some on **The Wild Bunch**, but more on **Pat Garrett** [**and Billy the Kid**]. But, if you will notice, each one of the characters—and you've got a pretty heavy load right there when you talk about Bob Ryan and Albert Dekker—notice their wardrobe, and then pay attention to what happens through the rest of the piece. He's very touchy about that."

In a wonderfully bizarre touch, L. Q.'s demented character wears his hair in two girlish ponytails. "For some dumb reason," L. Q. opines, "it'd take thirty, thirty-five minutes every morning to put them on. Also, I was wearing a collodion scar." The scar became an agonizing daily ordeal for L. Q. over the film's four-month shooting schedule. "Sam is such that, whether you work or not, he wants you there, wants you in wardrobe. And you may sit around all day and do nothing, but he wants you there. And you're made-up. And I had the collodion scar put on every day, and it almost did me in. I went for probably a year with that scar on my face before it finally smoothed out. That's one of the reasons, of course, we don't use collodion anymore, 'cause it tends to injure the tissue."

Following the film's final, epic battle sequence, L. Q. and Strother were originally supposed to die on-camera, a scene that was filmed, but remains unseen, thirty-five years later. "In the picture," L. Q. explains, "in most of the versions, you stay on Bob Ryan, who's seated at the door of the compound where everyone has just streamed out. And Eddie O'Brien rides up, and they have a conversation. You hear, in the distance, gunshots. There are three of 'em, and there's a slight break at that point. I've forgotten, exactly, whether it's slightly before Eddie gets there or just after he gets there, I'm not sure which.

"At any rate, what [Peckinpah] then did was to go out, and, of course, he looked for the rockiest place in the entire state of Mexico. And then we did the shooting of Strother, of Paul [Harper], and myself. He wanted to find out first if it was going to kill anybody, so he used me. And the way we rigged it, it would be the off-stage shot. We rigged a step on the saddle, and what I had to do was go up and back to clear the horse. I do that. Now, first off, I have to trigger a squib, so that you can see that I am shot. So, I triggered the squib, dropped the reins, dropped the rifle, went up, and back. Luckily, I went far enough in both directions to clear the horse, and then I started spinning in the air. My head went down, and I started rolling over. Well, I had the duster on and the pigtails, and now it becomes a ballet, because the duster fanned out in the air like a skirt. The pigtail stuck out like wings. I had to then trigger another squib, so that I got shot in mid-air, and I cartwheeled totally over on my side, hitting the rocks, of course. My head slammed to the ground—we're in extraordinary slow motion. The blood squirts out, because I triggered another one. The head slams to the ground, it comes up—you can see it—back down again, up again. Each time, going not quite so far, so that my head backed off the ground, like, at least three times, maybe four. But the way it worked out, and the way he had cut it, and they did the same thing with Strother, which wasn't quite as much, and Paul, which was less, by far, than either one of ours. Just the way it worked out, and when it was cut, it looked just totally like a ballet. You're coming off the horse, Strother's coming off the horse, the big blood spray is in the air, the pigtails are flyin', the duster's going; it was just really extraordinary to watch it. But then, the version got too long, and he couldn't leave it all in, so we pulled it out. It may have made it in a couple of versions, but I'm not sure."

With his expertise at portraying scumbags fine-tuned, it was unsurprising that L. Q. should play one of the western baddies who lynch Clint Eastwood in Ted Post's *Hang 'Em High* (1968). "*Hang 'Em High* was made here in answer to the spaghetti westerns," says L. Q. "It's in that style. It's a good western, if you will. It kind of found the better of both sides, and used them. It is a very strange picture, when you take it from top to bottom. Ed Begley, who's marvelous, Ben [Johnson] was in it, Pat Hingle was in it. Good people all over the place, and it just works." Eastwood and L. Q. had done several episodes of *Rawhide* together, previously. In an early 1990s issue of *Entertainment Weekly*, L. Q. spoke his mind on the  subject of modern westerns and Clint Eastwood: "The stuff they call westerns today, all you have to do is change the horses to Ferraris and you'd be doing Wall Street. I love Clint Eastwood, but he couldn't make a western if it bit him on the ass. *Unforgiven* is not a western."

The lyrical, gentle *Ballad of Cable Hogue* (1970) is a unique Peckinpah western that tends to grow on his admirers. Jason Robards, who was never better, starred as Cable, abandoned to die in the Nevada desert by Taggert and Bowen (L. Q. and Strother). "We are the ones that precipitate everything. Everything hangs on us…He [Cable] waits for us to come back. He knows we gotta come back.

"I'll tell you a Strother Martin story. Strother and I finished, 'cause we started with Jason, Strother, and myself. We did our stuff, and then left, Strother and I. Strother came back here [to Hollywood], I went back to Santa Fe to do *The McMasters*. And we, I think we're into a five—or six-week shoot, I forgot what it was. Sam and them went ahead with *Ballad*. And, towards the end of *McMasters*, Sam had Sheila…Now, Sheila Clegg was his production secretary, mine later. Super, super production lady. Had 'em call and talk to production on *McMasters* and say, 'We need L. Q. for…,' and they mentioned the date, which was, I don't know, four or five days hence. 'Can he be free?' And they checked with the producer, checked with the director, and both of 'em said, 'No! We've got a huge scene to shoot that day,' and he was right. They were bringing in, oh, they must have had 150 extras and all of the principals in the cast. And it was gonna be a tough two days to shoot it. And Sheila said, 'Okay,' and that was it.

"So, a couple of hours later, she called back and said, 'Is there any way you can schedule it so that L. Q. can get off at, let's say, two o'clock on Saturday afternoon?' And they said, 'No! We can't do it! We're not gonna screw up our picture for yours.' 'Okay.' Thirty minutes later, she calls back and said, 'Are you…' And they said, 'Okay, okay. Tell you what we'll do. We will try—we cannot be sure—we will try to shoot it so that L. Q. is free along about two o'clock. Now, I don't know what the hell you're gonna do, 'cause we're in Santa Fe and you're outside of Las Vegas.' And they said, 'Don't worry about it.' 'Okay.'

"That Saturday morning, a plane showed up, a private plane, at about nine thirty in the morning, and called up and said, 'I'm here to pick up L. Q.' And they said, 'You can't have him! You can't have him maybe at all, but surely not till two o'clock!' They said, 'Okay.' So they screwed things around and fixed it up, so they got rid of me along about 2:15. They had a car. I jumped in the car, rushed to the airport, jumped in the plane. We took off in a beeline, the weather was shitty, but we still got to Las Vegas, or at least where we were, out at Echo Bay. Probably, it was about thirty minutes before we lost the light. They had a limo at the private landing strip pick me up. Had the wardrobe in the back seat. I'm changing, we get to the location, and we're shooting a sequence we didn't anymore need than God needs little green apples. We already had it. But Sam was being the pain in the ass that he always wanted. He had brought Strother back from L. A. Strother is standing there. It is the scene where we abandon him [Robards], where we take over the mule. Okay? We already had it. That's the stuff we shot first. Sam says, 'Okay,' and [cinematographer] Lucien's [Ballard] saying, 'You're about to lose the light, Sam. You got maybe fifteen, maybe twenty minutes. That's it.'

"Well, in coming in, Strother screwed up, did something wrong. Sam went ape. Lucien standing there saying, 'Sam, you got about eight minutes left now, that's it.' 'Okay. Get back. Strother, I'll kill you if you do anything wrong.' We do it, we ride by the camera, and then I fucked up. I totally screwed up, but we went on. We didn't stop. Got all the way through with it. We could hear, because now we were a block-and-a-half away from the camera, and we hear, 'Cut!' [L. Q. wails madly] 'Strother, you stupid, ignorant, terrible person! You will never work in my pictures again. I will see to it that you are drummed out of the business!' And I said, 'Sam, listen, if those…' He said, 'L. Q., you keep out of this. Strother, you have worked in your last picture. You will never again make another dollar bill from this business. If I'm not restrained, I may kill you on the spot!' He was all over him. I now said, 'Sam…' He said, 'Stay out of this, L. Q.' I left, went over, picked up a cold drink. Took me about four or five minutes. I wandered back. He is calling Strother everything on the face of the earth. Finally, he hit a spot where he had to breathe, and I said, 'Sam.' He said, 'L. Q…' I said, 'Listen, Sam. Shut up. It was my fault. It was not Strother's.' 'Is that right?' 'That's right, Sam.' He turns back to Strother, 'You ignorant son of a bitch. You will never work in this business again. Why didn't you tell me it was L. Q. and not you?' And he was on his back for another thirty minutes. But that was Sam, and that was Strother. Aren't you getting tired here, yet? We've been at this an hour and a half. I charge by the minute! God, I hope I don't have to make it all the way from '61 to '94!"

One of L. Q.'s more offbeat film projects was *The Brotherhood of Satan* (1971). The film is a very nearly surreal account of a cult of aged witches attempting to transfer their spirits into children's bodies. Strother Martin was the cult's leader. Thought he was involved in every stage of the picture, L. Q. has mixed feelings about it. "I wrote the script for that, produced it, wrote a book, and published the book as a novel. *Brotherhood*'s one of those pictures that shows up on the ten best [lists] of the year. It is a very strange picture, if you look at it and realize what is happening. It's uneven. There's some good places in it, and some bad ones. But it really was a good attempt to work a story about witchcraft. It's stranger than first appears, and its one of the really enigmatic endings you will find in a motion picture.

"I don't know what they're doing with it. We sold it, we sold ten percent of it to Columbia. And I myself was talking, I was at a breakfast with Jimmy Coburn, and Budd Boetticher, Roddy MacDowall, and I fell in conversation with a guy who works around Columbia. And I said, 'For Christ's sake, find out what they're doing with that picture! I don't even have a copy of it!' Because we had tried before, and got over into Columbia and the hierarchy, and nobody knew where it was. So, we're still trying to locate it. We'll see. I don't own it anymore, because they had spent so much money on it. Of course, they didn't, but it looks that way. It's in debt, but who knows what's happening?"

In Peckinpah's laconic *Pat Garrett and Billy the Kid* (1973), L. Q. played Black Harris, a member of Billy's gang who is gunned down by Garrett (James Coburn). L. Q., like everyone who sees the film was impressed by Slim Pickens' moving death scene, shot by a small river. He explains that that sequence is a perfect example of the "diversity, the texture of the way Sam likes to work, with humongously busy, active violent scenes, buttressed by very soft, almost sweetness, so you get the impact of both." L. Q. never worked with the director again: "Tried to kill him. But, other than that, no." L. Q. did not speak at his funeral, he says, "but at a little gathering we had for him over at the Director's Guild. I think there were two thousand people there, or something." What is L. Q.'s opinion of his work with Peckinpah, after all these decades: "What do I think? I needed the money."

Easily the most unique film of L. Q.'s career was also his only official directorial credit: *A Boy and His Dog*. The film takes place in post-World War IV America in 2024. Vic (Don Johnson), a teenage boy, wanders the dusty wasteland with his companion, Blood, a telepathic, intelligent dog, scavenging for women and food. Harlan Ellison's Nebula award-winning novella fell into L. Q.'s hands very unexpectedly in the early '70s. "We were cutting on *The Brotherhood*," he says, "and you're always searching for something else to do. And my cameraman, John Morrill, brought in a copy of a book, and said, 'Hey, you might be interested in this. Might be something you want to do,' and left it on my secretary's desk. And we just kept working. And we hit a point where it was quiet, a month or so later, and she said, 'You better read this, so you can give John an answer.' 'Oh, God, yes.' So I took it home, and was busy on something else, I was working acting. And I was working on my part for the next day. I finally got through around one-thirty, two o'clock in the morning, and I had to get up at six, so I started to got to bed, and said, 'Ah, well.' So I started reading [Harlan Ellison's] *A Boy and His Dog*. And I read it about a third of the way through, and I stopped, and I said, 'This is gonna be a shame. This is a marvelous hypothesis. It is a gorgeous, developed story, a third of the way through, but he cannot sustain it. He durn sure cannot top it, and so it's gonna be a real shame to watch it deteriorate.' Read the next two-thirds of it, and had the same feeling. 'How has he possibly gotten it this good, this far, because the next page, the next line, it's got to just fall on its butt.' And, then, along about, what time was it? It must have been three-thirty, four o'clock in the morning, I read the last part of it. Closed the book, and sat there in hysterical laughter for ten or fifteen minutes, a), at the ending of the piece, and, b), with the fact that he truly managed to top everything that he had done in the preceding pages, and just enjoyment and awe at what he had pulled off. And I went to work the next morning, got through with that, walked into the office, threw the book up on the thing, and said, 'Call John.' Alvy was sitting there; I said, 'This is our next picture.' So he took it home and read it. Called me, and said, 'What are you…I don't understand what you're trying to do. How are you going to shoot this? You can't possibly shoot this.' And that's the way it was, and we went on, and we did put it together."

Adapting such a complex novel on a low-budget, L. Q. says, "you're looking for a way to adapt your money to your story so you don't hurt it. But, in my mind's eye, *A Boy and His Dog*, as a novella, holds and occupies a very high niche in science fiction. There are few stories any better." The director realized very early on that several earlier post-nuclear films had him far outdistanced, budget-wise: "I looked at *On The Beach*, and I said, 'I cannot possibly duplicate this, there is no way!'"

What he didn't have in funds, though, L. Q. made up for with all-consuming ingenuity: "We worked on the picture, getting it prepped, for about three-and-a-half years. And, so I read the story through three hundred, four hundred times, looking for something I hadn't seen before, going all the way through it. And I would call and talk to people with a scientific bent, trying to determine what I could do that would be right for the picture, that would make it unusual, but that would be true. And I couldn't find it. It was totally eluding me to the point that I had hired an artist to replicate what the bombed-out city would look like, and to start working on the props and building the set, and had just given up on what I wanted to do.

"One night, I waked up in the middle of the night—I have no reason to know why or what caused it—but one word stuck out, and that was 'mud.' And then I started making phone calls to people who are in and around the atomic structure. Had a good friend who worked at Los Alamos as a mathematician. He went back and found out that one of the theories advanced in a nuclear war, is that, if Russia had triggered x-number of the missiles, we were tipped to what was going on, and it triggered our missiles, that there was a good possibility that, at someplace on the globe, an inordinate number of bombs would have gone off simultaneously. If that happened, there was the chance, and a very good chance, that the spin of the earth would be affected. It would only be a millisecond that it would happen, but that millisecond would totally remove the restraints on everything. Oceans become tidal waves; rivers, the same thing. And that up to—they didn't know, they weren't even really prepared to guess—up to so many miles inland, the water from the ocean would rush, bury, crush—and, then, when it withdrew, which it probably would as it went back to its normal spin—cities on the coast and quite a ways inland would be totally buried in a sea of mud. I mean just buried. It would be twenty, thirty, forty feet deep. And, of course, it would have killed all the people, 'cause it would have drowned 'em. But then that would have dried, and what you have is a big sea of dried mud. Once I realized that, a) that it was true, b) what it would look like, then I went in and fashioned things, cars that were sticking up out of the mud, parts of buildings, the whole works.

"And then we stuck with that interior logic. We put things underground, where they had dug holes in looking for food and shelter, because food would have been trapped. Canned goods would have been there. Who knows how many years they would have lasted, we don't know. But, then, working with my cameraman [John Morrill], what we did was, if you notice in the picture, outside of underground in Topeka, there is not one blade of grass, not one tree. Nothing grows. Everything was manufactured. Our set covered four-and-a-half square miles of preparing the ground. We went out and leased and bought land out on a dry lakebed to accomplish the look that we wanted. And it took us, we worked on it, crew out working on the set for six, seven months...of course, before we started shooting. But it worked for the picture. Then, John and I worked it out. What did we want to do, we hadn't much money, so what would make the realistic approach to it? And I realized our point of view should always be from Blood's point of view. Blood is low to the ground. So, we shot almost everything— there are a few shots that violate that—but most of 'em are shot at either human or dog level. And that's our p.o.v. of the picture.

"Then, what John did, once we were through shooting, he went through it and the lab began to desaturate the color, so that you start out with, not a very bright color, but at least color. And frame-by-frame, sequence-by-sequence, color is withdrawn, until you get to where they go down, where he goes Downunder, there's almost black and white, using color film. And then once he goes in the drop shaft, everything changes. And once he steps out in Topeka, it's brilliant, candy apple colors. He pushed all of the colors, the greens, the reds, the blues. You never saw the sky, all you saw was dark, because we told you we were underground. But the grass is too green, the trees are too crisp, the blues are too blue. And, then, we dropped back to the almost colorless, when you come out of the drop-shaft with the two of 'em."

In the latter half of the film, Vic is led into Topeka, a sunken "Downunder" city. One of the most fascinating touches that L. Q. added to this repressive, subterranean world was the obscene, clown-like make-up that the Downunder-ites wear. This, like the rest of the film, was thought out thoroughly in advance: "Well, again, it's based on truth. I talked to people who they were consulting about the biosphere. I talked to people like that. And I said, 'What would happen if you moved people underground, and let 'em stay there for quite a while? Could be two years, five years, whatever.' Well, it was fun to them, because it was an interesting premise. And they came back to me and said, 'Well, the first thing you would notice is that the color of the skin changes. It would go from a ruddy or a brown, to first a tan, from a tan to a beige, from a beige to a white, from a white to a translucent. The body would not need to protect itself with coloration, and, so, that would cease, depending on how long you went. But, then, you would almost see the veins inside the body after a certain period of time.' We weren't going that far, but I said, 'Okay, if this is the case, here are people that are basically coming from an agrarian society.' That's why Michael— who, in the story, was originally called the 'green metal motherfucker'—which was a machine to protect the people…Well, I said, 'They would not allow a machine to have ascendancy over them, at least of the appearance. So, what would they accept?' They would accept another farmer. So, they made a machine in the shape of Michael, and they clothed him in overalls and a straw hat, and they would go along with that, being agrarian.

"And, being healthy, outdoors people, when their color started to fade, they probably, somewhere along the line, some lady first used just a little bit of rouge, or she pinched her cheeks, as they did back in the 1800s to get a little color. And, then, finally get tired of that, and she would add a little color, and then she would add a little lipstick, and the neighbors had begun to watch that, and they thought that glow was healthy. So each one started, each one picked up, and, finally, it just gets carried away, as it always will, to its extreme. With the blotchy faces, and the red glowing dots on the cheeks, and the smile painted, because you never, ever failed to smile in Topeka. Because, if you did, you were a candidate for The Farm. A lot of people think it's just a reach to make 'em look different. It is a reach to make 'em look different, but it's also based in what would happen." What exactly is the "Farm"? "That's where they do you in," L. Q. says. "You get in the way, you don't smile, you don't agree with The Committee, you go to The Farm."

A Boy and His Dog was shot in the Spring of 1973, on a 27-day shooting schedule. It premiered at the 1975 World Science Fiction Convention in Washington, D. C. The trailer L. Q. produced for the film's initial release is a masterpiece, in its own right, and a near-miracle of economy—it contains portions of every scene in the film reduced to ninety seconds of nearly subliminal cuts, set to a sped-up rendition of Sousa's "Stars and Stripes Forever." *Boy* was well received by critics, including Charles Champlin and Roger Ebert, and it won the Hugo Award for best (science fiction) dramatic presentation. When Harlan Ellison *kvetched* to L. Q. about how he had received no such trophy for *Boy*, L. Q. unscrewed the base off of his Hugo, and sent it to Ellison.

(A little *Boy* trivia: one of the films being shown at the makeshift post-nuclear theater in *Boy* is L. Q.'s own *The Devil's Bedroom*. L. Q. can be spotted briefly, exhorting a group of yokels in the film-within-a-film. Also, the song that the post-nuclear guitarist plays in *Boy* is by none other than Richard Ellis, the beloved composer of "Butterfly Mornings" and the other songs from *Cable Hogue*. Ray Manzarek, formerly of The Doors, can be heard playing on the film's soundtrack. These days, *Boy* is rarely revived in 35mm form because it was shot in Techniscope, a widescreen process with a sprocket-hole alignment that will not conform to most projectors.)

One of L. Q.'s showiest death scenes occurs in Steve Carver's 1983 hit, *Lone Wolf McQuade*, starring Chuck Norris as the titular Texas Ranger. The scene involves a *coup de grace* delivered by none other than David (*Kill Bill*) Carradine, whose character, Wilkes, snaps L. Q.'s neck with his foot. The scene, L. Q. relates, "was written slightly different than that. And the director, Steve [Carver], when we got ready to start, said, 'Can you come up with anything that will work better than the stuff we have written?' I said, 'That's not going to be a real problem at all. Let me do that.' And, then, I worked with David. And the object of the rewrites, plus the stuff we had already done, was to make you really like my character, Dakota." Before Carradine appears, Dakota (L. Q.) has a crowd-pleasing moment where he intimidates a loathsome captive, Snow (William Sanderson), with a machine gun. "[Dakota] was specifically designed so that, just prior to David showing up, I had done the thing with the guy tied to the tree with the machine gun, and audiences, for some reason, just fell in love with that sequence.

"...It's hard to tell when you start winging it with people who've worked together before who've been at it for a while. Let's assume it was David's idea, because his theory was—which is right—just to shoot Dakota isn't enough, you have to degrade him, and the way you do that is the way we ended up shooting the scene. So, we went in, did that. And, again, since David and I worked together so many times, we knew what we were trying to get out of it, and each one built to that. And it worked pretty well."

When this interview was conducted, L. Q.'s filmography ended with *River of Death* (1989), which he tersely looked back on with something less than affection: "Ah-ha-ha! That came very close to ending it!" Lamentably, L. Q. was very nearly out of circulation for several years: "There was a period of time along about '89, '90, '91, where I was having a problem that we didn't find out till later was caused by a pool next door that was leaking, and leaking under my house. And it caused a medical problem. And I said, 'Screw it, I'll manage my properties, and giggle, and snort, and do other things.' And, so, I did some other stuff, but I just kind of let it slide, for reasons I don't want to go into now." This occurred between 1988 and 1991. "In '92, [I] found out what the problem was, from the leak, and then it took me another six or seven months to start recovering from it. And, then, I was going through much things with that. And, then, I went and did the picture *Lightning Jack*, with Paul Hogan. And then I did a two-parter for *Renegades*, and a two-parter for *Walker* [*Texas Ranger*], and I'm starting to get back at it again, because I've realized just how much I've missed it. And people have been kind enough to say nice things. They don't know what they're talking about, but we press on with that. And so, I'll probably now start working again."

Following this 1994 interview, start working L. Q. did, indeed. He made quite a comeback, and popped up in a string of major movies: Martin Scorsese's *Casino* (1995) as the corrupt, gaudy County Commissioner Pat Webb, *The Patriot* (1998) with Steven Segal, and two movies in a row with Anthony Hopkins (or "Sir Tony," as L. Q. calls him), *The Edge* (1997) and *The Mask of Zorro* (1998). More recently, L. Q. has said that, since he is "independently poor," he can pick and choose what he appears in. Since he has been turning down an awfully large quantity of scripts lately, will somebody please send him a good one? Or finance that *Boy and His Dog* sequel, maybe?

THE FILMS OF L. Q. JONES

1954   *Battle Cry*

1955   *An Annapolis Story*
          Target Zero

1956   *Santiago*
          Love Me Tender
          Between Heaven and Hell
          Toward the Unknown

1957   *Men in War*
          Operation Mad Ball

1958   *Torpedo Run*
          The Naked and the Dead
          The Young Lions
          Buchanan Rides Alone

1959   *Hound Dog Man*

1959 (cont.)	*Battle of the Coral Sea* *Warlock*
1960	*Flaming Star* *Ten Who Dared* *Cimarron*
1962	*Ride the High Country* *Hell is for Heroes!*
1963	*Showdown*
1964	*The Devil's Bedroom* *Apache Rifles* *Iron Angel*
1965	*Major Dundee*
1968	*Counterfeit Killer* (aka: *Crack Shot*) *Hang 'Em High* *Stay Away, Joe*
1969	*The Wild Bunch* *The Witchmaker* *Backtrack* (Made from *Virginian* and *Laredo* episodes)
1970	*The Ballad of Cable Hogue* *The McMasters*
1971	*The Brotherhood of Satan* *The Hunting Party* *The Bravos* (tvm)
1972	*Fireball Forward* (tvm)
1973	*Pat Garrett and Billy the Kid*
1974	*The Petty Story* *The Strange and Deadly Occurrence* (tvm) *Manhunter* (tvm) *Mrs. Sundance* (tvm) *Riddle at 24,000 Feet* (tv pilot)
1975	*A Boy and His Dog* (aka: *Psycho Boy and His Killer Dog*) *White Line Fever* *Winterhawk* *Attack on Terror: The FBI vs. The KKK* (tvm) *Winner Takes All*
1976	*Mother, Jugs, and Speed* *Banjo Hackett: Roamin' Free* (tvm)
1978	*Standing Tall* (tvm) *Colorado C. I.* (tv pilot)

1979	*Fast Charlie, The Moonbeam Rider*
	The Sacketts (tvm)
	Wild Times (tvm)
	The Buffalo Soliders (tv pilot)
1982	*The Beast Within*
	Melanie
	Timerider: The Adventure of Lyle Swann
1983	*Lone Wolf McQuade*
	Sacred Ground
1988	*Bulletproof*
	Red River (tvm)
1989	*River of Death*
1990	*The Legend of Grizzly Adams*
1994	*Lightning Jack*
1995	*The Friends of Harry*
	Casino
1996	*Tornado!* (tvm)
	In Cold Blood (tvm)
1997	*The Edge*
1998	*Mask of Zorro*
	The Patriot
1999	*The Jack Bull* (tvm)
2001	*Route 666*
2006	*A Prairie Home Companion*

TELEVISION

L. Q. was a regular on *Cheyenne, Klondike,* and *The Virginian.* The rest of his unending list of tv credits include: *Dr. Vegas, Perry Mason, Playhouse 90, Black Saddle, Two Faces West, The Rebel, Gunsmoke, Laramie, The Lawman, Ben Casey, Route 66, Rawhide, The Big Valley, Kung Fu, Ironside, Cannon, Charlie's Angels, Columbo, CHiPs,* and *The Incredible Hulk.*

BUCK KARTALIAN

*"Most of the time, I really had to work my butt off to get a part.
I never got it easy, except now and then."*

Almost invariably, the 5', 2" Buck Kartalian has put across the same sort of charm as his fellow, diminutive comics, Henry Gibson and Arte Johnson. And like Gibson and Johnson, Buck is equally adept in serious roles. (A memorable **Cagney and Lacey** guest spot, as an Armenian who recalls the atrocities that his people have suffered, comes immediately to mind.) But, simply put, Buck is a born comic, and an immensely lovable one, at that.

Along with his other major roles—in films like **Mr. Roberts, Cool Hand Luke,** and **The Outlaw Josey Wales**—Buck is best remembered as Julius, the gorilla jailer who torments astronaut Taylor (Charlton Heston) in Franklin Schaffner's one-and-only **Planet of the Apes** (1968). It is truly unnerving, watching

Buck in his ape make-up, enthusiastically hosing down the beleaguered Heston, and maniacally giggling and 'Ook'-ing about the abuse he's heaping on his human charge. The peculiar intensity of that scene comes from the way that the two characters goad each other with an ever-increasingly furious, mutual hatred. Buck's rabid shriek of, "SHUT UP, YOU FREAK! I said *SHUT UP!*" is matched by Heston's "Julius, you hairy scum...," followed by his climactic howl, "IT'S A MADHOUSE! A MADHOUSE!" The talking ape is utterly disgusted by the alien talking human, and *vice versa*. It is a highly affecting scene, in a film full of them.

In his last scene in *Apes*, Buck smokes a cigar from underneath John Chambers' foam rubber distortion. That bit of business was Buck's idea, since he is an unrepentant cigar lover, which, in over-sensitive California, is looked upon as something akin to being an unrepentant cockfighter or an unrepentant hit-and-run driver.

Buck appeared in a bit part in the second-to-last *Apes* film, *Conquest of the Planet of the Apes* (1972), as Frank, a gorilla waiter. Another role, though, that required him to don almost as much make-up as he wore for either of the *Apes* movies has gone virtually unseen for the past twenty-five years. Without even having to audition, Buck was cast as Bruce W. Wolf, the wolfman portion of The *Monster Squad* (1976-77), a kid's tv series. His co-monsters were Dracula (Henry Polic) and Frank N. Stein (Mike Lane), with forehead—rather than neck—bolts, for once.

The show began with the three monsters as dummies in a wax museum, who then came to life and fought crime. Its producer has continually withheld the show from syndication, and whether or not it will emerge from obscurity anytime soon is anyone's guess. During the show's very brief merchandising run, a board game was produced, featuring Buck. (Other pieces of "Kartaliana" include a Japanese "Kubrick" (Lego) figure of Buck in the original *Apes*, a scarce *Acid Eaters* photo novel, and an exquisite bust of him as Julius, grinning away with his cigar, produced by Apemania.)

It is extremely fortunate that Buck is the good-humored pussycat that he is. Because as actor Dan Roebuck subtly pointed out, Buck could easily "kick all our asses." At his eightieth birthday party, as his friends counted down, Buck

did one hundred push-ups. He smokes, on average, a cigar a day, to boot. If he didn't smoke, I suspect that Buck would be swimming the length of the Pacific Ocean and back, seven or eight times a day.

Buck was the *clothed* lead in the first dirty movie that this writer ever saw, **Please Don't Eat My Mother** (1972), a smutty remake of Roger Corman's **The Little Shop of Horrors**. This has always amused him, mainly because I think he has difficulty believing that someone remembers having seen it in the last thirty years, and will 'fess up to that fact publicly.

Buck and his wife, Margaret, are two of the most adorable people to ever settle in the San Fernando Valley. I have often affectionately referred to him as my Armenian grandfather. I will never cease delighting in memories of scavenging through yard sales with the Kartalians, admiring their art collection, and dining with them in the supremely pleasant atmosphere of their home.

Buck's official website is www.buckkartalian.com.

Born Vahe Kartalian, Buck is the son of Armenian immigrants. His family settled on Third Avenue in Manhattan when Buck was very nearly a toddler. "When I was a kid," he reminisced, "there was an elevated train that ran by my house, the Third Avenue El. It went right by my window. If it stopped, I would wake up." Buck's mother was from Istanbul, which, at the time, had a large Armenian population. Out of all of the "young, eligible men" in her village, she chose his father, because "he had a nice smile."

"My father died when he was about thirty-nine years old," Buck recalls, "when I was about eleven. They never went to the doctor, really. We were out with him, and he just dropped dead in the street. My mother was stuck with six kids"— Four girls and two boys. Buck's brother is now deceased.

Immediately after finishing high school, Buck was drafted into the Navy. He served on a destroyer in the Pacific. "I saw a lot of action," he says, "a lot of stuff: planes shot down in flames. We sunk a cruiser, bombarded the shore. I was a gunner, a 40mm gun. It would shoot these big 40mm shells, this double-barreled gun. I was really lucky: we had one destroyer right above us sunk, torpedoed."

As a civilian, Buck soon drifted into show business. Buck took to eating with a friend at a massive automat, on 42nd Street, near 8th Avenue. Right above it, he says, there was an even bigger gymnasium. A retired, octogenarian wrestler, George Tregis, ran it. "He wrestled when wrestling was *real*," says Buck. "He used to come up there, two, three times a week. They had another fella running the place for him. I went up there with my friend, and I just stood in awe of the surroundings. It was the most incredible place! They had this enormous space where people rehearsed their acts, before the end of vaudeville. They'd have people on unicycles, somebody would have a monkey on their head, somebody would be doing ballet or juggling.

"On one side of the stage, they had a bunch of mats. And the wrestlers would come up and rehearse their wrestling, their acts. It was just like a three-ring circus. I said, 'This place is amazing!' I joined the gym right away. I wasn't working. I didn't know what I wanted to do. I had no idea. I'd hang around there. And I made a lot of friends, and everyone was very helpful." It was there that Buck learned theatrical skills, like juggling and acrobatics.

"They used to have a little vaudeville theater. Before the show, they'd have vaudeville and stuff. They'd have acrobatics, a juggler, little acts. This was towards the end of vaudeville, the last two or three years. Somebody got hurt in one of the acts. A guy busted his hand, so this guy says, 'Hey, buddy, one of the guys in this act sprained his wrist. You want to take his place. C'mon—you can do it. I've seen you around the place.' So, I rehearsed with them and, next thing you know, I'm doing a hand-balancing and tumbling act with a guy and a girl. I was the middle guy. I did a tumbling act up there."

Soon afterwards, Buck's life was permanently altered when he discovered weightlifting, which he took up as a kind of hobby. He remembers: "Before you know it, one of the guys comes over to me and says, 'Hey, Buck, you're getting some build!' I said, 'Yeah, I've just been fooling around with the weights, and I'm developing fast!' He says, 'You really are. They're having a contest. Why don't you go down and enter? They're looking for the best-built man in New York City.' I said, 'Well, I'm not that good.' He said, 'You are! You really are!' I had no idea. I went down there, and they showed me how to pose, and I did it, AND WON THE DAMN CONTEST!

"I'd enter weight-lifting contests, and I'd come in second or third. And they had the Mr. America Contest. At the gym, they said, 'You ought to enter.' I said, 'I don't know.' They said, 'Go ahead—enter. What have you got to lose?' So, I said, 'Yeah, it's kinda fun.' And, the thing is, I wasn't working out like these guys that I was watching work out, like, six hours a day: I'd work out like an hour. I was getting strong as hell. Different people's bodies develop differently, you know. I had the kind of body that looked good when it's developed. Even though I was short, I was very symmetrical. If you saw a picture of me in a pose, a muscular pose, you would never know how tall I was. So, I get to the contest, and I come out third in it! Mr. America, best-built man in every state and Canada. I won for best arms, best chest, and I got a couple of trophies. It was the end of 1949."

A short while later, Buck was challenged to a friendly wrestling match by George Tregis himself. "I said, 'Are you crazy? You want to kill me?' He says, 'C'mon!' He's about five-foot-ten, weighs 250 pounds. Back in those days, when I was really in great shape, the most I ever weighed was 150. I said, 'Okay.' I start wrestling with him, fooling around. And I saw that it was just starting then, this tv wrestling, wrestling for showmanship, the kind of wrestling where you flip around, you jump, you dive around. And I was kidding around with this guy, going under his legs, jumping over him, because I was like a feather. I said, 'This is fun!' And the guy's laughing, and he'd get him in a hold, he'd get mad, because I was making a fool out of him.

"Everybody'd watch, they'd laugh, and I'd say [jokingly], 'YOU'RE HURTING ME! You're hurting me on purpose! That ain't allowed! You know that!' So, one day, I was up there with another wrestler, and I was kidding around with him. And, after I finished, a guy comes over to me, and he says, 'Hey, kid, got a second? I was watchin' you. I've got an idea. I've got a strong troupe of wrestlers. I send them on little trips. They go from here to New Jersey, they go to Baltimore, Pennsylvania, and back. I haven't got anyone like you. You'd be making good money, and make it fast.' I said, 'Gee, I've never done any of this stuff before. Will I make any money?' And he said, 'Well, it's up to you. As soon as you start, you'll open for twenty-five dollars a match.' I said, 'It sounds good.' So, I started wrestling.

"There wasn't much tv, and I'd go in these little towns like Lansdale, Pennsylvania, and little towns in New Jersey. There was a little circuit we did. We'd wrestle Monday night here, Tuesday night [there], Wednesday night [there], and then we'd come back. I'd wrestle sometimes six, seven nights a week. We'd all get in a car together separately, so nobody would see us together, like we didn't even know each other, you know? And the wrestling was BIG. I became like a favorite in some of these little towns. I would make 'em laugh, and they're always for the little guy. That was a ball." First, he wrestled as "The Mighty Mouse," then as "Buck, The Professional Motion Man," then, once again, as "The Mighty Mouse."

"I'd just dive over the ropes instead of stepping in the ring," says Buck. All wrestlers have favorite moves, and his were the dropkick, and slipping underneath his opponents' legs. "The promoter didn't know whether I'd be the 'good guy' or the 'bad guy.' After one match, he said, 'You're the good guy. They love you. You're the little guy, and they love you.' So, I wrestled for about seven or eight months."

A jaw-dropping example of wrestling fanaticism occurred in a small town where Buck was a regular and a well-loved favorite. That evening, some new wrestlers were being trotted out. "This time, I was in the car with one guy who called himself 'The Lion Man.' He looked like a lion: huge, his hair flowing over his head and over his shoulders, fierce-looking. Everyone outweighed me by about a hundred pounds, at least. So, I was gonna wrestle him.

"There's a real skill to it. People say, 'Ah, it's fake.' You gotta be in great shape, and you've got to know how to work the audience. As long as the audience is howling and yelling and screaming, the match is going well. If they're quiet, you're dying.

"So, the Lion Man says, 'What's your favorite hold?' And I said, 'I don't have one, but I've got some funny things that I do, like I leap onto a guy's shoulders, I put my legs around his neck, and I flip him over. Then, there's my drop-kick with my legs out.' He says, 'I've got a terrific one. Here's what I do: I lift you up, and then I lift my knee, and I kick you right in the balls with my knee.' I said, 'Let's try it.' And we did it, and I said, 'Wow, that looks terrific!' I didn't feel anything. It's unbelievable how well he had it perfected. I said, 'You know, Mr. Lion Man, I'm a little concerned about your kicking me in the groin like that. I know you do it well. I'm not worried about getting hurt, I'm worried about the audience getting so wound-up.' They really liked me and they'd ever seen this guy before. 'I think they're really going to be too angry.' He said, 'Come on! That's the idea! Build up the heat, get them angry!' I said, 'I know, I know. Okay.' We go in, and we're wrestling, and we're doing a good job. They're yelling and screaming for me. He's the dirty guy, playing dirty, and I'm the little guy trying to get the best of him. We're about a quarter through the match, and he says, 'I'm gonna do it.' And I said, 'Go ahead.' So, he comes over, and lifts me up, kicks me right in the groin, and he did it beautifully. The knee comes up, and it's right in there. I went down, and went, 'OOOOOOOH! OOOOOOOH!' I was really selling it to the audience. And they're screaming to the ref', 'FOUL! FOUL!' And, when we did it, the ref' turned his head so he wouldn't see it, so he wouldn't see the dirty stuff.

"I got up. We'd talk to each other in the ring, and make it look like were cursing each other. He said, 'That was great!' I said, 'But they're angry.' He said, 'Let's do it again.' So, he does it again. And the crowd is SCREAMING, and I'm selling it. And we did it a third time, for the last time. And I just stayed there, and moaned, and groaned, and tried to get up, and fell down again. And I went down and stayed there, and I looked up. And when I looked up, the ring was full of people. There was nothing I could do, what could I do? What I did was visit him in the hospital, poor guy. He said, 'Yeah, well, Buck: that's part of the game.' They broke his ribs, knocked out his teeth.

"You'd go into towns where there were, say, 50,000 people, and 8,000 would show up for the wrestling match. It was very big then, after it first got started. After the first couple of years, it was big...There used to be wrestling tours going all over the place, all these little towns.

"I went back to the gym, and, one day, a bunch of actors were going out for a reading. Someone said, 'Hey, Buck, you want to come along?' And I said, 'Sure, why not?' I finished my workout, and I went along. So, I was standing in the back there, and there was a woman behind a desk. She was backstage, but not onstage, behind the curtain. So, my friends went in, and I'm just sitting there. So, the lady comes over to me, and she says, 'You're next.' She hands me a book, and I'm standing there, and these two guys I went with, they're laughing. I said, 'Okay, I'll go.'

"So I get onstage, I walk out, and, of course, it's pitch black out in the audience. I don't see a thing. There's just the light on me, and I was standing there. And the director was English, Peter Glenville. And he said, 'Are you ready?' I said, 'I don't know. I came with some friends of mine. I ended up here onstage. I don't know what I'm doing here.' He calls to me from the back, I couldn't even see him, 'Why don't you turn to page four?' or whatever page it was, 'and read for the part of Samson.' I said, 'Okay.' Some guy comes on, and I read with him. I finish reading, and the director says, 'All right. Thank you very much.' I stood there, and I said, 'What do you mean?' He said, 'We'll let you know. Thank you very much.' So, I'm leaving, and the lady says, 'Come here, come here. I want to check you off. I don't have your name.' She says, 'Give me your phone.' I said, 'I don't have a phone. I'll give you the gym number.' So, I gave it to her, everybody knew me at the gym.

"About two weeks pass, and I get a call at the gym. The lady says, 'Are you Buck Kartalian?' I said, 'Yeah.' 'Well, you've got the part, and we'd like to have you come in and meet someone. You can start fencing lessons and…' And I said, 'Ma'am, what are you talking about? What part?' Because I'd forgotten about it completely, and it was completely out of my mind. She said, 'You came to the theater and read.' I said, 'OH! That thing!' I didn't know what the hell I'd read. She said, 'They want you, and you've got the part, and you can come down.' So, I went down, and met these people. And, sure enough, I had fencing lessons for two weeks.

"And, you know what the play was? The first play I ever did in my life? *Romeo and Juliet* [1951]. Olivia De Havilland was Juliet, Jack Hawkins played Mercutio, and a wonderful actor, he's passed away now, did Romeo, Douglas Watson." Buck's dramatic bow was as Samson, one of the boastful medieval delinquents who rouses up the play's opening brawl. "I wasn't making a quarter of the money I was making wrestling. Later on, I was doing very well in wrestling. I was making $100, $125 a match. Here, I was gonna get fifty dollars a week to start with. But I said, 'Hey, I think I like this.'

"We went out of town for about two months. Then, we came back, and we ran for about two or three months. It was almost over, and one of the fellas, Robert Burr, a lovely, lovely actor, he said, 'What're you gonna do now, Buck?' I said, 'I don't know. I really like this.' He said, 'You've got a good feeling for acting. You're real.' I didn't know what to do after the show. I said, 'What am I going to do?' He said, 'You know what you do? I've got an idea. They're going on the road with *Mr. Roberts*. And he gave me the name of the person to see. He said, 'They'll give you Harvey Lembeck's part. It's a wonderful part. You look like him.' And that's how they cast on Broadway: if you looked like the character, you got the part. So I said, 'Okay.' I went to see one other person first, and they sent me down to the theater. So, I went down to the theater, and I met this guy, and I said, 'So-and-so sent me down.' And I saw the stage manager, and he said, 'See the show for about a week. Then you're gonna read. Watch Harvey Lembeck, and, when you come to read, I want you to imitate him.' I said, 'Okay.' That's the way they do it: if it's a big hit show, they don't want to lead it in any other directions. I imitated him, and I got the part. I can't believe I just fell into one thing after another. And I was with the show for two years. I traveled all over the country with it. Tod Andrews was the lead. He looked a little like [Henry] Fonda. The show was such a big hit, they didn't need a big star." Lembeck, a gifted comedian, is now probably best known for having played Eric Von Zipper, the hapless biker, in AIP's "Beach Party" movies.

In both the Broadway and film versions of the classic World War II naval play, **Mr. Roberts**, Buck was directed by film and theatre titan, Josh Logan (**South Pacific**, etc.). Buck repeated his real-life role as a sailor on Captain James Cagney's ship. "What happened was I had been in Hollywood for about a year. I'd done a little work, and I went back to New York again. And, when I was in California, they were doing **Mr. Roberts** (1955), the movie. So, I tried my agent. I said, 'Get me in! Get me in! Get me into see somebody!' And he said, 'I tried, Buck, but John Ford is directing it, and he's using a lot of people he knows. There's really no chance.' I said, 'Aw, okay.' They went to Hawaii; they made the picture. And, when they got back, Josh Logan saw the movie, and wanted some additional scenes—he wasn't too pleased, I guess—to give it a little more jazz. Ford got sick, and Mervyn LeRoy took over. Logan wanted to do a couple more days of shooting.

"My agent said, 'There'll be a 'cattle call' [open audition]. You want to go?' I went, and there were about a hundred guys there. Who do I see coming by, but Josh Logan with Mervyn LeRoy. I didn't know LeRoy. Of course, Logan knew me. He sees me, and I thought, 'I hope he recognizes me! [laughs] It's been a while.' He sees me, and he comes over, and gives me a big hug, and I knew it: I was hired. They wrote a scene for me, with the soapsuds. Remember when the soapsuds were all over the play, and I'm in the passageway? The laundry blew up, and all the soap's all over the place. Henry Fonda sees the soapsuds, and says, 'What happened?' And I say, 'I don't know, but I'm gonna find out!' While I'm talking to him, the soap gets higher and higher, and, finally, goes over my head. They had to do that in one take: that was all the soap they had. It was fun. I didn't have any scenes at all with [James] Cagney. In fact, I never met him. He was through with his part."

The actor refers to Logan as "a sweetheart. He had the loveliest wife. They used to come see the show about every two, three months, to see that it was up to par. He had a certain level that he always wanted it to be at. He came over to me one time, and said [in a mock-threatening voice], 'You're not performing like Harvey Lembeck anymore!' I said, 'I know! I'm performing like Buck Kartalian! [laughs] I'm getting all his laughs and more!' He said, 'That's all we want, and we want the feeling of the show.' He knew I knew it by heart.

"When I came back after the two years, everybody wanted me in summer stock to do the show, because I knew it, and because I could give them ideas about how to do it, because I knew the show so well. Then I'd do the show, and they'd ask me to stay for another show. That's where I got all my great experience: doing summer stock. I would be rehearsing a show in the daytime, and doing another one at night. We do seven, sometimes eight shows during a summer. It was great. I never sang, and I did about five or six musicals. There was a director; his name was George Lipton. One day, he said, 'Okay, Buck, you're going to sing in this one.' I said, 'Oh, no, I'm not! I don't even sing in the shower!' He said,

'No, Buck, it's really easy.' It was **Kiss Me, Kate**. And there's two gangsters in it, and they sing this marvelous song: [sings] 'The girls today in society/ Go for classical poetry/ So, to win their hearts, you must quote with ease/ Aeschylus and Euripides.' It just goes on, and then we do a little dance, a little shuffle with a tap dance. It's a funny, crazy song, but I was scared to death, because I never sang, ever. He said, 'Don't worry, Buck.' Lipton used to slap a show together in amazing time, in no time. The first day, he'd block everything, and, the second, he was having run-throughs [laughs]. He was a magician. He knew he had good people to work with, and that they knew what the hell they were doing."

Lipton reassured Buck, and had a talk with their piano player. Buck then had to face the nerve-wracking ordeal of his first singing rehearsal. "The piano player says, 'Start in: 'The girls...'" And I go, [off-key] 'The GIRLS.' He says, 'No, no, no. 'The girls...' And I go, 'The GIRLS.' He says, 'No, no, no...' So, I said, 'Aw, shit. Excuse me. I have to go to the bathroom.' So, I leave, and I'm looking for the director. And he said, 'What happened?' I said, 'I never got past 'The girls!' I said, 'I can't hit right on the head the notes! I'm not trained!' He said, 'Let me talk to him.' I guess he told him, 'Let Buck do anything he wants. Just follow him.' [Laughs]

Buck relates that the play's female lead was a major opera star at the time, Patrice Munsel. "Here she is, doing the lead, and I'm comin' on with, 'The GIRLS today in SOCIETY...' I decided I was just going to do me. I'm gonna sell the song, and do some funny stuff. After we did our number, me and this guy, we'd get together work, we brought the house down. Really, they screamed and yelled. And Patrice Munsel came to me after our number, and she started laughing, and said, 'Buck, I never met anyone who could sing so badly, and be so good!'"

Buck eventually grew accustomed to singing, and did so again in **Guys and Dolls**, and as his first of several gangsters in **The Threepenny Opera**. "There were full houses all the time; we used to make about seventy-five, eighty dollars a week. This was off-broadway. We never had any dressing rooms, we had this long hallway area behind the stage. Men, women, everybody would undress there, everybody would be on top of each other [laughs]. It was a riot. At that time, I'd just gotten married. I had a little loft on 56th Street, and lived there.

"Then I went back, and I did a play with Geraldine Page, called **The Empress**. It didn't last very long. I had a lovely scene with her. She's a sweetheart." On Broadway, Buck appeared in **Wonderful Town, One More River,** and **Golden Fleecing** [ca. 1960] with Tom Poston, among others. "I did some stock. Then, I came out here, and the first picture I did was with Ernie Kovacs [**Sail a Crooked Ship** (1962)]. I'd only been here two weeks, and I got a movie right away. I did a lot of television. I don't even remember some of the shows I did."

Briefly, Buck can be seen as, once again, a sailor in **Morituri** (1965) with Marlon Brando. "We shot it off Catalina Island on a German cargo ship. We stayed on Catalina Island for about five or six weeks. We played American prisoners who were picked up when a submarine sank a ship. We had a scene with Brando, and I remember we worked much longer than we had to. Brando was having some problems with his personal life, and he'd walk off, and we wouldn't see him for a while. I think they changed the title to something else. I know that, at that time, it wasn't a big hit or anything. I know I had a nice time on Catalina Island, off-season. We had the whole island to ourselves."

In a movie thick with character actors, *Cool Hand Luke* (1967), Buck has a fairly sizeable, silent role as "Dynamite," a member of the film's Southern chain gang. At one point, he can memorably be seen playing "double Dutch" with some jump-roping fellow inmates. "I worked with [director] Stuart Rosenberg on a couple of the early *Untouchables*. Stuart Rosenberg knew a lot of actors, he knew hundreds of actors, because he directed a lot of television shows." Buck recalls, "We shot that out in Stockton, California, though, actually it took place in Florida."

The author of the book *Cool Hand Luke* was based on, Donald Pearce, appeared "as an extra in the movie," Buck says, with a trace of distaste. "I remember he wasn't very nice. We almost got in a fight, one day. [laughs] He was kind of a jerk. He wrote this thing, because he was a prisoner. He wrote about his story. I guess Rosenberg saw something in it: here's a hero who's a loser, you know? I was 'Dynamite.' I had a lot of little scenes. The movie wound up being very, very long, so they cut it. I had a couple of nice little scenes that were cut out, but I was in enough of the picture, anyway.

"One day, we're out in Stockton and Rosenberg says, 'Do you know how I cast you guys? I'll tell you. I know so many actors, on Friday, I put a character's name up on the wall, and I put five pictures underneath each one. And I said, 'Gee, they're all so good! I can't tell who I'm going to pick! How am I going to pick this?' So, I walked down the row, picked up one picture, threw it in the wastebasket, picked up another one, just at random. And whoever was left Friday got the part!'

"Conrad Hall was the cameraman on that one, brilliant cameraman. We rehearsed with the camera for a whole week on the set. We had an outdoor set. We shot all the stuff indoors at Warner Brothers. We went down to Stockton for all the exteriors. They built the whole prison. One of my kids, Jason, was born during *Cool Hand Luke*. He's made his own film recently."

The irreplaceable Strother Martin played the chain gang's straw boss to perfection. "He was a funny, funny, funny man, just a wonderful, lovely man. He always had a funny joke. And he was a great diver. There was a pool there, and, one day, he got up and started diving. He said, 'I was a pretty good diver when I was younger.' [He was doing] incredible dives. He was a sweet, sweet man."

Whenever his movie roles began thinning out, Buck would do more plays. "I didn't make much money at them, but I loved the theater so much. I loved it, I enjoyed it, like candy to a baby. I did a play called *The Wall*, and I got just fantastic reviews from it. It was set in the Warsaw Ghetto. A lot of people thought I'd actually been in a concentration camp, a lot of the Jewish people that came to see it. I played a marvelous character, called Fishel Shpunt. I did Paddy Chayefsky's play, *The Tenth Man*, that takes place in a synagogue, out here for about two months. Then somebody wanted us to do it in Florida at the Coconut Grove Playhouse. It stayed there three weeks...I don't even remember a lot of the plays I did!"

In *Devil's Angels* (1967), Buck played "Funky," a member of the Skulls biker gang. Lead John Cassavetes, scrounging up money to finance his own films with, played their chieftain. The film was directed by Roger Corman's former art director, Daniel Haller (*The Dunwich Horror*). The film was made as an immediate follow-up to/cash-in a Corman hit, *The Wild Angels* (also '67). Buck's "wonderful agent" at the time, Hal Schaefer, sent him out, Buck explains. "He said, 'Buck, can you ride a motorcycle?' I said, 'I've never been on one in my life. Forget it.' He said, 'Come on, Buck, go see the guy anyway.' So, I go see this guy, and he hires me. He says, 'Can you ride a motorcycle?' I said, 'Well, uh [clears throat].... Years ago, I was on one...' He kind of looked at me like he knew I'd lied. I got hired. Here I am. Oh, shoot. What am I gonna do?

"I met one of the guys who was bringing the motorcycles down to Arizona, to Nogales—that's where we did it. He said, 'You've never been on a motorcycle in your life? Come on over to my place. I've got motorcycles, and you can use one of them.' So, I got on one for the first time, and I'm going around the block. And what happened was, all of a sudden, a car comes in the driveway, and I didn't know which was the brake, and I squeezed the gas. And, of course, I went right underneath, and I hung with my hand, I tore a muscle in my right hand. I said, 'It's all right. I've got a torn muscle. I can live with it.' [laughs] We went out to Nogales, and, it was so stupid of me. Out there in the wide, open spaces, in a couple of days, I was riding a motorcycle like I was an old pro at it."

Kartalian and Cassavetes.

At the time, Cassavetes had been nearly unemployed for several years from being "gray-listed." "I got along very well with Cassavetes," Buck enthuses. "We used to sit and talk. He was just a very, very deep kind of person. Sometimes he was high when he talked to me. He'd lose me every once in a while, then he'd come back. He was a marvelous, funny man.

"We had a couple of scenes together. About this one scene, he said, 'This is a stupid scene.' I said, 'Yeah, it is.' He said, 'Hey, Buck, why don't we rewrite it?' I said, 'Can we do that?' At that time, Cassavetes was having ups and downs, and this was one of his low periods, so he took this movie. American International was doing the movie, and the producer [Burt Topper] wasn't very nice to us. We tolerated him, he tolerated us, I guess. So, we stayed up all night one night, figuring out what we were gonna do, and we came up with several very interesting moments in the scene, we changed it.

"The next morning, we told the director [Daniel Haller], 'Hey, look at what we did. Can we do it.' And the director stands there and looks at us, and says, 'Wow. That's marvelous. It's funny, and very poignant. It's terrific. It's two guys who really like each other.' And we said, 'Well, that's what we are. We're buddies.' He said, 'I can't do anything without the producer seeing it.' The producer comes over, and watches us do the scene. And everybody was hanging around, and they all applauded after we were through. The producer comes over and says, 'Listen, John, Buck: that's OUT. We don't do that kind of stuff here. I want VIOLENCE. I want BURNING. That's what this picture's about!' [laughs] I just laughed. We just took it. We were working for them, they're the boss. But it was a nice experience. I spent several weeks in Nogales. A funny thing: I was there, and I went across the border one day. We came back, and the border guards held Cassavetes and me back. They wouldn't let us go back to the States. John said, 'We're in a movie! Here, call this number.' And they searched us. Someone must have told them we had drugs on us. I never did drugs. Some of the guys used to smoke pot. I never even smoked one puff. The worst thing I ever did was I smoked a cigar [laughs]. They held us for a couple of hours, John made some calls, and they let us go."

One of Buck's most absurd credits was in a dual role as Artie, one of the vacationers who experiments with LSD, and the devil (in long johns!), in the no-budget cult classic, ***The Acid Eaters*** (1967). In the course of the improvised plot, Buck showers outdoors, makes out with a topless, buxom co-star, paints, and distributes drugs! "WHOA! That's one of those things…. You know more about me than I do! Somebody gave my name to this guy. They needed somebody to do a play, and he said, "Buck's around here. He loves to do plays. This guy called me in. His name was Carl Monson. He ran a little theater, it's not there anymore, down on Magnolia and Lankershim. Now, the big television center is there. He directed some plays; it was his theater, and he did some very good work. He directed a lot of stuff, and he had a great imagination. My God, way out, WAY OUT, crazy guy. I did about five or six plays with him. He said to me, 'You know, Buck, I'm gonna do movies one day. You're gonna be in all of my movies.' He calls me up [later], and says, 'I'm gonna do some movies.' I said, 'You're kidding.' 'Yeah, it's not exactly what I wanted, but it's movies. It's for the

Pink Pussycat Theaters…' I said, 'All right, as long as I don't fool around with the naked ladies. I'm married. I can't do that.' He says, 'No, no. You'll be a gangster, a funnyman, whatever. There'll always be a part for you. You know that.' That's when we did **The Acid Eaters**. I played the Devil in that [laughs]. I did about four or five movies with him. I don't remember the others' names.

"I'll tell you what Carl used to do. He had his cameraman, and a couple of other people, and the actors. He'd have about three, four cars, and we'd be driving. I'd figure Carl knows where he's going. I'd be sitting with him in the first car, and I said, 'Hey, Carl, where are we going?' 'Location, Buck. Location.' And I said, 'Where?' And he said, 'I don't know yet.' [laughs]"

Producer Arthur P. Jacobs' **Planet of the Apes** (1968) was a surprise science fiction hit, with Buck in a plum supporting, simian role. Buck vividly remembers reading for the part of Julius with director Franklin J. Schaffner: "He looked at me and says, 'I'll give you a choice: you can have that part, or some other part. You'll work about six weeks with the other part, but with Julius, you'll only work two weeks.' Julius was a much better part; that's what I wanted. I said, 'I'll play Julius.'"

About the copious amounts of make-up he wore, Buck says, "I didn't mind it too much. [Twentieth Century-Fox make-up chief] John Chambers made a mask of my face out of plaster. The principals [lead apes] all had masks that were tailor-made. The extras just had hoods, they just put them on. At a distance, you couldn't tell. For close-ups, Schaffner was always afraid it would look like a masquerade, you know? He wanted to make it real, real as hell. That was the whole thrust of the movie: make it real. I remember I was saying a line one time, and he said, 'Buck, stop trying to be funny.' And I said, 'I'm not trying to be funny. It's a funny line!'

"We'd go in at like four in the morning to make-up. And, after a while, they had sixty—I don't know how many—make-up men. I had one guy who always took care of me. To put the appliance on, he'd first do around the eyes, the nose, and the jaw with the teeth in it. Then, he'd put the little hairs in all around it, blue them slowly all around. I took a good four hours to put it on. By eight o'clock, we'd be ready to go on the set." The ape make-up gave Buck "this strange, strange feeling, like I didn't exist, like I could see everybody, and nobody could see me. You notice every little thing when you have a mask on like that, because you're hiding, you know?"

Like Don Pedro Colley after him, Buck noted his co-star, Charlton Heston's, taciturn on-set manner. "He was okay. He was a very quiet, very somber actor. He wasn't a jokester or anything. A very serious worker. The funny part was there was a part where I'm hitting him over the head with a club. When we were done with rehearsals, he said, 'Julius'—he always called me Julius—'Hit me harder.' I said, 'Okay. [laughs] You asked for it.'

"We had one scene where I'm just sitting there, and there's a gate, and the other fellow [Lou Wagner] comes in with orders to release the human. [Schaffner] said, 'Okay, for this scene, the camera will open up on Julius here.'

My ears went up: 'The cameras will open on me. I can't just be sitting there doing nothing. I've got to be doing something.' Then I said, 'Ooh! Ah! Schaffner, why don't I be smoking a cigar!' And he gave me a look like, 'What the hell are you talking about?' He didn't say anything. So, he said, 'Let's rehearse it once.' So, we rehearsed it. Then he said, 'Okay, let's shoot it. Somebody get Julius a cigar.' It's strange now, when I think of it, I never remember, when I was younger, learning lines. I just looked at them, and I knew them. Today, I really have to work like hell to learn 'em. Son of a bitch, I don't understand why I can't absorb 'em faster! For five minutes, I'd look at a page, and I just knew it. I never thought of a line: it came."

Most of Buck's scenes involved Julius' chimpanzee superior, Dr. Zira (Kim Hunter). "She was a very sweet, nice lady," he recalls. "The funniest, strangest part of the whole thing is that I never saw Kim Hunter without her make-up on [laughs]. She was a chimp, as far as I knew!"

The actor had a fascinating "inter-species" run-in with Kim Hunter's lighting double, who worked in street clothes, with no make-up. "When we'd come in," Buck says, "all the extra apes or whatever, we'd all march in together onto the set. And I'd sit down. One day, I was just talking to her, I don't know how it happened, just gabbing away. And, the next day, I came in, and she comes right over to me. I said, 'How the heck did you know it was me?' And she said, 'Your eyes.' The only part of me you could see was my eyes. And we'd talk, kid around together, laugh. Then, one day, she looked at me, and she put her hand on my hairy paw, and kind of looked at me lovingly. Holy shit, the girl liked me! [laughs] She never got to know what I looked like, ever. I said, 'I can't. I'm married.' But she really liked me! 'My God,' I said, 'Beauty is really only skin deep.' [laughs] Falling for a gorilla."

Only a few of the ridiculously miscast American Indian impersonators starring in the wacky MGM (nominal) comedy, *Stay Away, Joe* (1968), were Buck, L. Q. Jones, and Burgess Meredith. Perhaps most miscast of all was Elvis Presley as Joe, an Indian rodeo rider. "I really liked [Elvis]. I was three months with him. Poor guy, he always had to have his five, six, seven guys with him, hanging around, lighting his little cigarillos, running around getting things for him. Basically, he was a very shy guy.

"He really didn't do much acting; he was playing himself. I remember we did one scene where we're supposed to be having a party, and everybody's happy. He looked at me like he didn't know what to do. I said, 'Have a good time. Just joke around.' And I gave him a little tap, and we started kidding around, and he loosened up. The scene turned out nice. When we did the movie, he was young and in his prime, he was in great shape. He did a lot of karate and stuff. He was very introverted. Some actors are like that. Like Douglas Watson in *Romeo and Juliet*. He was the shyest guy you'd ever want to meet! But he'd get onstage, and just glow, be radiant, dynamic. It was a really silly picture. I don't think it came out the way they expected it to. I think Elvis got his million dollars, anyway. He was a sweet young man."

Luckily for him, Buck remembers very little about working on the sleazy, campy *Myra Breckinridge* (1969). The film tells the sordid tale of what happens when doctor John Carradine turns Myron Breckinridge (Rex Reed) into Myra (Raquel Welch). "The only thing I remember was, I went in to see about it with Bob Fryer. I remembered him from New York years ago. He was always a casting director. Nice man. He had something to do with the casting. They had this really young director [Michael Sarne], really young guy. I saw him, and he said, 'Okay, I want you to read for the Acting Teacher.' And Bob Fryer says, 'Isn't he too young for the Acting Teacher?' And he said, 'How old is an acting teacher? Go read with this young lady.' So, I went aside, and I read with her. And we read, and he says, 'You've got the part.' That was it. I've never seen it. I don't know what the heck I do in it.

"I never did see Mae West. There were signs on the set that said, 'No Smoking,' because Mae West didn't like smoking. The thing that I remember about it is that every day, they'd do about a page of it, and every day, they'd give me new pages. They kept changing it and changing it."

Octaman (1971) was an ultra-low-budget remake of *Creature From the Black Lagoon*, written and directed by *Black Lagoon* screenwriter, Harry Essex. It featured a decent monster costume by a very young Rick Baker. "I don't even remember doing it," says Buck. He played one of the titular monster's first victims, a Mexican.

The infamous *Please Don't Eat My Mother* (1972), from Box Office International, needs no introduction. "I knew [Carl] Monson, I would say, five, six years. He's passed away now. He was much younger than me. One day, he calls me over, and he's doing a take-off on *Little Shop of Horrors*. He said, 'Pick up a script. We'll start shooting tomorrow.' 'Pick up a script? Why don't you give me a little time [to learn lines]?' He said, 'Well, pick up a script anyway. Maybe we'll pull it off in a couple of days.' I go up there, and he hands me two pages. I said, 'What's this? Is this my part?' He said, 'Oh, no! You have the lead in it!' I said, 'There's just two pages here!' 'Buck,' he says, 'As we go along, we'll make it up.' With two pages. I said, 'Is it short?' He said, 'No, it's a full-length feature.' And with that crew, we made *Please Don't Eat My Mother*." Buck plays a voyeuristic shlmiel who views the film's many, spliced-in, borderline hardcore sex scenes. *PDEMM* played in grindhouse theaters for years under a variety of misleading new titles.

Fox's *Conquest of the Planet of the Apes* (1972) was the fourth film in their rabidly popular *Apes* series. Buck played a gorilla waiter, Frank, in two brief scenes. "My agent sent me down there to meet the director [J. Lee Thompson], and he said, 'Ah! You're Julius! You're in the picture!' I said, 'Oh, good. Great.' The agent said, 'Great. You've got a five-week guarantee.' I said, 'But what kind of a part have I got?' And he said, 'I don't know, but you've got a five-week guarantee.' That means I get paid for five weeks, no matter what I do."

The film, about an ape revolt in near-future America, was shot at the recently constructed Century City complex. On his first day of work, Buck showed up, and got his script. But after looking through it, he couldn't find his part. He then

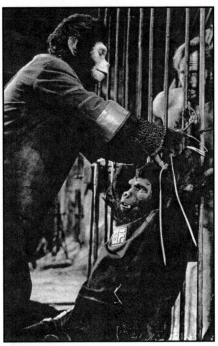
Planet of the Apes.

reported in for his extensive make-up. "The thing is, I had a nice appliance because they still had my old appliance. I got all ready to go, and I went up to the AD [assistant director], and I said, 'Where do I go? What do I do?' And he said, 'You're Frank. It's not in the script, but you're Frank. When it comes to your scene, I'll let you know.' Then we came to it, and he said, 'You go over to the lady sitting there, and she whispers something to you, and somebody else gives you a note to give to her,' and I don't know what the hell else. And that was it.

"[We shot it and] I came over and said, 'That's it?' He said, 'Yeah, that's it. That was good.' And I waited until the end of the day, and I said, 'When's my call tomorrow? I'm not on the call sheet.' They said, 'You're on hold.' And they're paying me, I had a five-weeks guarantee, anyway. I was available the whole five weeks. The next thing you know, the whole fives weeks went by, and they never called me in again. That was it. I got paid every week. [laughs] I knew one actor, John Anderson, and he was doing very well. But when a job was over, he would panic. He didn't know if he was ever going to work again in his life. I'd tell him, 'Would you give me a break!' You also have to realize that [getting parts] isn't the only thing in your life. They say, 'Go see this guy! Go knock on this door! Go knock on that door!' But, sometimes, you make a nuisance of yourself, and they throw you out. Sometimes, they say, 'I like this guy. I admire his guts.' YOU NEVER KNOW."

As a shopkeeper in Clint Eastwood's *The Outlaw Josey Wales* (1976), Buck had several good scenes with Eastwood. "This is another thing that's interesting. Originally, when I first came out here, when you did plays, now and then you'd get a movie from it. Somebody would come and see it [and give you a part]. I was doing this play, called *The Wall.* I had a wonderful role. I play a jokester, a buffoon, who dealt with both the Jews and the Nazis. He used to actually help the Jews, get them information and stuff. At the end, the audience thinks I'm dead. The Nazis arrest me and take me away, and they think that's the end of me. But at the end of the play, I show up again. I got out of it. And the audience…[Buck heaves a massive sigh of relief] You can hear them breathing. It was such a wonderful experience, one of the highlights of my doing plays. The character was so true. So, the agent sent me down to see about *Outlaw Josey*

Wales. The casting director and I are old friends. Of course, I didn't know him from Adam then. I just walked in to see him. He said, 'Did you do a play, called *The Wall?*' I said, 'Yeah, a few years ago.' He said, 'You don't have to read for me.' And I got the part.

"Most of the time, I really had to work my butt off to get a part. I never got it easy, except now and then. I remember when I got *Monster Squad.* It was produced by a man named Phil D'Angelo. Hal Schaefer was my agent, and he'd sent me out on a couple of things. I'd done a war show, *The Gallant Men*, I think he was producer of that. I worked with him one or two other times on a couple of other shows. One day, he calls me in. So, I go in, and there's three other guys there. He says, 'Okay, on the new series, called *Monster Squad*, you're the Wolfman, you're Frankenstein, and you're…[laughs]' And I'm looking at him, and I said, 'What? Are you playing games here? What do you mean 'I am?'" He says, 'You are.' I said, 'You don't want me to read?' And he said, 'What read? You got the part!' Of course, I was in total shock the next couple of days. No one comes over and says, 'Hey, you got the part.' If you want to read for one line, you've got to read."

Buck was briefly seen in the popular action film *The Rock* (1996), starring Sean Connery and Nicholas Cage, "just in the very end of it," he says. "Cage was very nice, very lovely. We shot that scene many times, over and over again: this way, that way. They'd shoot just my feet, then my

hands, then my head, then from overhead. They did a lot of coverage."

Like most actors, Buck refuses to retire, and still often reads for parts. His son, Jason, is an aspiring filmmaker, and cast Buck in his film, *The Pedestrian*. "I've got three auditions Monday," Buck said, when I originally interviewed him. "Casting directors don't know what to do with me because my hair's not white. They want a real old man. If I got the part, anyway, they'll change the part from an old, old man, to a younger man." He is also now the doting grandfather of twins. Having seen the kind of grandfather he can be, I can definitively say that two more fortunate grandchildren, you would hard-pressed to find.

THE FILMS OF BUCK KARTALIAN

1955	*Cell 2455, Death Row* *Mister Roberts*
1960	*Sail A Crooked Ship*
1967	*Cool Hand Luke* *Devil's Angels* *The Acid Eaters* *The Young Warriors*
1968	*Planet of the Apes* *Stay Away, Joe* *The Wild Females*
1969	*Myra Breckinridge*
1971	*Octaman* *Legacy of Blood* (aka: *Blood Legacy*)
1972	*Conquest of the Planet of the Apes* *Please Don't Eat My Mother* (aka: *Glump, Hungry Pets*)
1976	*The Outlaw Josey Wales*
1980	*The Man With Bogart's Face*
1985	*Gymkata*
1987	*Real Men* *Checkpoint*
1991	*Big Girls Don't Cry*
1995	*Josh Kirby: Time Warrior 3*
1996	*The Rock*
1997	*Eight Days a Week*
1999	*My Favorite Martian*
2000	*Flintstones in Viva Rock Vegas* *Pedestrian*

TELEVISION

Clips of Buck as the Devil in *The Acid Eaters* was used in a hallucination scene in John Waters' *A Dirty Shame* (2004). Buck's television credits include: *The Untouchables, Gallant Men, The Munsters, Batman,* a regular stint on *Here Come the Brides, Cagney and Lacey, The Judge, E. R., Curb Your Enthusiasm,* and *Life With Roger.*

PAUL KOSLO

"I coined this phrase years and years ago, and I've heard other people use it that know me: 'Hollywood makes you forget about everything, but yourself.' And that's not the most important thing. It's not more important than family and friends. And if you're so blessed that you get paid do something you love, and you get to do it—I feel really fortunate to have done that."

Whether playing a hero or a heavy, the lanky Paul Koslo always seemed on-edge, seething with pent-up energy. His long hair was almost inevitably unkempt, and his laconic delivery was unmistakable. Each of his characters seemed— whatever their cause might have been—possessed by a nearly manic fervor.

The Koslo performance that seems to have garnered the biggest response from his fans is "Dutch," one of the few healthy humans left in *The Omega Man* (1971). He makes a stunning entrance, dashing to Neville's (Charlton Heston) aid, decked out in a leather jacket, emblazoned with a hand flipping the bird on its back. When Neville dies during the film's climax, it is Paul's "Dutch" who is left to lead what may be the final remnants of humanity.

Try watching a steady diet of the extraordinary action cinema of the '70s. Sooner or later, you will begin to think that Paul Koslo was in every last *policier*, biker movie, or western shot during that decade. Just a few of his period credits: three films with Charles Bronson, John Sturges' *Joe Kidd* (1972), *The Laughing Policeman, Freebie and the Bean* (both '74), and *The Drowning Pool* (1976).

Paul as Dutch, in *The Omega Man*.

He was a regular in the films of Stuart Rosenberg, Richard Sarafian, and the late exploitation director/actor Jack Starrett. Two standout Starrett/Koslo collaborations between them were the absurd Hell's Angels-Vs.-The-Entire-North-Vietnamese-Army cult favorite, *The Losers* (1971), and the equally absurd black action gem, *Cleopatra Jones* (1973). Paul played every conceivable kind of part in these films, from a foppish British gangster to a drug-dealing, lowlife snitch, sporting hideous dyed-blonde hair.

But Paul's career was far from limited to action. He appeared in countless, disparate films, playing a startling variety of roles. There were several sweeping dramas, like the star-studded *Voyage of the Damned* (1976), where he portrayed a concentration camp survivor, and *Roots II* (tv; 1979), where he was cast as a redneck founding father of the Ku Klux Klan.

From there, Paul joined the massive ranks of talent who appeared in Michael Cimino's gargantuan *Heaven's Gate* (1980), the biggest money-loser of its day. He played the late River Phoenix's father in *A Night in the Life of Jimmy Reardon* (1988), and, more recently, had a role that hearkened back to his '70s roughneck *metier* in the Jean-Claude Van Damme vehicle, *Desert Heat* (1999). Like most character folk, Paul has also done a slue of tv work.

Director Richard Fleischer fondly remembered directing Paul in *Mr. Majestyk*. He was so pleased with Paul's performance that he allowed his character to survive the film's final shootout. Fleischer recalled the crew and most of the people on the set—excepting Charles Bronson—laughing hysterically at Paul's work. After over thirty years, Fleischer was still delighted to have done the favor for his young protégé.

Paul has wisely shielded himself from the deleterious effects of Hollywood life by distancing himself from L. A. in the safety of rural California. He has increasingly focused on producing and directing for the theater, along with his partner, Ed Harris.

By the time this book sees publication, Paul's first feature film as producer, *Y. M. I.*, will probably be complete and available for viewing. *Y. M. I.* follows a group of nihilistic teenagers who pledge a suicide pact together. From some footage I saw in its early stages, it looks to be an intense little work. Paul assembled a terrific cast for it from among his peers, including stalwarts William Smith, Peter Brown, and R. Lee Ermey.

Several years ago, Paul and his wife, actress Allaire Paterson, became the proud parents of a "very opinionated" (so says Paul) little girl, Chloe.

Paul was born Manfred Koslowski (pronounced "Kos-lov-ski") on June 27, 1944 in Germany, the son of a Prussian soldier. His grandparents were Polish and Russian. When Paul was around four, he and the other children couldn't help but be aware of the Sherman tanks rumbling down the nearby streets. "You couldn't miss it, because the earth would shake for miles around. And we'd be out there in awe, me and my other friends in the neighborhood. We—and other people— would be standing there, watching. And the GIs would be throwing out Wrigley's chewing gum, and Hershey's chocolate bars, and kids would be there in droves, fighting for them."

Post-War, Occupied Germany was, needless to say, devastated. As the adults tried to rebuild their lives and homeland, Paul recollects, "a lot of us kids were left on our own for long periods of time. So what I did was I started to daydream and I found out about cowboys and Indians from the Americans. So we used to play cowboys and Indians. It was a natural progression from the Americans, since nobody else had cowboys and Indians, and we were really intrigued by that."

In the '50s, Paul's father immigrated to Regina, Saskatchewan in Canada, says Paul, "Which, at that time, was like Podunk [laughs]."

"My native tongue was German, and it was really tough trying to adjust. But, when you're a kid, you can learn another language really easily. It took, I'd say, a couple of years to adjust.

"My mother was a homemaker, until later, when she used to run a deli in a big Safeway supermarket up in Canada. And my dad did a bunch of different things. When we first moved to Regina, he worked for a German newspaper, he swept floors in Simpson's [the Canadian equivalent of Sear's], and he was a private detective, and he built his own home, all at the same time. So he was definitely doing twenty-four hour days for the first couple of years. I think that's probably what eventually killed him, because he died when he was about fifty-seven of emphysema. He was a smoker, so it was probably all the pressure. He got asthma, and it turned to emphysema. He actually died in the hospital bed, with a lit cigarette burning in his fingers."

It was in Regina that young Paul saw his first film: a Gordon Scott Tarzan movie. Admission: five cents. "When I saw a picture, like another world on a wall, y'know, I couldn't fathom that. But I related to it instantly, because it was like inside my mind when I imagined things, playing cowboys and Indians. And then I knew, right then and there, that I wanted to be an actor, from then on.

"I guess I was about eight years old. I couldn't relate to people, although I knew I was a person, because I could talk like they could. But, usually, we [kids] were just pushed out of the way, because our parents were busy trying to build a new life." Paul thinks that it was this uncertainty that drove his father to relocate the family to Canada.

"And it was natural from when I saw that [movie] for me to want to go into that, or want to act. Actually, we moved from Regina to West Vancouver, British Columbia, probably in '57 or '58. I went to school in Horseshoe Bay Elementary School, and then I went to junior [high] and high school at West Vancouver High.

As a boy, Paul relates, he was a prize mischief-maker: "I was like one of the two-percenters [laughs]. We'd do all kinds of silly stuff, like, when the principal would be about to start the hundred-yard dash—he'd always be the one to fire the starter's gun—we'd throw a dead, plucked chicken onto the track. Or, if I was running on the track team, if they were doing the mile race or something, one side of the track was on the slope of a hill. So I would get to the outside lane and, after a couple of rounds, I would just duck down on the side of the hill on the far side of the track. And, then, when it came to the last lap, I would pop back up [laughs] and be like a hundred yards ahead of everybody. Of course, I got reprimanded pretty badly. There was sort of like a gang of us." The boys' hell-raising was harmless, though. "We'd have "best leg" contests, boys against the girls. We'd wear panty hose, we'd shave our legs. It was a hoot.

"My dad and I never got along, unfortunately," Paul says. "We had a lot of problems. I guess, right from their soul, kids rebel a lot. It's been like that since the beginning of time, father rebelling against son…We didn't see eye-to-eye, and there were a lot of different reasons for it. In his upbringing, he never got along with his dad, so he didn't know how to act with me. So I left home when I was really, really young, when I was about twelve."

At "Victoria, British Columbia, on Vancouver Island," Paul worked for around a year for his "brother-in-law-to-be," a fellow German, "building apartment kitchens in a big shop."

The following summer, on the mainland, Paul "was travelling a little bit, just to see the country, and I got commandeered by the Mounties to fight a big forest fire. And I did that for four months, all summer long. They paid me seventy-five cents an hour, twenty-four hours a day. I think I amassed about thirty-two hundred dollars, which was a fortune at that time." With his newfound wealth, Paul spent over a year, hitchhiking across North America twice. "Then, I finished high school. As a matter of fact, I went back to West Vancouver High. They had what was called 'The Great Thirteen,' which was like a first year junior college, but I'd been out in the world too much and just couldn't get back into the regimentation of it.

"I'd heard about this great acting school in Montreal, so I decided to audition. My parents didn't know where I was." Once again, Paul's father disapproved: "He never encouraged me at all. He kind of laughed at me, when I told him I wanted to be an actor. I didn't have any support whatsoever, so there was a lot of negative feelings about that."

Following high school, Paul decided to head east to the National Theater School in Montreal, a "sister school to the National Theater in London. I'd been doing a few little acting jobs on television, small parts, a couple of lines here and there. I did just to see if I liked it. I LOVED IT. It drove me to keep on going, but I realized that I needed training. I auditioned for the National Theater School, and I got in. And I got a Ford Foundation Scholarship."

After studying in Montreal for a year, Paul took menial jobs like waiting tables and pumping gas in the interim. He graduated from high school a year late, so he was already nineteen. During his next year at the Theater School, Paul was booted out. "The first year there, you learn the technique of acting: you learn diction, interpretation, improvisation, voice, dance, music, broadswords, fencing with foils, rhythm, everything. And the third year, you study plays and put them on for the public. My thing was, again, I was sort of the two-percenter type. I was asking too many questions. I was saying, 'Well, it could be like this couldn't it? I mean, it doesn't have to be.'

"We were in Stratford, Ontario, which is about five hundred miles from Montreal, where we'd go during the summer to put on plays. And that first summer, after we had been at Stratford, the artistic director called me in and said, 'You may be really talented, but I don't want you back next year. You're outta here.' It was like a mule had kicked me in the head. I just turned around on my heel, and I never said anything to him. I just walked out. Then, the assistant artistic director called me, and said, 'This is probably the best thing that could've happened to you, Paul, because you've got a lot of talent, and you'll be out there, learning what it's all about. Take your talent, and go out there, and get jobs. Get work, and learn in the business. You don't have to do plays for two years.'

"I got out, and, about a month later, I was walking across the parking lot of CBC, the Canadian Broadcasting Corporation. Four guys, business types, were walking across the parking lot the other way. As we passed each other, a guy says, 'HEY! You look Russian—can you act?' I said, 'Well, as a matter of fact, I just finished at Stratford this year.' He said, 'Oh, good, man. Come on up to my office. Here's my card. I'm casting the lead in this *Festival* series,' which is like a *Kraft Playhouse* for Canada. I said, 'What is it about? Is it a good part?' He says, 'It's the LEAD, man. It's the part of Raskolnikov in *Crime and Punishment* by Fyodor Dostoevsky.' FUCK!

"So, I went there about three months later. I didn't know anything about it. I didn't have enough time to get any information so I could be prepared, somehow.

But I didn't need to, because they had everything there. Actually, Michael Sarrazin, Rudolf Nuryev, and all these other guys were up for the same part." Opposite Paul in the film was Genevieve Bujold.

"I just happened to be in the right place at the right time. It was made-for-tv. It played on PBS on the East Coast outlet, because New York's not far from Montreal. Somebody from William Morris [Agency] in New York saw it, and they asked me if I wanted to be represented. I met the guy from the William Morris office, and they signed me. By that time, after I did that show, I got another show out of that, about Dylan Thomas. I was living in Toronto, and now I had the William Morris Agency behind me. And they said, 'Listen, Paul we want you to meet guys on the West Coast, too.' So, I went there and I met them, and [then] I came back to Toronto. Then I decided to move to Hollywood in 1966.

Despite rumors to the contrary, Paul was *not* in the spaghetti western, *Django* (1966). "In '66, there was a Spanish film crew that came and did an interview on me, and I was supposed to go do a spaghetti western. I don't know if that had anything to do with it." In reality, Paul appeared in *Hair* on Broadway for most of 1967.

"The first movie I did here, Jack Starrett directed. He did *The Dion Brothers, Cleopatra Jones*. He was an actor. He was 'Gabby Johnson' in *Blazing Saddles*. He was a hell of a director. He was actually a really good director, but he was a real renegade. He didn't like the big studio system, and he bucked them and they didn't like him for it. So, he never really made it to be a big, major director."

In 1971, Paul was "Limpy," a hobbling Hell's Angel, recruited, along with his buddies, to save a government agent from the Viet Cong in Starrett's *The Losers*. "I had the chance, of course, to leave the country to go to Manila, to see part of the world I'd never been to. And that was really interesting for me. Jack cast me because I'd done the lead for him in **The Zodiac Killers**. And I realized that Jack had a lot of talent, because, man, this guy would shoot beautiful stuff! He was really a talented guy. William Smith and myself were sort of the leads. William Smith is the king of the biker movies. Actually, I just saw him a while ago. He's a little crazy, but he's a good guy."

After their long flight to Manila, Koslo and his co-stars (who he described as "five reprobates from Los Angeles") began shooting. The twenty-five-year-old Paul loved his part. "I rode the three-wheeler; the other [bikes] were like Yamahas. We converted them. Some of the movie plot was us reworking our bikes with machine guns on the handlebars...I reworked this three-wheeler, which was actually a Harley frame with a Volkswagen rear end and a roll cage. We had a big rocket launcher on top of the roll cage, then fifty-caliber machine guns on either side of that. And they actually worked. All I had to do was press a button and blanks would come out of there. So did the rocket launcher—it shot dummy rockets. All that stuff was really exciting to me. That was the first time I'd ever had to learn to ride a motorcycle."

Prolific stuntman Gary McLarty, who Paul describes as the "best in the business" at bike stunts, "taught me to ride." But the location shooting wasn't all back-breaking labor, Paul confesses: "The women were hot and heavy, and the drinks were cold and strong, and we were stayin' there in the jungle." After the first three weeks of the six-week shoot, says Paul, "We found out that the producer of this show wasn't paying us, back in Hollywood. So, we went on strike. We made some calls from where we were staying, the Manila Hilton, and the agency got some money over there for everybody for the first three weeks [work]. Bill [Smith] instigated that. He said—pardon my French—'If that motherfucker comes around, I'll throttle his fucking neck! How dare he not fucking pay us!'

"But Bill is a very genteel guy, he really is. Did you know that he speaks seven languages fluently? He was an interpreter in part of the Diplomatic Corps in the Korean War. He's always been a dear friend, and I'll always support him. He's got nineteen-and-a-half inch arms. A regular person's neck is only about fifteen-and-a-quarter [inches], or so. He's really lean, but he's all muscle.

"We had people cook, these Filipinos who live in the Jungle, [in] these small villages and stuff. And they used all the natural stuff for cooking, parts of the natural habitat that were edible, fruits and coconuts they got off the trees. It's something you'd never think of now, because we're so automated and we've become technologically advanced. They'd have wild game that they'd cook up, and raised chickens and hogs and things. They'd just slaughter them and cook 'em up. It sounds kind of primitive, but it was really romantic. It's so nice to go to another country and you don't understand them, and they act so helpful and nice. I fell in love with the Filipino people, I really did. They were so nice. I mean, in any big city, you're gonna get some idiots. But everyone, to a fault, was just perfect. I couldn't have asked for a better experience...Other that that we didn't get paid for the first three weeks. And then, later, when we got back home,

we had so much overtime, we hit him [producer Joe Soloman] up for that, too.

"My next picture was *The Omega Man*, and [star] Charlton Heston was then president of the Screen Actors' Guild. I said, 'Hey, by the way, I just got back from the Phillipines and this guy owes me about forty-two hundred bucks in overtime.' And he made some calls to the legal department, and they got this guy, and I had my check within about two weeks. So, that worked out really well.

Omega Man, directed by the late Boris Sagal, was a very loose adaptation of Richard Matheson's stunning novel, *I am Legend*. The science fiction cult classic, set in Los Angeles after an accidental chemical war, follows the battle between the healthy survivors, lead by Neville (Charlton Heston), and a swarm of deranged mutants, "The Family," led by Matthias (Anthony Zerbe). "I had a lot of trouble with [*The Omega Man*]. I'm just starting out, remember, and I have about three or four movies under my belt, and I don't want to step on anybody's toes. I want to be a consummate professional, and Rosalind Cash took me under her wing."

At that time, Charlton Heston was incredibly busy—acting, presiding over SAG, and aiding then-governor Ronald Reagan. "He'd have limos standing by," Paul remembers. "So, all the stuff that I did with Heston, which was quite a bit of work, when it came to my close-ups, I did them with a mop. They had a mop, and they set the wooden part of it down on the floor, and the mop part was where Heston's head was. They had this mop handle—say, about six foot-three—and I would do all my acting, all my close-ups, with the mop. And the script girl held the script and would say the lines, and the mop would be in front of her head. So, I got very disconcerted, I got very insecure. That was just his thing, when he thought it wasn't important for him to be there. He never did that with Rosalind Cash, of course—you wouldn't do that: they had a plot-line relationship."

"So, Roz kind of took me under her wing. And she explained to me that I was doing a great job, and for me to keep it up, and for me to not lose faith in myself. Because it was a big movie for me. There was basically Lincoln Kilpatrick, Anthony Zerbe, Roz, and him and myself were basically it, as far as [the leads]. I thought, 'This will be great. Hopefully, I can do a good job.' And, then, when it came to my close-ups, he wasn't there. I wasn't getting anything [reaction]. It was very disconcerting. It was strange.

"Boris Sagal, the director, was really gracious. As a matter of fact, one time he invited me and Roz over for dinner, and that's when he apologized for Heston's behavior. He said, 'He doesn't mean to be that way.' And, sure enough, before the movie came out, Heston invited me over to his house, and out for dinner at Chasen's one night. He was really gracious. He didn't actually say, 'Hey, listen: I'm sorry I wasn't there for the close-ups.' But, in his own way, in a roundabout kind of way, he apologized.

Koslo's character wears a unique brown leather jacket, emblazoned with a hand giving "the finger" on its back. "You know what? I had that jacket lying around in a box in the barn. And I gave it to the guy that's been working for me for about fifteen years—his name is Lee Harper. He's like a Gary Cooper kind of guy: he never says much, you know? And animals flock to him! And he found the jacket in the barn, and said, 'Oh, wow, man!' I gave it to him and he wears it sometimes. [laughs] I went to Western Costume one time and they had a sale where you could buy different costumes. And they had Gary Cooper's boots and I bought 'em for about twenty bucks. This was years and years ago. It was funny—they were just a little bit tight, and I'd wear them and get cramps in my feet. They'd fall asleep and stuff. [laughs]

Koslo in *Soldier Boys*, 1972.
(above and right)

Also in 1971 was Richard Sarafian's ***Vanishing Point***, an infinitely more interesting "counter-culture" film than the similar ***Easy Rider*** (1968). ***VP*** follows Kowalski (Barry Newman), a bitter Vietnam vet and ex-cop, trying to make it from Denver to 'Frisco in a little over twelve hours. (Upping the ante—no pun intended— his Dodge Challenger has a trunk-full of uppers.)

Paul refers to ***VP*** as "sort of the first road picture, where people went on the road and they drove. The whole crew and all the equipment and all the trucks would drive from town to town. It was like on ***The Losers***, when we lived in the jungle. And, now, when the company moves, the actors just fly. It was like a caravan…

"I read for the director [Richard C. Sarafian]. And what happened was, on the way to Fox, I was on my motorcycle and I was wearing an American flag shirt. In the '70s, it wasn't done, because people were burning the flag because of Vietnam being so unpopular. Man, I got a ticket on the way over to the studio by this cop for wearing an American flag shirt! For desecrating the flag! I couldn't believe it, man! So, I was pissed. It kinda made me late, and, in those days, you didn't have cell phones, and I didn't have the studio number. I was about twenty minutes late. So, I started to recall to the director what had happened to me. And I was so pissed, so full of emotion, he said, 'You know what? You're gonna play that cop. I don't even have to have you read for me. And that's how I want you to play him, just like you are right now, the emotion you're feeling. Because you want to get the guy [Kowalski], and you're gonna be feeling emphatic about trying to get this son of a bitch.' He cast me in that.

"We started in Denver, Colorado. *Vanishing Point* had an incredible cast. And Kowalski was Barry Newman. He was more like a Charles Bronson-type character. Newman was a really nice guy. He always had a good thing to say about everything. Cheerful. It's funny, because he wasn't like [Kowalski] at all. He was like a nice Jewish boy [laughs]."

Koslo in *Roots II*.

In one scene, Paul brutally clubs the blind, black disc jockey, Super Soul (Cleavon Little), the film's Greek chorus. "He was a nice guy," Paul recalls. "You know, I did ***Roots II*** (1979), working with African Americans. And I've never had any personal problems with racial prejudice myself, ever. And, yet, when I did Roots, I played this guy that started the Ku Klux Klan—Earl Crowther was his name. I took my work home because I thought I needed to. The character went from his mid-20's, up to about seventy-seven years old. I had about four hours of make-up ever morning. So, everybody hated me, but they were gracious enough to know that that [character] wasn't like me, but that I was preparing all the time. When you put pressure on people like that, and it's about the racial situation to begin with—the point I'm trying to make about Cleavon is that he said, 'C'mon man. Do whatever you want. In a general scale, we have a race issue, but, one-on-one, that's how we can make a difference.' And that just opened everything up for me, you know what I mean? Again, he was a really talented, gifted guy. When he smiled the whole world lit up. You can see that in ***Blazing Saddles***. Great eyes, just so black and white. And he was good in ***Vanishing Point,*** too."

Koslo in *Joe Kidd*, above and right.

In John (*The Magnificent Seven*) Sturges' *Joe Kidd* (1972), starring Clint Eastwood, Paul boned-up on his marksmanship in his role as a western sharpshooter. "That was a western, and it was big for me because I'd never actually been on a horse. They were behind [schedule] at Paramount, so I was driven straight from there, all the way up to Lone Pine. And, when I got up there, Clint [Eastwood] and the guys were so gracious—they knew I couldn't ride that well. So, they let me ride all the time that I wasn't working. And they showed me how to holster a gun, how to quick-draw, how to do some spinning with the .45, slide back down in the holster like all the showboat guys do, which I thought was really nice of them.

"I was working with guys like Don Stroud, John Saxon, and, of course, Bobby Duvall. We were a mess, us guys [laughs]. Bobby is so incorrigible. There's a scene of just Clint riding, and we're in the Alabama Hills, way up there in the Sierra Nevadas. And the wind is just blowing like crazy, and everybody's got their hats tied down. The whole crew is standing there, and we're all watching Clint do this ride through the sagebrush, and the wind was howling and it was really loud. Then, all of a sudden—it was right after lunch—Bobby let out this hellacious fart—you could hear it through the whole valley! I mean, it was louder than the wind! And, at the same instant, this wrangler's hat blew off his head right in front of us. We were all cracking up, and, then, Bobby says, 'I blew his brains out!' And Clint was about twenty feet away, riding, and he heard the fart! I've never heard such a loud fart. I'll never forget that as long as I live. This cowboy's hat just blew off his head, right in front of him, and it was gone. He tried to get it, but it went like four hundred feet through the air, like it was propelled out of a rocket ship. And that's kind of how everybody treated each other. Base humor. Boy's locker room stuff."

Lolly Madonna XXX (1973) (aka: *The Lolly Madonna War*) centered on feuding hillbilly families; it was also directed by Sarafian. In one of his final roles, Robert Ryan played one of the clans' patriarchs, Paul's father. Rod Steiger headed the opposing family.

Robert Ryan, says Paul, "was great. You know, I've done—what?—130 movies and television shows. And I've got to say that he was probably the best out of everybody I've worked with. I really mean that. We went to Knoxville, Tennessee, to make that movie. We played a family, and the first thing he did was to invite us to his room, and he made dinner for us. And the lady who was playing his wife, an actress from New York [Teresa Hughes], just fell right in, and, within a half-hour, we were a real family. It was just such a beautiful gesture that everything just fell right into place. He was like a father and a confessor. He was like a sage and everything to us. He was really, really sweet—genuine. I'll tell you, man, he was incredible. He still makes that impression on me when I think about him. And he was a hell of an actor, too. He never became a gigantic star, but he was a big star in his day. You didn't have the Arnold Scwarzeneggers, then."

Starrett's *Cleopatra Jones* (1973) was a wacky blaxploitation movie, starring the ridiculously-attired Tamara Dobson as the crime-fighting Cleopatra. Paul played an English gangster working for the nefarious crime czarina, "Mommy" (Shelley Winters). In a jaw-dropping death scene, Paul's character is squashed alive in a car compactor, leaving only his signature ring behind. "I remember Shelley Winters being a pain in the ass. She was really jealous of me, for some reason. Finally, Jack [Starrett] had to put the clamps on her. She'd say things like, 'What's this guy doing behind my back?' because she was so insecure. Jack would say, 'Hey, you just take care of your stuff and don't worry about anybody else. Just do what you've got to do.' Finally, she threw a fit and he lit into her. He said, 'Don't you ever, EVER do that on my set again!' Rosalind Cash used to come down and visit, because she was friend with the girl that played Cleopatra Jones, Tamara Dobson." Sadly, Cash died in 1995. "It was the last time I saw her."

The singular Antonio Fargas also appeared as one of Winters' scuzzy associates, "Doodlebug." "Yeah, man, he was a fun guy. He's a good actor, too. Really an interesting guy, because he looks so weird, you know? He has that strange look: the nose, the eyes. But he was really a sweet guy, really a nice guy, really talented, really respected. We'd go out and party and stuff. But, for me, going through the

'60s and '70s, with peace, love, and flower power and all that stuff—tune in, turn on, and drop out—I did my share of partying. But I was always serious about wanting to be somebody. It was more a social thing, really, because I'd see friends later, and drugs had really gotten to them.

"I just feel fortunate that I have the longevity, the sense not to destroy everything. You can't lose your humanity. Life is tough enough, we've all got skeletons in the closet, and we've all got hopes and dreams. This *business* is so tough—and the business of the business. It can really fuck you up, the insecurity. I coined this phrase years and years ago, and I've heard other people use it that know me: 'Hollywood makes you forget about everything, but yourself.' And that's not the most important thing. It's not more important than family and friends. And if you're so blessed that you get paid do something you love, and you get to do it— I feel really fortunate to have done that."

English director Michael (***Death Wish***) Winner's ***The Stone Killer*** (1973) was Paul's first encounter with superstar Charles Bronson. "I remember that wasn't a pleasant experience. I always try to make my work experience pleasant. I try to have fun. I try to be a professional. I get there early, and I leave late. I love to mingle with the crew. I even like to help out, to pull a cable or give a hand. I have that attitude for film and television. It was just [a clash of] personalities, again. Michael Winner was the director of that movie. I sat down in somebody's chair, and it was his chair and he kicked me out of it. Not that it's a big deal, but it's the WAY he acted.

"I saw something Bronson did that I thought was really despicable. Bronson doesn't like people, yet he sits in the middle of downtown intersections in his chair for everybody to see. And, then, people come and bother him, and he tells them to fuck off. Apparently, there had been an elderly lady that was driving by, and she wanted to know what all the hubbub was about, because they had traffic controlled. And they said, 'Oh, it's a Charles Bronson movie.' So, she went home to change and get her autograph book, because he was her favorite actor. She brought her camera with her, too. He told her to fuck off when she asked for his autograph. She was so shocked that she just took a picture of him, right there, while he was there, when she was leaving. He had the cops take the camera from her, take the film out, and give her the camera back. That wasn't nice. I'm just concerned about when the camera's rolling, but these things affect you when you've seen these guys all your life that you work with, like I've seen Bronson. And I've always respected his work. So, you go on and say, 'Hey, you respect the guy's talent, but that doesn't mean you necessarily have to like him.'"

Amazingly, Paul made two more films with Bronson, the first of which was ***Mr. Majestyk*** (1974), based on an Elmore Leonard novel. It was directed by one of the last of the old guard Hollywood storytellers, Richard Fleischer. "Oh, he was the greatest. He and Robert Ryan were kind of in the same vein, as far as taking you under their wing and going out of their way to make you feel comfortable in these movies and doing things for you. Like Fleischer let me live at the end of the movie, because I was supposed to die. He said, 'There's so many guys getting blown away, this is ludicrous. Let's see if we can work out the ending, because I want you to live.' At the end of the movie, we're in this hunting lodge. He said, 'Charley, you know what? Everybody's dying here, and I think Koslo's character is so funny, maybe we can build on this and we'll let him live. Let's see if we can work the end of this out now. He's not going to be dying.' And Bronson says, [Paul beautifully imitates Bronson] 'What, are you crazy? I'm not here to make a star out of Paul Koslo. I'll be in my dressing room.' And Richard says, 'Charley, I need you to work this out. He's going to be in the scene with you.' He says, 'YOU work it out. When you're finished, you call me.'

"Richard came right over and said, 'Paul, I apologize for Charley. I'm sorry he's put you in the middle of this.' I said, 'No, it's all right. I feel really, really honored that you're doing this, because it's really great for me.' It was a wonderful compliment. [Fleischer] was a big-time guy. But he was a little tiny guy; he was probably about five foot-three or -four and he weighed like ninety pounds. He was so fragile, but he was so wonderful and intelligent and wise and witty and so gracious. I was on his side, obviously.

"So, then, we worked this thing out and the a.d. [assistant director] got Charley back out. Richard said, 'Charley, this is the way we've worked it out. . .' Bronson cut in. 'I don't care. Let him do whatever he wants. I'll take care of him,' just like that. When he said, 'I'll take care of him,' I thought, 'What the fuck does that mean?' He says, 'What are you gonna be doin'? You gonna be comin' runnin' through that door?' 'Yeah, I'm gonna be coming. Al Lettieri's inside and the scene now is he's gonna tell me to go out under gunpoint, so that he can draw you out, trying to get me.' I said that to Charley. He says, 'Okay, you come out and I'll take care of you. Just do what would come naturally.' Al Lettieri gives me the sign, and says, 'Get out! Get out or I'll blow your brains out!' or whatever his line is. I come through that screen door and I'm GONE! I'm like two hundred yards into the forest! [laughs] Charley didn't have time to react or do anything. There was a horse hitch rail in front of the lodge, which was like three feet high, so I just jumped over it and kept running.

"Charley says, 'Hey, you think that's funny?' I said, 'You told me to do what comes natural. Sorry.' 'You come SLOW next time, and do what comes natural.' So, he's hiding behind the door, he's got this shotgun, and I come out slow this time and the shotgun was just staring me in the face, so I just grabbed it out of his hands and got the drop on Charley. He said, 'You do that again, you'll be sorry you ever saw me.' I thought, 'Wow, man.'

"Again, Richard said, 'Charley, we've got to work this out with you.' I said, 'When I do this, I come out the door, then I turn right, because you're behind the door, and you get the drop on me.' I kind of had to [to placate Bronson]. He says, 'Oh, okay.' So that's what we did. I went out and kind of crouched behind the horse rail and he got the drop on me, and we took it from there. It was really a bad experience. That night, I went and partied with all my buddies, all the other guys, you know: Al Lettieri, Taylor Lacher, and Lee Purcell. They were all talking about it, you know. When you come into this motel, there's the registration desk, it's right there. To the left are the dining room and bar, and to the right are the rooms. And you go down a long, long way—I don't know, a city block. And Charley had the first eight rooms off the lobby, because he had a big entourage. Then, you go past that and turn to the left and it's got about a two-block row of rooms. And I'm down in the last room, like two-hundred-and-fifty feet from the lobby. That next morning, I'm going back to the lobby. I wasn't working until the afternoon—it was just night shooting or something. And Charley's coming towards me, and I noticed one of his room doors was open. I noticed Jill Ireland in there, like crocheting or knitting or something. I go past Charley and we pass each other. And I hear, 'Hey, you!' That's how he always called me, or anybody. He doesn't say, 'Hey, Bill,' or whatever; he says, 'Hey, you!' I stopped, and I turned around, and I looked at him like, 'Are you talkin' to me?' I did one of those, and I'm the only guy there. So, he says, 'Yeah, you. You're the trouble-maker. I hear your voice every night, screamin', yellin', keepin' me up and keepin' my family up.' And, all of a sudden, we hear, 'Hey, Charley—who're you talking to?' It was Jill Ireland—she heard us in her room there. He says, 'It's that Paul Koslo guy. He's one of them.' Oh, man. I didn't say anything. I just turned around and I walked away. He couldn't have heard me, because my room was so far away.

"At the end, when we were moving to the next city, to Canyon City, Colorado, we were all paying our bills. We were in that lobby area and it had stairs going back upstairs. So some people were sitting on the stairs, waiting to pay their bills. There was Charley, right there on the stairs. People had to go around him. He just sat there, big as life. I got to pay my bill, and he says, 'Hey, you.' I turn around and it's Charley sitting there. 'C'mere.' He pushed somebody aside and said, 'Siddown.' And I felt like an idiot because everybody's watching us, because everybody hates his guts! He says, 'My wife thinks I should apologize to you. I don't apologize to nobody. Next to me, you're the best actor in this movie.' I said, 'Don't count on it, Charley,' and I just got up and walked away. Then he asked me for his next movie after that! That was a really weird relationship.

"Al Lettieri was the real Mr. Majestic on *Mr. Majestyk*. He was great. This is a true story. We were outside of—I think it was Canyon City. It could have been another city we were at. We were in this cornfield. There was nothing but corn for miles around and this gravel road. Lettieri was like seven days late because he was doing a film in London, so they were shooting around him. We'd just had lunch. It was just some of the crew and some of the actors standing around and stuff. Charley's off by himself, pouting somewhere down the road. We look down the road and see this cloud coming towards us. And it gets bigger and bigger, until it's just a few feet away and we realize it's a big, super-stretch limo. And it pulls up, the driver gets out, he opens the backdoor, and two young, little chicks come out, you know, like twenty, twenty-two years old. And out comes Al

Lettieri, this warthog of a guy. This guy's from Sicily, you know: the original *Godfather*-type guy. He says, 'Hey, where's the honey wagons?' [Note: a "honey wagon" is a long trailer with bathrooms for the cast and crew and cubicles for the actors. It's called a honey wagon because it's always surrounded by flies.—JH] Somebody pointed them out. 'The actors—they're around?' Somebody said, 'Yeah.' [Lettieri said] 'All right, girls, do the honey wagons first!' He'd brought these two girls to blow everybody in the honey wagons! [laughs] We thought this was great.

"He says, 'Hey, is that Charley over there?' We said, 'Yeah.' You know, *Mr. Majestyk* is about a melon-grower. This is unbelievable. If I had a picture of this, I would have made a billion dollars. Here, this little warthog of a guy, short guy—not any taller than Bronson, but twice as wide—Lettieri, says, 'That's him over there?' We said, 'Yeah.' He walks up to Bronson, right next to him, and he puts his arm around him, his shoulder, and grabs him by his right arm. And he squeezes him to his right side, and he lifts him right off the ground! He turns around and he's walking past us, singing [to the tune of "Melancholy Baby"] 'Don't you be by MELON-CHARLEY baaaaaaaaby!' He carries him like this— Bronson's feet are of the ground—and Bronson didn't know what to do, because he had this death grip on him—it was like a vice. And he walked him down this road, past the limo, about two blocks, carrying him like this. To this day, nobody knows what they talked about." Richard Fleischer recalled Lettieri having severe drinking and drug problems on the set. In his autobiography, Fleischer also described how Bronson so incensed the crew, they were prepared to quit on the very first day of shooting.

"There were lots of stories on that one," says Paul, "about Bronson being belligerent to the hosts of this big dude ranch they were staying at. The food was incredible, and Bronson would send his driver off for some bologna and white bread and say, 'It's because me and my wife can't eat this shit,' the food which they were serving, which was incredible food. Stuff like that. But the guy was a gigantic star. What are you gonna do? Just chalk it off to oddity, to personality, I don't know. You just do the best you can. Richard Fleischer made it all worthwhile."

In the follow-up to *True Grit* (1969), *Rooster Cogburn* (1975), Paul acted in support to acting royalty: John Wayne, in the title role, and Katharine Hepburn. "Ah, the Duke. Yeah. [laughs] Again, that was one of the highlights, when I think about some of my movies, I think about him and Katharine Hepburn. He had some sort of a lunch that he set up for everybody, for the crew and for the actors to all get acquainted with him and Katharine Hepburn. And he says to me, [Imitating Wayne] 'What part 'ya playin', kid?' My character's name was Luke, so I said, 'I'm playing Luke the Duke.' And he says, 'No, you're not—you're playin' Luke the Puke. There's only one Duke around here!' I said [obsequiously] 'Yes, sir! Yes, sir! You're absolutely right!' That night, back at the hotel, some of his grandkids were playing guitar and I had my guitar. He came over and said, 'Anybody my grandkids like can't be all bad,' and he shook my hand and sort of made me feel at ease.

"He was a great man. He WAS bigger than life. He was a living legend, more so than Clint Eastwood. I mean, I was impressed by Clint, because he was a big star, but he wasn't a legend. When you were in the Duke's presence, you couldn't take your eyes off of him. I don't know how to compare anybody to him, as far as formidable legends go.

"If you were screwing up, like if you hadn't done your homework, he'd come down on you hard—real hard. But if he saw that you were working, that you were lending a hand, then he wanted to have a beer with you—he was like a regular guy. He was always making jokes and stuff.

"That's one of the highlights of my career, working with that guy and Katharine Hepburn. She's another one—she's the flip-side of that legend. For all the macho things he'd do, she'd do macho female things. Like, she'd ride on the tailgate of a pickup truck, bouncing around, messing with the kids, whatever. Of course [producer] Hal Wallis was having a heart attack." *Cogburn* was Wallis' last credit.

"There was a running competition between the two of them [Wayne and Hepburn]. It was really just great. You felt really secure being part of that. I felt like I was blessed, like I was chosen or something. I felt really comfortable being in it. We had Anthony Zerbe in that movie, and Richard Jordan. All the outlaws were a bunch of reprobates from Hollywood. There wasn't a class distinction or anything like that, working with these big stars, these legends. We were not as close as the Robert Ryan thing, but it was a pleasant and a pleasurable experience, and you felt like you were one of the team instead of just another actor on the job."

Reprising his role in the detective thriller, *Harper* (1966), Paul Newman starred in *The Drowning Pool* (1976). Paul also appeared. "[laughs] Paul Newman. He and I—man, it looked like we were gonna go into fisticuffs, right at the beginning. We were in Louisiana, and we were in a swamp hovercraft going through the swamp. They had a pilot that steers and runs it, and then behind him was this little seat that would barely fit two guys in it. So, [Newman] always kept pushing me off of it, he kept crowding me. I didn't know why, but it got to be really old pretty quick. On the third day, the hovercraft was next to the wharf. We're on the water. Then, all of a sudden, he goes to push me in the water. And at the last second, I grabbed the seat of the hovercraft and I grabbed him. And I got to push him, and he's gonna go in, but at the last minute, I just pulled him back inside. And he saw that I wasn't going to take any shit from him, that I'd prevented him and myself from going into the drink. After that, I could do no wrong with him.

"He used to drink these little cans of Coors, they were only about eight ounces or maybe six, and he had those specially made for him. The Coors Company made those especially for him. He would give me a couple of six packs every few days of his special brew. He'd let me use his phone, his little cell phone. In those days, they were like batteries, where the phone was clipped on top."

The Drowning Pool co-starred another budding '70s talent, Andy (*Dirty Harry*) Robinson: "He's great. I've known Andy since then. He does a lot of theater, all the time. He's a very dynamic actor—very gifted. [He's] like a lot of good actors: they start in the theater, and that's where they go back to. You've got to build your craft. It's a whole different animal, acting in front of a camera, or in front of a live audience."

Paul's next film for Stuart Rosenberg was *Voyage of the Damned* (1976), an all-star, epic tragedy, based on Gordon Thomas and Max Gordon Witt's best-seller. It chronicled the epic tragedy of a luxury liner with nearly 1,000 German Jews aboard, seeking refuge wherever it could be found, only to be shipped back home to their doom. Paul and Jonathan Pryce played brothers, both concentration camp survivors. "Like I said, I feel very, very privileged to have worked with these people in some of these movies because they'll never make movies like that anymore. The only thing, maybe, I wish I could have been part of were some of these big [movie] experiences...of the *Star Wars* trilogy, for instance. But I feel this way about some of these movies that I've done, and certainly *Voyage of the Damned* is one of those movies.

"First of all, we got to travel a lot in Europe. We actually shot this thing on a big, pop-rivet, old 1933 ocean liner. I don't know how you could get another cast like that. You were with giants. Royalty. I was on that movie for about three months. It was another experience like *Heaven's Gate*: big, big cast, incredible talent. And it's an experience, a part of your life that you'll never forget. And it's not a thing that you think about consciously, but, once in a while, you'll cross its path somewhere. I still know people from those movies. I keep in touch with them—there were a couple of people that didn't have big parts that you'd probably remember: Georgina Hale—she's an English actress—and Jonathan Pryce. We played brothers in that movie. It was great. we really got along great. Since we were both [playing] Jews with the shaved heads, we got really close.

"Faye Dunaway was not my type of person. She's just too much. The only other guy who was like that on that film was Oskar Werner, who was always my hero. *Jules and Jim* is one of my favorite movies. Werner was a fucking drunk. He was so drunk, he couldn't work.

"They would have to try and dry him out to sober him up. It took like six or seven hours, so he could only work at like the end of the day, because he was too fucked-up. And, then, he had a nasty streak when he drank, and he always drank, so I never knew what he was like any other way. And I did spend time with him to try and get inside his head, and see why he was like that. We went to a concert, a classical violin concert at St. Paul's Cathedral in London. But he had a mean streak in him. When I heard he was in that movie, it just made my whole year. And when I met him, it was just frightening.

"But, that having been said, working with those people was working with royalty. They're the old guard, and they're legends." The young actor was stunned to be in the company of "acting royalty" like James Mason, Max Von Sydow, Julie

Harris, Luther Adler, "and Dame Wendy Hiller, who really WAS royalty." Reflecting back on them, Paul thinks of them as "all great, great pillars of inspiration."

The aged, obese Orson Welles was also an outstanding member of the cast. "We never got that close to him, because he was in a different location of the film. We shot in Barcelona, and we shot on different locations, although we were in the same city and stayed at the same hotel. We did kind of chum with him a couple of times. One was he was going to go out to eat and he wanted us to join him. We were going to go out sightseeing, Jonathan Pryce and some of the younger members of the cast and stuff. When we ran into him, he had this cake, the size of a birthday cake: I swear it was about four or five inches high and about a foot across. So, we thought, 'Oh, good: we're gonna have some cake with him.' And he says, 'Are you going to order anything?' He was totally serious. He had two valets with him, because he was so big, he had to have help sitting up off of a chair, to put his shoes on, to sit down on a chair. Of course, we were like in the presence of the Pope or something. And he made you feel that way. He had that power. Then we decided to go sightseeing. We said we'd be back and eat with him. We came back about an hour-and-a-half later, and he was still sitting there with those two guys. And he had one piece of cake left, and he was working on that! We didn't have the guts to go back in, [laughs] because we knew we wouldn't be getting any of his cake. We ate something, anyway, when we were gone. But he'd give me a cigar every once in a while. I did four films with Stuart Rosenberg. He was a big cigar fan, too. Because Stuart gave me some, Orson kind of took me under his wing when it came time for a cigar.

"It was really a great experience, although it was hard for me, because Jonathan Pryce, although I was skinny and lanky, he was a little skinnier than me. I had made a plan to go on fasts, which I did. By the time I got to Barcelona, I had already been fasting eight days. And I went on a sixteen-day fast, believe it or not. And, then, because it was such a long shot, I would fast for five, six, seven, eight days, depending. We were shooting for almost four months, so I was down from like 160 to about 137 pounds. I kind of hurt myself, kind of overdid it. I would actually astral project myself out of my body and see the silver cord. I was seeing my spirit leaving my body through a silver cord, and I'd be looking down at the Earth. It probably sounds crazy to you, but it happened to me about three, four times."

Michael Cimino's lavish western **Heaven's Gate** (1980) was an infamous box-office flop, rivaled, at the time, only by the likes of **Howard the Duck** (1986). The film is much better than its reputation would lead viewers to expect, and flopped mainly because of Cimino's disregard for any kind of budgetary considerations. "That was another of those things where we had, I think, like seventy-some principal actors. Big actors. That was a great experience, except that the director was a little weird. After like the first nine days of work, he had twelve hundred extras every day for six months. Twelve hundred extras a day, being made-up? Can you imagine? Then, it got to the point, after the first week-and-a-half, [that] the twelve hundred extras would say [in mocking sing-song] 'Good morning, Mr. Cimino.'" As the film neared its close, Kris Kristofferson's stand-in decked Cimino, breaking the director's nose.

"I did a scene with Kristofferson, where they had eight cameras rolling at once for fifty-eight takes, every camera, every time. They shot over a million-and-a-half feet of film on that movie. You could make, literally, fifty films from just the footage that got shot. That's unbelievable. I know that England loved that movie, for some reason. It was a big hit in England. It's still playing in first-run art houses there.

"I played the mayor of the German town. I wore this big raccoon coat all the time. I had a little daughter and a wife. One of the other women immigrants, who was having problems in her family life, finally blew my brains out towards the end of the movie. There were so many parts in the movie, so many principal actors in it. I've never seen *Heaven's Gate*. That's another thing: other than some stuff I've seen lately because my wife's got it, I would say, I haven't seen eighty percent of my work."

Screen fantasist Stuart Gordon (*Re-Animator*) helmed *Robotjox* (1987), about an Olympian bout between massive, robotic American and Soviet gladiators. "We did that in Rome, with Anne-Marie Johnson. That was a good experience because I hadn't done too much sci-fi, and I have, since then. He [Stuart Gordon] is a very, very gifted guy, very nice guy. He's the co-author of *Bleacher Bums*, which is a play that's played in Chicago for almost thirty years now. He's a very good writer and a very talented director.

"You know, a lot of directors, they've got their minds made up about what they want. But Stuart allows the actors a lot of time. He'll give you a lot of leeway to bring something to the table. That's rare in directors. Starrett would let you do that, Stuart Rosenberg, too. Not all directors will let you do that; maybe two out of ten. And that's good, because you could see his roots from the theater.

"He has more of a theatrical process, where you rehearse a lot more before you actually shoot. We actually rehearsed for about a week before we shot. We would go to the sets and they would have it taped out, where the things would be, and would have different props for us. And we'd know where we were going, and what we were doing. We'd actually build up some relationships between the characters, which is so rare nowadays, which you hardly ever hear of. That's really great."

The all-star Japanese science fiction film, *Solar Crisis*, was the last of a long string of movies Paul was in that were directed by Richard Sarafian, who had his name removed from the finished feature. "I did another movie with Heston in '91. So, we rekindled whatever relationship we had before then. You know I'm Canadian, right? And I had a marijuana arrest in 1968, for possession of marijuana—it was like a long roach, about half a joint. And that came back to haunt me four years ago. Can you imagine: They tried to deport me. So,

Charlton wrote a letter. I've paid millions of dollars to the American government, and I've got every tax return since 1967. They treated me with carte blanche. When that immigration thing happened, he wrote a great letter for me to the government. As it turned out, a lot of people stepped up to bat for me, people that I've worked with in the industry, people that are really high profile. But I didn't need it: they let me go on my own merits. It was like a computer [error] thing. I'd been coming and going, back and forth, hundreds of times. They must have checked on me all the way back in Washington. I couldn't believe it. All over a roach. That just goes to show you the power of the government, and where your name might be, you know what I mean? It was a horrifying experience. We got through it, though. It's just too bad that everybody sorta had to suffer."

Desert Heat (1997) brought Paul back to the kinds of action movie roles he had done to such perfection in the '70s. Paul had come all the way from working with John Wayne and Robert Ryan, to Jean-Claude Van Damme. "I'd heard all these things about him [Van Damme]: that he was difficult, that he threw tantrums. I didn't have any problem with him, he was really nice to me. Really nice to everybody, actually. I really got respect for the guy on this job that I did with him because he was really concerned about his product. Even though it's hard to understand him sometimes—he speaks with an accent—he really went out of his way to try and be clear and lucid, because he was one of the producers. He took his time, so that different gags with the stunt guys would work, or so that pieces of comedy would work well. That was really nice to see. A lot of guys will let the stunt guys work things out with actors; they'll use their double. But he did it himself, which was really nice. Most of the time, guys will shoot the back of somebody's head, and it [blatantly] looks like someone else. I think it's the best job he's ever done acting.

"*Desert Heat* has been the number nine most-rented video these last six months. I can tell, too, because they sent me two healthy checks. Which is weird, because I've done so many other movies, recent movies that I've done, that I've gotten a piece of the action on video sales, and I've never gotten the kind of money that I've gotten off of this. So, it's gotta be doing good."

Like his late father, Koslo has asthma, which forced him to quit his recreational running, "although I'm busy doing stuff all the time," he says. "I had a farm; I had horses for years and years. Just got rid of the horses—too much work. I stay pretty active." Koslo was in the midst of directing a play, *Stamped*, starring James Gammon and Margaret Blye, when this interview was conducted. "Directing is a very strenuous thing. You have to keep your mind and body sharp. It's like 24/7—you wake up thinkin' about it, then you think about it all day. Then, when you're drivin' home—I live about ninety miles out of LA—you spend a great deal of time thinkin' about it."

Like many of his fellow actors, Paul is untroubled by nostalgia about his career. "I had a poster for *The Losers*. I don't know what happened to it. It's probably down in the barn, all rotted away, probably full of peacock dung. I had

The Losers.

one to *The Omega Man*, too [the artwork features Koslo, on his bike in the movie.] But, you know what the problem was? Until I got married, I never did have an eight-by-ten of me, all these years. Until the last two or three years, when my wife diligently and lovingly got my stuff together.

"She didn't know who I was. She's an actress, she's done two hundred plays, but she'd never heard of me. Then, we met at the theater, and I produced her show and stuff, and she started to find out. I didn't tell her I was an actor or anything, and she started finding out more and more about me. Curiosity got the best of her, and she started doing research. Now, I guess she's got about half of my films [on video]."

The movie industry that even a relatively young actor like Paul knew two or three decades ago has soured badly. "I don't know, man. For me, it's gotten to be looking across at the other side to a bunch of business people. I'm still doing a few good independents. I'll do like a couple or three films a year, and a couple of television shows, although I'm not pushing my career and I'm really entrenched in directing and producing in the theater. My love is still acting and directing— they run hand-in-hand. But, as far as the [movie] business, the business has really gotten shitty now. It's gotten terrible. Our union is terrible. It's all money, man, IT'S ALL MONEY.

"There's no representation, nobody really stands up for the actors. The producers are making all the money. The creative process has gone to accountants and lawyers and agents. It's all about marketing: where the market is and what they can do with it. And the guys like me, the character actors, who were there in the past, like the '70s and '80s, are still around in the '90s and working—we're

not making the money we used to
make. Because they're going to the
Jim Carreys.

"And the guys like Ed Harris,
who's been my theater partner for
five years, they're making money, but
they're not making the money they
used to, either. The money that's
there basically goes to the star, and
that's it. No matter where you are,
unless you're a Carrey or a gigantic
superstar, like a Gibson or a
Schwarzenegger, you're not going to
get any money.

"And it's a youth-oriented market,
so people that are getting older now,
that are in their forties and fifties,
never mind sixties and seventies: that
window closes drastically, especially
for actresses. And I hear it from everybody: people are making nothing. We're
doing better with independents, because they think we've got some kind of cash
value, as far as recognizability and stuff. So if you were getting twenty to fifty
grand a week from the majors, you can still get that in an independent. But you
won't be getting that in a Schwarzenegger movie. You'll be getting ten or fifteen.
There are twenty thousand guys in that same demographic that'll do it for the
same price. That's why so many people are doing their own movies."

THE FILMS OF PAUL KOSLO

1967	*Crime and Punishment* (Canadian tvm)
	Dylan Thomas: A Portrait
1970	*The Zodiac Killers* (aka: *Flux, Maniac*)
	The Losers
1971	*Scandalous John*
	The Omega Man
	Vanishing Point
	(Escape of) The Birdmen (ABC tvm)
1972	*Welcome Home, Soldier Boys*
	Joe Kidd
	The Daughters of Joshua Cabe (ABC tvm)
1973	*The Lolly Madonna War* (aka: *Lolly Madonna XXX*)
	Cleopatra Jones

1973 (cont.)	*The Stone Killer*
1974	*The Laughing Policeman* *Freebie and the Bean* *Bootleggers* *Mr. Majestyk*
1975	*Rooster Cogburn*
1976	*The Drowning Pool* *Voyage of the Damned* *Scott Free* (NBC tvm)
1977	*Maniac!* (aka: *Assault on Paradise, Tomorrow Never Comes*)
1978	*Love and Bullets* *Down Home* (tv pilot)
1979	*Roots II: The Next Generation* (ABC mini-series) *The Sacketts* (NBC mini-series)
1980	*Heaven's Gate* *Rape and Marriage: The Rideout Case* (CBS tvm)
1981	*Inmates, A Love Story* (ABC tvm)
1983	*The Gambler Part II–The Adventure Continues*
1984	*Hambone and Hillie* *The Glitter Dome*
1985	*The Annihilators*
1987	*Robotjox* *Caribe*
1988	*A Night in the Life of Jimmy Reardon*
1990	*Loose Cannons* *Solar Crisis* *Xtro II* *The Peace Officer*
1991	*Conagher*
1992	*Project Shadowchaser* *Drive Like Lightning* (tvm)
1993	*Chained Heat II*
1996	*Downdraft*
1997	*Judge and Jury*
1999	*Desert Heat*
2002	*Y. M. I.*

Supposedly, *The Losers* was also released as *'Nam's Angels*. This has not been verified.

TELEVISION

Some of Paul's many television appearances were on: *Mission: Impossible, Cannon, Ironside, Gunsmoke, Hawaii 5-0, Dallas, CHiPs, The Rockford Files, The Incredible Hulk, Battlestar Galactica, Buck Rogers, Knight Rider, The Hitchhiker, The Flash,* and *Walker, Texas Ranger.*

He was also a regular on *The Outsiders.*

Shock Cinema Magazine also ran an interview with Paul.

MARC LAWRENCE

"What else? Long fucking interview, kid. A lot of shit you're gonna write. Who reads this shit?!"

In 1938, Ed Sullivan wrote:

"In 18 years of reporting, I met quite a lot of gangsters, quite a few of whom were exploded out of circulation. The screen has attempted to portray gangsters, and some [sic] experts as Edward G. Robinson, Clark Gable, James Cagney, and Humphrey Bogart have gone to their make-up boxes to dig out a resemblance. None of them, from a mobster standpoint, has been successful. The only screen gangster who actually could pass in the mobster assembly is Marc Lawrence in *I am the Law*. In fact, he is so close to the real thing that you can wonder how he got hired."

In spite of such effusive praise, Marc Lawrence has trouble understanding how anyone could ever think of him as an outstanding character actor. "I have no sense of evaluation there," he confessed. To him, acting is merely a job.

During the interview that follows, he tended more towards somberly recriminating himself: "If I knew what the mask meant to me, to other people, I would have held onto the mask," he said, of his famous face. "Because after this fuckin' [HUAC] investigation, I hated myself so much, I wanted to change my face. So I had my scars removed, I had my nose lifted, cut some of my nose off, I had my eyes tightened up. It's like if you take Jack Palance. You see those high cheekbones? If you took those high cheekbones away, he wouldn't have been Jack

Palance. So I did the same thing to my face, like a fuckin' idiot. I hated myself so much that I wanted to change my face. So that's interesting?" he growled.

Perhaps the best way to really introduce Lawrence is with a tangential anecdote. The actor who played Lawrence's fellow heavy in *Foul Play* (1978), William Frankfather, did the last acting of his career on-stage at the University of Virginia, starring in a production of *King Lear*. After a performance, I went up and introduced myself, and mentioned that I was acquainted with Lawrence. Astonished, Frankfather replied, "He's still alive?" His wife asked who we were talking about, and Frankfather told her, "Remember, in *Foul Play*...The face?" and gesticulated towards his face. Her memories of Lawrence—pockmarks, glowering eyes, and all—swelled back immediately. "Oh! *THE FACE!*" she burst out.

Marc Lawrence's face is *instantly* recognizable. Gaunt and sharp-featured, Lawrence was perenially typed as gangsters and assorted other villains. And, as *The Illustrated Who's Who of the Cinema* put it, he has gotten "even more sinister with age." That is a matter of opinion. As many thugs as he has played, Lawrence can be disarming as hell. He referred to this interviewer, on a number of occasions, as "bubbie."

His gentle side notwithstanding, it seemed like we couldn't go fifteen minutes during this interview without Lawrence reminding me that I was "a fucking nut." Only afterwards did he reveal his vast sweetness. And he also has tremendous comic potential that remains virtually untapped to this day. During the interview, he mentioned that he was about to appear on an episode of *E.R.* "I play a dying old man," he said. "The story of my life."

This interview was quite a toboggan ride. At one point, he gave me a little quiz in interviewing: "Get me to the fuckin' point! What's the most leading question, which I'll never answer? Why have I lived this long? Who the fuck knows? What's the secret of being alive?" There followed a dramatic pause: "BREATHING," he barked back at me, and then laughed hysterically.

Marc Lawrence has gotten to the wonderful stage in life that some lucky older people reach, where he is ready and willing to tell you his unvarnished opinions about *anything*. Will he work less because of it? Will his comments push someone to kill him? What does he have to lose? He is a master of letting his mouth run amok. Some of his finest comments are unprintable. **For the faint of heart or easily-offended, I recommend skipping this interview.**

Astonishingly, Lawrence has appeared in well over one hundred movies in the last seventy years. He has acted in support to almost every major actor, during that colossal span of time, from John Gilbert to Kevin Spacey. His extraordinary life's-worth of anecdotes became the basis for his grueling autobiography, *Long Time No See*. For example, Lawrence recalls how he and Richard Burton used to be drinking buddies. The two related well, because they had both been left pockmarked from childhood illnesses. Understandably, Lawrence seems to have always regretted the time that he told Burton that he didn't think he was much of an actor: Burton held back too much, he said. On another occasion, Lawrence was decked by one of the Epstein brothers, the screenwriters of *Casablanca,* because he thought Lawrence was fooling around with his wife. *Long Time No See* comes highly recommended, if it can be found.

During the '30s and '40s, Marc Lawrence established himself as one of the cinema's preeminent gangsters. In Italy, over lunch, dead-eyed "Lucky" Luciano told Lawrence what a convincing job he was doing playing "us." The actor also worked-out at the same gym as "Bugsy" Siegel. One day during the '40s, Lawrence jovially mentioned to Siegel that he was playing a character named Slugsy Biegel in his newest movie. The next day, his character's name had been changed. Besides containing many fascinating recollections of his fellow actors, directors, and other co-workers, Lawrence's book stands as one of the most un-self-serving actors' autobiographies since his co-star and friend Edward G. Robinson's *All My Yesterdays*.

Lawrence began his movie acting career in 1932, as a convict in the "Death Cell" episode of *If I Had a Million* starring Gene Raymond and directed by James Cruze. Some of his other early roles were in *White Woman* (1933), starring Charles Laughton and Carole Lombard; *G-Men* (1935), starring James Cagney; and *Dr. Socrates* (also '35), with Paul Muni, the first of at least six times that Lawrence was cast as characters named "Lefty." He worked on several films each with directors Henry Hathaway, John Huston, and William Wellman. Lawrence bears a strange resemblance to Boris Karloff, which was partially the reason he was cast in *Penitentiary* (1938), in the role Karloff had originated in the film it was a remake of, Howard Hawks' *The Criminal Code* (1932). Lawrence also acted opposite Karloff in Cecil B. DeMille's *Unconquered* (1947), in which the two were, respectively, unlikely Jewish and British American Indians.

He made recurring appearances in two extremely popular movie series, the Charlie Chan and James Bond films. In *Diamonds Are Forever* (1971), he had a memorable role as one of the many crooks after the titular diamonds. The eyes of the gangster he plays in *Diamonds* have the same deadness that Lawrence often adopted on-screen, the same kind of mordant stare that "Lucky" Luciano had given him.

In *The Man With the Golden Gun* (1974), he played Rodney, a hit man shipped in to Christopher Lee's private island for a deadly pistol duel. Lee told Lawrence that he had the funniest line in the picture. It comes when Lawrence prowls through Lee's lair, and a mechanized wax figure of Al Capone suddenly springs to life, firing a prop tommy gun. Lawrence shoots the dummy. As he realizes "who" he has just shot, he humbly repents. "Big Al," he says. "Wherever you are: I'm sorry!" In *Marathon Man* (1976), he plays one of Laurence Olivier's murderous thugs, and straps in Dustin Hoffman for the infamous "Is it safe?" scene.

During Senator Joe McCarthy's House Committee on Un-American Activities witch hunts, Lawrence was pressured into testifying about some Communist

Lawrence and Olivier in *Marathon Man*.

party meetings that he had attended. Under extreme duress, he bought himself years of misery by naming the names of several other actors, writers, and directors whom he had noticed attending the meetings. From the unsparing descriptions he has given elsewhere of the McCarthy hearings, the period that came in their wake was easily the worst of his life. Not only did the actors whom he had "fingered" find themselves blacklisted, he was, too. Lawrence would not work again in Hollywood for over a decade.

He went through a state of such profound shock and sadness that he was committed to a sanatorium briefly, and was nearly given shock treatment by an overzealous doctor. With the help of actor George (*Air Force*) Tobias, he escaped the deranged quack's ministrations.

He relocated his family to Italy for many years, where he worked regularly as an actor and directed his first film, ***Nightmare in the Sun*** (1964). I purposefully avoid bringing up his involvement in the McCarthy trials during the interview, not only because of its depressing connotations for him, but also because the rest of his career was so much more interesting. For a full account of this major chapter in his life, refer to Lawrence's autobiography. On that note, let it be said that, as long as this interview is, it scarcely scratches the surface of Lawrence's astounding career.

Amazingly enough, in his nineties, Lawrence is still more active than most actors of half his years. He was in the Disney musical, ***Newsies*** (1991), and also had minor roles in two of director Robert (*El Mariachi*) Rodriguez's movies, playing the bellman Tim Roth replaced in ***Four Rooms*** (1995), and a surly motel clerk in ***From Dusk Till Dawn*** (1996). More recently, he was featured in a scene with Arnold Schwarzenegger in the forgettable, mega-budget ***End of Days*** (1999), and was also in the somber drama, ***The Shipping News*** (2002). His latest theatrical film to date was Joe Dante's ***Looney Tunes: Back in Action*** (2003), as Steve Martin's father, a member of the board of the Acme Corporation of Warner Brothers' cartoon fame. Like most of the people who suffered through Martin's dismal performance, Lawrence was appalled: "He has no *humor*," he opines.

Lawrence's final word on the acting profession: "*Everybody's* a good actor, kid! If you can pay the bills, then you're a good actor!" Lawrence died on November 27, 2005.

In 1997, Lee Server did a very fine interview with Lawrence for *Film Comment*, entitled "The Last Gangster." Mort Drucker's expert caricature of Lawrence is seen throughout *Mad* Magazine's illustrated parody of *Marathon Man*. Lawrence was rightfully angered by ABC's *The Century* documentary miniseries. ABC interviewed him about the HUAC trials, and entirely against Lawrence's wishes, fell back on the cheap journalist's trick of using some footage that they had of him crying. That series is available on video.

Marc Lawrence was born Max Goldsmith: "My father's name was Israel Goldsmith. That's my name, Goldsmith. My mother's name was Minnie Sugarman. She was born in Poland; my father was born in Russia. I was born in the Bronx, December 17, 1909. Glad I got that right.

"I don't remember my childhood. All I remember is [I was] a frightened little kid, Jewish kid. Scared to death. There was an explosion in New Jersey, I was thrown out of bed—I was about three, four years old. Then I was held, pushed, marched to the middle of a field with my parents. There's an explosion in the town, of an ammunition factory. We saw all of the flames and the noise and explosions, and it was a frightening experience. All right, that was it. [laughs]

"When I was a young kid, about eleven years old, I remember sleeping in a graveyard for horses, something like that. And I caught the St. Vitus' Dance, which turned out to be rheumatic fever. And since I was thirteen, I've had rheumatic fever. Consequently, that became the 'Gangster Me.' The gangster psychology was born then, 'cause with a bad heart, nobody will hurt you. My brother used to whack me every now and then, when nobody was looking [laughs].

The actor never served in the armed forces: "No, I couldn't. I had a bad heart."

The first stirring of interest in acting Lawrence felt came from seeing his brother, Jay Goldsmith, act. "And my uncle [Jechial Goldsmith], he was a star in the Yiddish theater," Lawrence vividly recalls. "My father's brother. And my brother was acting in this other show. He was very good. And I kind of envied him. He was a much better actor than I was. He became my stand-in, later on, because he became a plumber, he didn't become an actor. It was a pity, because he had a lot of talent.

"I don't think I was very much of an actor. I envy a lot of actors. That's the story of my life: envy. I guess a lot of actors have this. 'You're doing something I wish I could do as good. How do you do that, eh? I'd like to try that. Why not?' Want to do everything else that somebody else does. It's a childish pursuit. That's what makes you act.

"I did high school, I did college [City College, New York City]. While I was in college, I went to Davenport's Free Theater, where I acted in Sir Henry Irving's *The Bells*, which was a classic. There was a guy who looked like John Carradine that was [in it], forgot his name. And the smell of backstage was a little disgusting [laughs]. He was an old man, but was interesting. He played the lead and I got one of the characters...

"Then, I did a play called *Thomas Paine*, written by Hans Josef, in 1930. I must have been eighteen or nineteen years old. Lionel Stander was in it. He played George Washington with a Brooklyn accent. I played Thomas Paine with a Bronx accent. One critic said, 'It's just too much Paine.' [laughs] It was almost the end of my career, but I got a nice notice.

"And the producer of the place was a guy called Joe Lagatuga. He gave me the name of Marc Lawrence. My name was Max Goldsmith. And when I went to high school, I was taught by a guy to be a good mathematician. And he gave me the name of Lawrence. He said, 'You need a middle name.' So I used to sign my name 'M. Lawrence Goldsmith' when I entered the theater. Then, this producer put in the name 'Marc Lawrence,' and Marc Lawrence got very good notices. Outside of that, too much pain. I kept the name.

"I did lots of plays," he says, and it was there he received invaluable training in using "Voice techniques. Screen actors don't ever use voice technique. I was with Eve Le Gallienne. She was a famous lady who had a theater, on 14th Street, called Pacific Repertory Theater, and many great actors worked there. Jacob Ben Ami, way before your time. And she had a repertory theater: Burgess Meredith was a student, one year ahead of me. Howard De Silva was one year ahead of me, and a lot of other people like that. And John Garfield was in my class. I did little plays with him. Nice boy, sweet guy. It was a very unfortunate death. Richard Waring and I were chosen out of thirty apprentices to be a member of the company. I came to California while I was waiting. And Eve La Gallienne had an accident with her face. So I failed to go back, because she postponed her company for one year. And Waring went with her and I didn't. I came here, fell in love with a gal, decided to do pictures, [rapidly] and so on, and so on, and so on..." When he first arrived in Los Angeles, Lawrence's roommate was Lee Sabinson, who later produced *Finian's Rainbow* on Broadway.

From 1936-39, Lawrence had a contract with Columbia. He appeared in *White Woman* (1933), which also featured Charles Laughton. "I didn't work with him, sweetie. I got to know him later on. He was a very imposing actor. The English actors have a way of speaking [does English accent] that makes you a little intimidated, because their articulation is very precise. They hit their consonants and they elongate their vowels, where we don't do that. We swallow our consonants and forget about our vowels. [Illustrates by doing Bronx accent] 'Whattayadoin', Whattayadoin'? I got somethin' to tell ya! I'm talkin' ta' 'ya!' [Then reverts back to British accent] 'What am I doing? I'm talking to you!' [He also didn't get to work with Carole Lombard, who was in the same film.] No, I didn't. I wish to hell I could. She was a gal with four-letter words. She's the only woman I know that could use the word 'fuck' with delicious eloquence. Everybody enjoyed when she said, 'What the fuck are you doing?' She did it so deliciously, everybody enjoyed hearing the words. All the kids use it now: 'What the fuck are you doin'?' 'Goin' to the fuckin' party.' And everyone says 'fuck.'

"But she was absolutely wonderful. She had a marvelous kind of happy disposition. I suppose it destroyed a great deal of Clark Gable's desire to live." Lombard died in 1942 in a plane crash. "When something special comes into your life, it's a great loss when you lose it. I didn't know her. I think I did another picture with her. I don't remember. I'm eighty-eight years old, you're asking me to remember exactly where? I just remember an incident. I remember her laughing, I remember her saying the word, I remember being on the set with her. I don't remember the fucking picture. I don't know what the hell I did yesterday, and you're asking me to remember the fucking picture? What the hell are you talkin' about? What did I do this morning? I'm gonna do an *E. R.* on Tuesday. A scene, an old man dying. The story of my life. I do a nice little scene, *E. R.*"

Lawrence was an extra in the immortal *G-Men* (1935) with James Cagney. "They were shooting real bullets," Lawrence says, a shockingly common practice of the cinema's first forty years. "I remember we were sitting behind a barricade, and they were shooting real bullets in the barricade…It was a stupid idea. I remember, once, I got a scene in *Bonanza*, and the shmuck director [Robert Altman?] had somebody throw a hard-boiled egg right at my eye. It almost blinded me. Stupid guy. Some of these guys are stupid. Okay, next question."

He had a cameo appearance in Josef Von Sternberg's *Desire* (1936) with Marlene Dietrich. "Played a chauffeur. I got the chauffeur because it was the beginning of my career. It was after I did *If I Had a Million*. They noticed in the second unit in Paris that there was a chauffeur that looked something like me. So, I became a chauffeur, opened up the door [in the movie]. On the set came John Gilbert to visit Marlene Dietrich. *Holy Jesus*. I shit in my pants. There's John Gilbert. You see, I then understood, as I do now, what a fan means. I didn't know what the hell a fan means. When a guy says to me, 'Gee, I like everything you done, Marc,' I look at him and say, 'What the fuck are you talking about? What is he talking about?' I didn't know what it means, 'fan,' unless you're a big star. Like John Gilbert was a big star for me, as a kid, Eddie Polo was a big star for me as a kid, because I worshipped him. But I can understand why people have a certain feeling about me, despite the fact I'm not a big star. They say, 'I'm a fan of yours.' I can see that right away. I felt that way about John Gilbert. My God, being that close. If I could tell the guys back in the Bronx I was looking at John Gilbert like I'm looking at my own shoe. Holy cow, like I'm looking in a mirror, like I'm looking at myself, it was John Gilbert. I could almost rub shoulders with the guy. That feeling. I can understand people saying, 'Gee, I wish I'd taken a picture with this guy.' That was my experience when I saw him. Marlene Dietrich, I wasn't a fan of her's. I was a fan of John Gilbert. Gary Cooper, I wasn't a fan of him, and I did three pictures with him. [laughs] It's interesting. I'm outside of that, you know? I could say, 'I'm a fan of yours,' but I'm not really a fan. It's interesting. I'm not an outsider looking in."

He worked on a number of occasions with director William (*Wings*) Wellman. "I enjoyed William Wellman. I loved him, because he loved actors. And he loved to act himself, and I enjoyed his acting, because I know he enjoyed me, you know? So, it was a kind of general sense of, 'We all accept each other. I accept you, and you accept me, and we embrace each other. And we make other people feel good.' And he gave you that. He was a wonderful man. I adored him.

"He was a wild man, and an exciting man. It was a thrill working for him. He saw me in a play, he saw me in [Clifford Odets'] *Waiting For Lefty*. I did it on stage. And I came over to the studio to see him. And he said, 'Jesus Christ, you're a great fucking actor. You're a great fucking little actor. Goddamn it! Goddamn it!'"

The budding actor found himself forced to choose between taking a part in a movie that would have meant eighteen weeks' work, or a smaller role in *The Robin Hood of El Dorado* (1936) that would only take three days to shoot. "[Wellman] says, 'I've got a better part than they offer you. Goddamn it!' I said, 'I'll take the eighteen weeks!' 'NO! You take the three days. It's a great scene. The other is shit.' I said, 'But it's eighteen weeks. Eighteen weeks, I need.' He says, 'Never mind. Three days.' I did the three days and stayed three weeks. He kept me on there, this skinny kid. He kept me there for three weeks! Beautiful guy, and when I went to see the fucking thing, he cut the whole scene out.

"It was a scene with Warner Baxter. I play one of the gang, I fall off a horse, and I go over there, take a cigarette and start to smoke it. And he comes over to me, Warner Baxter, and says [in Mexican accent], 'Why you no break horse like I tell you?' And I say, 'I'm through.' And I'm smoking my cigarette. And he says, 'Since when are you through?' 'Since five minutes ago.' That's all. And he says, 'You can't be through. We need you. We're short of men.' 'That's too bad for you.' Like this, this kind of shit. And then he says, 'You know what that means at my command?' 'No, what it means?' 'It means death.' So I'm dead. And we both take our guns and we both shoot. I fall of course, since it's Warner Baxter. [laughs] Then he says, 'Hey, Juan! Dig a nice big hole, and push him in.' And it's a marvelous scene. And it broke my heart that he never used it."

He was a gangster in *San Quentin* (1937), featuring Humphrey Bogart. "On the set, I remember driving in a car with Bogie. Bogie said to me, 'Listen, Marc. When I talk fast, I have a tendency to lisp. Would you watch my lisp?' I didn't know what the hell he was talking about. I had no idea. I didn't realize that he lisps. I didn't pay any attention to his speech [laughs]. I said, 'You want me to do that?' 'Yeah, do it, do it, do it for me.' [laughs] So, I said, 'That's alright.' He might have been kidding me, I don't know. What else? Long fucking interview, kid. A lot of shit you're gonna write. Who reads this shit, anyway? You're a fuckin' nut."

Charlie Chan on Broadway (also '37) was the first of several Charlie Chan films that he acted in. "I did one with Warner Oland. He was on Broadway.

Warner Oland played Charlie Chan. I made a couple with Sidney Toler, nice man. Warner Oland would fall asleep sometimes on a scene. He used to do that [laughs]. And he was kind of a laid-back man. He was a Swede, wasn't he? He had this marvelous mask [face] that was very Chinese, actually."

In '37, Lawrence made his first two of six Columbia "B" pictures, each of which ran approximately an hour, where he acted opposite Rita Hayworth. Born Rita Cansino, Lawrence was in the first film where she was billed under her new "nom-de-screen." "I did three or four with Rita. She was a little baby, a frightened little baby. A little child. I looked at her, and, I said, 'Who is this little kid?' [She had a] Kid quality. I liked her. Very nice. I think she liked me, because she called me, when I left the studio, and asked me, 'Who was your business manager?' That's how it goes, flirting with me. She wanted me to be her business manager. Very sweet girl, but she married the wrong guys. She married an older guy first, Ed Judson. Then she married Orson Welles. It was an absolute fraud. He's marrying an image on a screen. And the other guy is marrying an image on the screen, too.

"I wrote a nasty article about fucking newspaper guys that were interviewing her when she was sixty or something, and they asked her, 'What does it feel like to be a goddess at fifty-nine?' or something. And I said, 'Go fuck yourself. How dare you say that?' She was a frightened little girl. She was frightened; that's why she had Alzheimer's. She's been fighting all her life. When she was a child, she was beaten by her father. Her father would say, 'Dance! You know how to dance!' She'd dance, not with the energy or love or with affection or with joy. There was no joy in her dancing. She did it because she was told to do it, like you whip a horse. It was fuckin' awful. What kind of life did she have? She married Orson Welles, who was a theatrical giant, who was too much for anybody! He was the kind of guy who you'd say, 'I'll go to the circus, but I can't join the circus. I'll watch it. Too much going on [with Welles].'

"What the hell for? It was like Arthur Miller marrying Marilyn Monroe. What the fuck for? What's an intellectual shit doing with this glamour goddess? Same shit. And Marilyn herself was a lovely gal. Bewildered girl, too. All this attention she's getting…She had too many toys to play with. It's terrible."

The Shadow (1937) was unrelated to the radio show and character of the same name. The actor's recollections of the many hastily ground-out studio films he made are hazy, but certain details remain vividly: "I know I never memorized any lines, because the script was about two feet thick." Lawrence told the film's makers: "'You want me to read this shit? Just tell me what to do, and I'll make up my own lines.' That's what I did. 'Get over there—Don't move! Alright, this guy…Watch me here. I'll do that! Yah? You understand? Okay! That's good.' This kinda shit's easy to do [laughs hard]. What are you going to do? That's the only memory I have of it. I don't even remember seeing it."

In the prison drama, *Penitentiary* (1938), Lawrence played a part that Boris Karloff had originated in Howard Hawks' *The Criminal Code*. "Harry Cohn liked me, because he was sitting with Johnny Rizzelli one day. Johnny Rizzelli that was the gangster hired to knock off Castro by the FBI. And he was a pal of Harry Cohn. Harry Cohn loved gangsters. I liked Harry Cohn, too. And he was sitting with Harry Cohn watching a screen. And [Rizzelli] looks up and says, 'You know, the kid up there on the screen there could be one of the mob.' Harry Cohn was impressed that he compared me with one of the mob. So he gave me the remake of *Criminal Code*, which was the original picture.

"So, Boris Karloff did the original part. I imitated Boris Karloff, that's what it was. A very bad imitation; I walked the way he did. Mind you, we had a German director [John Brahm], who I despised. I hated the cocksucker. Because all an actor needs when he's acting for the screen is a director that enjoys his performance and encourages him, you know. But if he criticizes him, fuck you, Joe. Get the fuck out of my sight, I say to me, psychologically. Like Fritz Lang when we did *Cloak and Dagger.* He was a monster. He would scream at Lilli Palmer. Poor Lilli Palmer. Oh, my God, in German he would do that, too. It was as if the German government was judging her. It was horrible. There was another German director, too. Ah, fuck him. He's dead now, so God bless. Okay, next question."

Then there was **Who Killed Gail Preston?** "Who the hell killed him? I don't know. [laughs]" He remembers nothing about making it. "No! [laughs] Nothing at all! These names don't mean a thing to me. What else was I in?"

Lawrence reminisced rapidly and tersely. **Convicted** (also '38) featured Rita Hayworth and was based on a Cornell Woolrich story. "With Rita Hayworth. It was shmucky. I saw that. I had a stupid performance. I didn't like it much."

I Am The Law (also '38) was the first time Lawrence worked with Edward G. Robinson. "I've never seen it, so I don't know how great it is," Lawrence relates. "I loved Eddie Robinson, though. I adored the man. I was frightened of him at first, because I never thought about him as Eddie Robinson, nice man. I thought about him as Little Caesar. His image of being Caesar is so strong and vital and terrifying, when I spoke to him personally and he was gentle to me, I was very suspicious, very trustless. And I didn't believe anything he said to me when he said nice things! [laughs] I think he'd jump down my throat any minute. And I think his son felt the same way. I don't think his son ever knew him. He saw him as that tough guy on the screen. In a way, I understand it, because my kids have that same feeling about me. They don't see my humor. My wife didn't see my humor, either. Certain people do, certain people don't. I don't know."

The Housekeeper's Daughter (1939) was directed by the great Hal Roach. "He's an interesting man. A very nice man. He was used to doing two lines at a time, and say, 'Cut.' I don't know why, but he would. I liked him. He was a very gentle man. Sometimes, you enjoy such people."

Beware, Spooks! (also '39) starred satchel-mouthed comedian Joe E. Brown. "Oh, yeah, I liked Joe E., even though he was a crazy guy. Nice man. Sweet man. I don't remember anything about him."

Also in 1939 was **Invisible Stripes,** starring a very young William Holden, Humphrey Bogart, and George Raft. "George [Raft] hit me in the Adam's apple," Lawrence glumly recollects. "Well, he was supposed to slap me, the shmuck. He's a fighter. So he shot me, hit me, a sneaky shot, in the Adam's apple. I couldn't talk for ten minutes. He apologized of course. That's all. What else, what else, what else?"

Brigham Young, Frontiersman (also '40) had another outstanding cast, including Tyrone Power, Vincent Price, and John Carradine. In this biopic of the Mormon pioneer, Lawrence says, "I played a district attorney. Six o'clock at night, they called me and asked me if I would do eight pages of dialogue by the next morning. And I stupidly said, 'Yeah, sure, sure!' So, at two o'clock in the morning, I knew the lines. I got up at six o'clock in the morning to go to the studio. I did it, and that was suicide. You can't do that. It's impossible to do, because you're too tight emotionally. You're not free. And I saw the performance; it was shit, shit. Tight—no looseness." Also present during Lawrence's scene were Vincent Price and John Carradine. He was also in a later film about Brigham Young, the title of which Lawrence couldn't recall: "I played an old Indian, but they cut that out. Marvelous part. They cut the whole fucking thing out, for Phil Yordan, years later."

The Great Profile was one of John Barrymore's final films. But, laments Lawrence, "I never saw Barrymore. It was just a phone call. All I remember was a phone call. That's all. I wish to fuck I could work for the guy. I thought he was great. Fantastic presence, dynamic. Very good, marvelous actor."

Abbott and Costello starred in **Hold That Ghost!** (also '41), one of their earliest vehicles. "Aw, come on. Enough with it! They were a couple of comics, vaudevillians, what do you want me to say? When you work with comics, it's their show. You're just a spectator."

MGM's **Nazi Agent** (also '41) starred one of the screen's perennial Nazis, Conrad Veidt. "Nice guy," Lawrence says of Veidt. "I liked him. I didn't like the director [Jules Dassin]…He was full of shit. You can quote me on that: full of shit."

Surprisingly, a major, Paramount, released **The Monster and The Girl** (also '41), a very low—"B" monster picture. Along with various Three Stooges shorts, **Monster** remains one of the earliest examples of the ever-popular pulp idea of a human brain being transplanted into a gorilla. "That was with my friend Jack Moss, before I did **Shepherd of the Hills**," recalls Lawrence. "The story of Jack Moss is very interesting. Jack Moss was a fat man who became Orson Welles' manager. Prior to that, he was the manager of Henry Hathaway, George Raft, Charles Laughton, Gary Cooper, and a couple of other guys. When Jack Moss took a liking to me, I became his buddy.

This Gun for Hire, 1942.

"So, from **Monster and The Girl,** he was telling me, 'I have difficulty casting a character of a mute, and the name of the picture is **Shepherd of the Hills**.' So, he tells me the story, and I told him a story about Steinbeck, about a mute. And when I told him the story, he kind of liked the way I gave him the interpretation. He says, 'I want you to play the mute.' Henry Hathaway says, "How can he play a mute? He's Jewish! How can he play the hillbilly? He's Jewish!' This kind of shit. Anyway, I played it. And while we're doing the picture, they were writing it.

And [Moss] would read scenes to me, asking for my approval. So I didn't understand it: Why this interest in Marc Lawrence? I remember when we were on the set, he would tell me stories of his youth. When he was about six years old, he had a buddy. And you hang on to a buddy when you're very young, like a kid hangs on to a toy, automatically holds, this closeness. This buddy moved from his neighborhood. He felt lost, so he kept looking for his buddy, but he never could find him. So, all his life, he's kind of looking for his buddy, and I became this little toy, this toy buddy. He sort of leaned on me for the moment. I believed his fanciful story. I remember meeting Charles Laughton. He said to me, 'Marc, Marc, how can I reach Jack? I know you're close to Jack Moss. How can I reach him?' I said, 'I don't know. If Jack doesn't want to talk to you, he doesn't talk to you.' I said, 'I'm sorry. I can't help you.' And then when Jack wouldn't talk to me, I said, 'I'd love to call Charles Laughton and ask him whether he could help me.' So we both had a kind of feeling about the closeness to this guy, but we couldn't be fraternity brothers then, you know?

"Anyway, when I finished the job of the mute, they ran a preview and most of the comments were about this mute. And I remember going to Jack's office. The head of the studio was William LeBaron. And LeBaron was leaving the studio, and he wanted Jack to take his job as head of the studio. And when he left the office, Jack turned him down. He turned to me and said, 'What do you want to be Marc? A great director? A great actor? Whatever you want to be, I'll back you.' Like this. This is Fairyland, Incorporated. We

The Ox-Bow Incident, 1943

had this kind of relationship. Never happened. Went to Orson Welles and I never worked for him again. Never saw him again. Years later, I came back from Europe, I ran into Jack, and we renewed our acquaintance again. But he was then out of the business. It was all dealing in ghosts, ghost ideas, ghost images, ghost past. And the final hand, as Burgess Meredith says in his book, 'My past is much longer than my future. My future's much shorter than my past.' Nothing else to tell you. What else can I say? I would like to end with a story about *Shepherd of the Hills*, which is lovely, cause it's the story of a man looking for his own past. It's a story of Harry Carey coming back, searching his past. Can't do that. You can look at it, but you can't go back to it."

For his first decade in films, Lawrence worked almost exclusively for Warner Brothers, Columbia, and Paramount. But by the early '40s, Lawrence was working prolifically at nearly every studio and independent in Hollywood. Monogram Pictures' **Dillinger** (1945) starred Lawrence Tierney as Public Enemy #1 John Dillinger. His gang was played by Lawrence, Elisha Cook, Jr., and Eduardo Ciannelli. Lawrence confirmed most of the late Lawrence Tierney's co-workers' opinion of the man: "Out of fucking his mind. Still out of his fucking mind. You know, any major studio, would have fired him on the first fucking day, because he walked through it as if he didn't give a shit as to what was happening.

He said his lines as if he was taking a piss somewhere. Pissing in places he had didn't have any right to piss in, but he didn't give a shit. The third day, there were two old people on the phone. He was supposed to shoot at them. And, so, he goes [quietly, staccato], 'Bang, bang.'

"Now the director was a little guy named Max Nosseck. Max Nosseck was a little tiger. He goes up to Tierney, who is about six foot-something, and says, 'You shit! You dirty bastard shit! You shit bastard! What did you do?! What is 'Bang,

bang?!' What is 'Bang, bang?!' Jesus Christ, you stupid bastard! You shoot 'Bang. [long pause] Bang.' What is this 'Bang, bang' shit, you son of a bitch bastard?' And, for the first time, Tierney got his Irish up. From that fucking time on, he was a terror. This little Jewish guy was fantastic. Scared the shit out of the big Irish asshole, and he was a terror from that time on. He [Tierney] was sensational. As an actor, I take my hat off to Lawrence Tierney. But as a person, you could shove him up somebody's ass…Not my ass. Fuck him! He's a pain in the ass.

For his co-star, Elisha Cook, Jr., Lawrence had nothing but praise: "Little 'Cookie' was great. I loved him. He's a fantastic actor. I remember little Nosseck saying to him in the long shot, he had a three-, four-day growth of beard, on his face. And when it came to the close-up, he shaved. So Nosseck said, 'Why you shave?' And [Cook] says, 'It made me feel better.' [laughs] So Nosseck gave him a look, and he said something in German, which we all understood: 'Son of a bitch bastard,' we both understood.

"But that was Cookie. Cookie was another character, but a lovable character. Nothing vicious about Cookie. Lovely man. I worked with him again. Cookie was a drinker—he drank a lot. He lived up in Bishop [California]. He'd sleep in the dressing rooms, where he worked.

"I think you've got enough there to write fifteen articles," Lawrence suddenly groused. "What else do you want?"

Fritz Lang's ***Cloak and Dagger*** (1946) starred Gary Cooper as an American scientist, caught up in World War II-era intrigue in Europe. Lawrence played an Italian Nazi, and speaks no English in the film. There is an extended, brutal fight scene between Lawrence and Cooper, which sprang from very basic origins: "It was one line in the script: 'Someone starts a fight with so-and-so.' Took six days to shoot. All the details and close-ups, of pulling his face, his pulling my face, I'm putting my dirty fingers into his mouth. I apologized, because I said, "I'm a fan of yours, Gary. I hate to do this, but this is in the script." And I grabbed him. [laughs] Sweet guy. I loved Gary. He was a gentle, laid-back man. Beautiful look, beautiful face. 'I hate to put my dirty fingers in his beautiful face. But there it is, kid, it's in the script.' [laughs]"

The two actor/combatants were reunited for far less hostile roles the next year, in Cecil B. De Mille's frontier drama, **Unconquered**. "I played this Indian," he said. Then, Lawrence mumbled some improvised gibberish, his simulation of an Indian tongue—"This kind of shit. So the Indian interpreter went to De Mille and said, 'He speak better Indian than I do.' I was doing just 'Mumble, mumble' shit.' He invited me to his Christmas party, De Mille. After my investigation, he never invited me again."

Briefly, Lawrence shows up as "Ziggy" in the Warner Brothers gangster classic, **Key Largo** (1948). The film, which needs no introduction, was directed by John Huston, and starred Humphrey Bogart, Lauren Bacall, Edward G. Robinson, and Thomas Gomez. It was scripted by future director Richard (**The Professionals**) Brooks. "I did a play in New York," Lawrence says, "called Survivors by Irwin Shaw—another prick. And Richard Brooks saw me in that. I met Brooks before, but he came back and told John Huston about it. And John asked me to do some scenes in **Key Largo**. One day's work. And I did it.

"Huston's a pretty unusual guy. Very unusual. He loved to live. Living is more important than working, it's as important as fucking is to some people. Living was primary with John. John was a character, that guy. He was strange to me, strange to everybody, because his manner of speech was not particularly English, but had a way of a playing a character that made you say, 'Well, he's not talking to me. He's talking to somebody else.' [Lawrence imitates Huston] 'That's quite good, you know. I like that. Yes, that's good.' This kind of articulation, like, 'What, are you talking to me?' [Imitating Huston again] 'Cause he would say certain things, and he had a strange way in which he spoke to you. That's John.

"Very nice guy. I liked him. Very warm guy, in many ways. He had to live every fucking moment. He was right. I'm afraid to live. A lot of people are afraid to live. John was not afraid to live. I've been a cripple since I was thirteen, so I've been afraid to live. But John had no such fault. I envied that, the ability to say, 'I take life in, as I take in my breath.' 'Cause that's living. Because, without taking in living, you're a dead man. And John never wanted to be dead, he wanted to live. 'But by Christ, if I'm alive, I want everybody to know that I'm alive, 'cause I know fuckin' well I am.' It was unfortunate that he had the emphysema. The smoking killed him. John was a really heroic character. He was the devil, he was devilish, he was inventive, he was [giggles] incorrigible, he was warm, he was dirty, he was animalistic, he was a monkey, he was everything, he was a horseman. John was everything. God bless him."

Marc Lawrence and Sam Jaffe in The Asphalt Jungle

Then Lawrence was the bookie, "Cobby," in Huston's classic story of an unsuccessful Diamond heist, *The Asphalt Jungle* (1950). "I was doing a picture called *The Black Hand* (1949) at Metro. After I did *Key Largo*, I ran into John. He said, 'Marc, do me a favor. I'm testing two people. They're not actors. I want you to work with them.' One was Edward Bemmelman. The other was Tom Reed. They were both writers, so I worked with them. Bemmelman had one credo: that no man should work more than ten minutes a day. So, after ten minutes work, he said, 'That's enough. Ten minutes are up.' And Tom Reed was a nice guy. But then we he started to do the scene, I was cueing Bemmelman off-scene. And Bemmelman started to fall asleep in the scene. So John pushed me into the scene. I said, 'What are you doin'? What are you doin'! Get your hands off there! You understand what I'm sayin'?" Like that. I got through it, and John says to me, 'You're going to play the part.' 'What part?' 'Cobby.' I said, 'You're crazy. He's a short little runt of a man.' He said, 'You're gonna play the part.' That's how I got the part."

(Author's note: Lawrence was none too pleased that I hadn't read his autobiography, prior to this interview: "You haven't read my book? Why are you asking me questions? Why didn't you get my book, you shmuck? What do you know about me? I could be full of shit when I tell you all these stories. The book tells

Lawrence and Brando.

the story. But you're not interested. You're just interested in superficial things, right? The outside, not the inside. The inside is terrible. It's full of a lot of tragedy. Oh, forget about it. I don't feel like talking about that. What else? What's the end of this shit? How much more do you want to ask me?")

As Orson Welles once pointed out, gangsters were big movie fans, and often emulated the actors who played them on-screen. Lawrence ran into various hoods on a number of occasions, including Lucky Luciano. "They adored any guy who played gangsters. And they'd say, 'This guy, he's a good one or he's a bad one.' Well, I was a good one to these guys. Since I was a good one, they liked me. I was very close to the real guys. I didn't fake 'em. I was glamorizing 'em, and they liked that a little better. Lucky Luciano liked me, because for some reason or another, we both had dead stares. Dead stares mean when you stare a guy out. Like when you're playin' poker, you never know when the other guy's bluffing. 'Is he bluffing? He's not bluffing?'"

After being blacklisted, Lawrence found his career revitalized in Italy, where came to be known as "The Italian Bogart"—"I signed to do six pictures with [producer Dino] De Laurentiis, as a result of that," Lawrence states. "[De Laurentiis] was a terrifying little fucker. He was hiring gals at a dance marathon, but he was selling them as female fodder to other countries. He was a tough guy. He treated women like some would treat goods: 'I have this kind of goods, and that kind of goods. I can give you four of this, and twelve of that.' What can I say?" It is a little-known fact that, while in Italy, Lawrence used to play chess with screenwriter Charles B. Griffith, the creator of *The Little Shop of Horrors* (1960).

In United Artists' *Johnny Cool* (1963), Lawrence portrayed one of the breed of exiled gangsters he was personally encountering in Italy. The fim's astounding supporting cast included John McGiver, Elisha Cook, Telly Savalas, and Sammy Davis, Jr., who sang the theme song. Though Lawrence enjoyed working with actor Henry Silva on the film, he was much less enthusiastic about its director:

"William Asher was a pusher, which I didn't like. I don't like directors that push. Because directing is a fraud.

"You know, in the theater, they never had directors. Do you know who the director was? The star of the theater play. Hear me? Directors only become important because they call it 'the Lubitsch touch,' 'the Frank Capra touch,' all engineered by 'P. R.' 'P. R.' shit. You don't need these directors, because you don't teach anybody how to act when you're directing a picture. You get the guy, get the star, get the characters that you know. Today, in tv the stars are made overnight because the personality stands out, you get to be a star. The whole genius of motion pictures is that the invention of the motion picture itself is a piece of genius. So if you're at home in what you do, and you have enough personality, you become a star. If you have the kind of personality that people really like, you become a big star, exploited either by the studios, or exploited by publicity, or exploited by the amount of fan mail a guy or woman gets.

"What makes Tom Cruise a star? What makes John Travolta a star? Who the fuck knows? I don't know. I think they both stink, as far as I'm concerned, but I'm not the judge of all that. [laughs] If they want to make 'em a star, they make 'em a star. It's all bullshit. There are very few actors. I mean, to me, Laurence Olivier was a star, Bogart was a star, Cagney was definitely a star. Cagney had a very special face. There was a delicious quality to Cagney. You enjoyed his evil. He was like a little kid, he got away with everything. I loved it."

Among modern actors, Lawrence strongly admires Al Pacino, whom he calls a "Little guy loaded with talent. Beautiful. It's a pleasure watching him. There's an openness about him. He accepts, accepts the weakness and strength of everybody. He accepts, he doesn't resist. It makes him a human being. And he has a broad vision of so many things. Not like Robert De Niro, who is limited. Robert De Niro is a *heavy*, and Tommy Lee Jones is a *heavy*. They're not leading men. They're one note, which is very strong. They hit that note very hard."

Custer of the West (1967) was one of the final films of *film noir* master Robert (**The Killers**) Siodmak. It reunited Lawrence with Lawrence Tierney, who was deported from Spain during **Custer**'s production. The role came about Lawrence says, from his having "worked for Phil Yordan. I did some writing for him. Tierney was so violent a character that he was kept out of two countries. He couldn't go back to England. He couldn't go back to Spain. They wouldn't let him in. He's that violent a guy. So, they wanted me to redo his whole fucking part, a picture he made for Phil in Spain. I was in Spain then. I looked at the thing and said, "Jesus Christ, this guy's great. What the fuck do you want me to do?' 'There's a couple of things I don't understand, a couple of lines here, a couple there. That's nothing.' But here was a New York voice. I have a New York voice. I could dub in that voice and you wouldn't know whether it was he or I. So, I dubbed in five or six lines. That was all. So, I did that. I never told him. I wouldn't want tell him, I wouldn't even want to talk to the cocksucker. He's crazy. Out of his fucking mind. So is his brother [Scott Brady], so's the whole family.

Something's wrong with 'em."

Boxoffice International's *Dream No Evil* (also '70) was a low-budget horror movie featuring the marvelous Edmond O'Brien. Marc appears as a mortician, moonlighting as a pimp! "I liked Eddie O'Brien very much," Lawrence says. "He was a very sweet man. His death was unfortunate. His decline was very unfortunate." O'Brien wasted away from Alzheimer's, and died in 1985. "Marvelous actor. Great voice, great presence, wonderful head, wonderful brain. I had a great feeling about Eddie."

Pigs (1972) was an independent horror movie, and one of Lawrence's few excursions into directing features. He also starred in the murky-looking film as a deranged ex-clown, along with his daughter, Toni. The plot revolved around pigs that eat people. He described it tersely: "It was a picture I produced with my own money." About the title, Lawrence quipped, "Nothing to do with the personalities I've met in Hollywood." During the film's theatrical run, the first ticket buyers to arrive were rewarded with packages of bacon.

More recently, Lawrence acted in two movies written by and starring Quentin Tarantino. As usual, Lawrence didn't mince words when describing him: "*Oy gevalt!* Tarantino is a headline. You know what a headline is? Tomorrow, it's forgotten. Yesterday's headline. He's a clever little bastard. He's glib. He knows the answers to everything—You know, even before you ask him, he's got the answer. He's too clever. Not as talented as they think he is. Glib."

Though he may loathe Tarantino, Lawrence got along considerably better with Tarantino's occasional partner, Robert Rodriguez: "He's very free and lucid, very gentle, the proper approach to directing. He gently persuades you. He's like a warm embrace. He'll say, 'Do it nicely.' So you do it, you know? Very bright, extremely bright. I enjoyed the little scene I had and I did other scenes, which they didn't print, but that's all right. I enjoyed working with Rodriguez. As I enjoyed even [George] Clooney. I'm going to work with Clooney on Tuesday on *E. R.*"

At one point, Lawrence demanded, "Are you taking all

this down? Are you gonna mention all the shit that I say? All the dirty words? Are you going to any of this censor this shit? If you censor, I'll kick the shit out of you! 'Cause that's the real me." "My editor never censors anything," I told him. "Well, fuck him. Tell him from me to leave the fucking thing alone." But Lawrence's poker face slipped, and he warmly tipped his hand: "Give him my best," he laughed.

"I think that'll do it," I said, after the last question.

"Well, thank God!" said Lawrence. "Longest fuckin' interview I've ever had."

THE FILMS OF MARC LAWRENCE (MORE OR LESS)

1932	*If I Had a Million*
1933	*White Woman*
	Gambling Ship
1934	*Death on the Diamond*
1935	*G-Men*
	Dr. Socrates
	Little Big Shot
	Man of the Hour
	Don't Bet on Blondes
	Go Into Your Dance
1936	*Desire*
	Trapped by Television
	Counterfeit
	Night Waitress
	The Road Gang
	The Final Hour
	Love on a Bet
	Under Two Flags
	The Cowboy Star
1937	*Charlie Chan on Broadway*
	San Quentin
	Criminals of the Air
	The Shadow
	I Promise to Pay
	Racketeers in Exile
	Counsel for Crime
	Murder in Greenwich Village
	Motor Madness
	What Price Vengeance
	A Dangerous Adventure

1938	*I am the Law*
	The Spider's Web
	Charlie Chan in Honolulu
	Penitentiary
	Convicted
	Who Killed Gail Preston?
	Adventure in Sahara
	There's That Woman Again
	Squadron of Honor
	While New York Sleeps
1939	*Blind Alley*
	Invisible Stripes
	SOS–Tidal Wave
	Beware Spooks!
	The Lone Wolf Spy Hunt
	Sergeant Madden
	Homicide Bureau
	Romance of the Redwoods
	Ex-Champ
	The Housekeeper's Daughter
	Dust Be My Destiny
	Code of the Streets
1940	*Johnny Apollo*
	Brigham Young, Frontiersman
	Charlie Chan at the Wax Museum
	The Man Who Talked Too Much
	The Great Profile
	Love, Honor, and Oh, Baby!
	The Golden Fleecing
1941	*The Monster and the Girl*
	The Shepherd of the Hills
	Lady Scarface
	Hold That Ghost!
	Sundown
	Public Enemies
	Nazi Agent
	Tall, Dark, and Handsome
	A Dangerous Game
	The Man Who Lost Himself
	Blossoms in the Dust
1942	*This Gun For Hire*
	Call of the Canyon

1942 (cont.)	*Yokel Boy* *'Neath Brooklyn Bridge*
1943	*The Ox-Bow Incident* *Submarine Alert* *Hit the Ice* *Eyes of the Underworld* *Calaboose*
1944	*The Princess and the Pirate* *Tampico* *Rainbow Island*
1945	*Dillinger* *Club Havana* *Flame of the Barbary Coast* *Don't Fence Me In*
1946	*Cloak and Dagger* *The Virginian* *Life With Blondie* *Blonde Alibi*
1947	*Unconquered* *The Captain from Castille* *Yankee Fakir* *Joe Palooka in The Knockout* *I Walk Alone*
1948	*Key Largo* *Out of the Storm*
1949	*Black Hand* *Jigsaw* (aka: *Gun Moll*) *Calamity Jane and Sam Bass* *Tough Assignment*
1950	*The Asphalt Jungle* *Abbott and Costello in the Foreign Legion* *The Desert Hawk*
1951	*My Favorite Spy* *Hurricane Island* *Vacanze Col Gangster*
1952	*La Tratta Delle Bianche* (translation: *White Slavery*) *I Tre Cosari*
1953	*Noi Peccatori* *Fratelli d'Italia*

1953 *(cont.)*	*Jolanda, La Figlia Del Corsaro Nero*
	I Pui Comico Spettacolo Del Mondo
	Legion Staniera (*Foreign Legion*)
	Ballata Tragica (*Love Without Tomorrow*)
1954	*La Catena Dell'Odio*
1955	*Helen of Troy*
1956	*Jubal*
	Suor Maria
1957	*Kill Her Gently*
1962	*Recoil*
1963	*Johnny Cool*
1964	*Nightmare in the Sun* (Director and co-producer)
1965	*Pampa Selvaje* (*Savage Pampas*)
1966	*Johnny Tiger*
	Duo Mafisi Contra Al Capone
	Deux Tueurs (aka: *Du Mou Dans La Gachette*)
1967	*Custer of the West*
1968	*Krakatoa, East of Java*
	Eve (aka: *King of Kong Island*)
1969	*Un Escercito de 5 Uomini* (*The Five-Man Army*)
1970	*The Kremlin Letter*
1971	*Diamonds Are Forever*
	Dream No Evil (aka: *Now I Lay Me Down to Die*)
1972	*Pigs* (aka: *Daddy's Deadly Darlings; The Strange Exorcism of Lynn Hart*)
	Honor Thy Father (CBS tvm)
	Fraser, the Sensuous Lion
1974	*The Man With the Golden Gun*
1975	*Switch* (aka: *Las Vegas Roundabout*; CBS pilot)
1976	*Marathon Man*
1977	*A Piece of the Action*
1978	*Going Coconuts*
	Foul Play
1979	*Cataclysm* (aka: *The Nightmare Never Ends, Satan's Super*)
	Revenge of the Pink Panther
	Hot Stuff
1981	*Super Fuzz*

1982	*Terror at Alcatraz* (NBC pilot)
1985	*Night Train to Terror* (Condensed version of *Cataclysm*)
	Family Ties Vacation (Co-producer, act?)
1986	*The Big Easy*
	Blood Red
1990	*Donor* (tvm)
1991	*Ruby*
	Newsies
1995	*Four Rooms*
1996	*Gotti*
	From Dusk Till Dawn
1999	*End of Days*
2002	*The Shipping News*
2003	*Looney Tunes: Back in Action*

A clip of Lawrence and Laird Cregar in *This Gun For Hire* was used in Woody Allen's *Crimes and Misdemeanors* (1989). Lawrence was not in *The Big Sleep* (1947), as has been reported elsewhere.

In the '50s, Lawrence made a short subject about the cats of Rome, as personified by a cat named Uncle Harry. It was released as *Romans of Rome* (*Romani di Roma*) by MGM.

TELEVISION

Lawrence's tv work includes having acted and/or directed on: *Bronco, The Rifleman, Wagon Train, The Deputy, Lawman, CHiPs, Bonanza, Nichols, Wonder Woman, Star Trek: The Next Generation,* and *E. R.*

BIBLIOGRAPHY

Kennedy, Burt. "Burt Kennedy Interviews John Ford." In: Thomas, Bob, editor. *Directors in Action.* Indianapolis, New York: The Bobbs Merrill Co. 1973.

Lawrence, Marc. *Long Time No See.* Palm Springs, CA: Ursus Press. 1991.

Lloyd, Ann and Graham Fuller, Editors. *The Illustrated Who's Who of the Cinema.* New York: Macmillan Publishing. 1983.

Maltin, Leonard, Ed. *The Real Stars.* New York: Popular Library. 1979.

Meyerson, Harold. "The Case of the Vanishing Character Actor." *Film Comment* magazine. November/December, 1977. pp. 6-15.

Sarris, Andrew. *"You Ain't Heard Nothin' Yet": The American Talking Film, History and Memory, 1927-1949.* New York: Oxford University Press. 1998.

Vale, V. and Andrea Juno, Editors. *Re/Search #10: Incredibly Strange Films.* San Francisco, CA: Re/Search Publications. 1986.

Young, Jordan R. *Reel Characters.* Beverly Hills, CA: Moonstone Press. 1986.

CPSIA information can be obtained at www.ICGtesting.com
Printed in the USA
BVOW01s0059270814

364339BV00001B/151/P